Eight Great Reasons to Buy This New Edition of *Short Takes*

If you're wondering why to buy this new edition, here are eight good reasons!

1. **An expanded "Freeze Frame" section** models critical reading and writing by annotating a sample paragraph with marginal comments.

2. **Twenty new essays** (of 50) focus on engaging topical subjects ranging from popular culture and media to science and technology.

3. **Useful strategies for writing** include guidelines for journaling, clustering, timed writing, asking questions, listing, and working in groups.

4. **New examples clarify distinctions** between revising, editing, and proofreading—and offer reasons for why writers make changes.

5. **Revised chapter introductions** focus more clearly on patterns of organization.

6. **New images—cartoons and comics**—comment on and enhance the essays, showing how the same analytical skills can be applied to other forms of expression.

7. **New readings reflect diverse perspectives,** including race, culture, profession, and gender.

8. **A new chapter sequence** places definition after description and narration, so that each chapter builds on the previous one, leading to argument as the culmination.

D0011633

PEARSON

Short Takes

MODEL ESSAYS FOR COMPOSITION

Tenth Edition

Elizabeth Penfield

University of New Orleans

Longman

New York   San Francisco   Boston
London   Toronto   Sydney   Tokyo   Singapore   Madrid
Mexico City   Munich   Paris   Cape Town   Hong Kong   Montreal

Executive Editor: Lynn M. Huddon
Senior Supplements Editor: Donna Campion
Senior Marketing Manager: Sandra McGuire
Production Manager: Jacqueline A. Martin
Project Coordination and Electronic Page Makeup: Elm Street Publishing Services/
 Integra Software Services Pvt. Ltd.
Cover Design Manager: Wendy Ann Fredericks
Cover Designer: Kay Petronio
Cover Photos: (from top to bottom) Crystal Cartier Photography/Brand X Pictures/Jupiter
 Images; Justin Sullivan/Getty Images, Inc.—Liaison; and Carl Purcell/Corbis
Photo Researcher: Cindy Joyce
Senior Manufacturing Buyer: Alfred C. Dorsey
Printer and Binder: Courier Corporation/Westford
Cover Printer: Phoenix Color Corporation/Hagerstown

For permission to use copyrighted material, grateful acknowledgment is made to the copyright holders on pp. 295–297, which are hereby made part of this copyright page.

Library of Congress Cataloging-in-Publication Data

Penfield, Elizabeth.
 Short takes : model essays for composition/Elizabeth Penfield.—10th ed.
  p. cm.
 Includes bibliographical references and index.
 ISBN-13: 978-0-205-72547-2
 ISBN-10: 0-205-72547-3
 1. College readers. 2. English language—Composition and exercises. 3. English
language—Rhetoric—Problems, exercises, etc. 4. Report writing—Problems,
exercises, etc. I. Title.
 PE1417.P43 2009
 808'.0427—dc22   2009010654

4 5 6 7 8 9 10—CRW—12 11

Longman
is an imprint of

ISBN-13: 978-0-205-72547-2

www.pearsonhighered.com   ISBN-10: 0-205-72547-3

CONTENTS

2 On Using Narration   40

3 On Using Example 69

4 On Using Definition 97

5 On Using Comparison and Contrast   126

8   On Using Cause and Effect   202

10 Multiple Modes: Two Topics, Six Views **276**

THEMATIC GUIDE

Science and Technology

Language and Education

Popular Culture and the Media

PREFACE

This book combines the old and the new. When the first edition was only an idea, I was teaching freshman English in a structured program that emphasized rhetorical modes and final product. My dilemma then was one that many teachers still face: how to incorporate the modes with the whole tangle of the writing process. But once I focused on the aims of discourse, the modes fell into place as means, not ends, and as patterns of organization used in combination, not just singly. There remained the problem of the textbooks, many of which contained essays of imposing length and complexity that intimidated and overwhelmed many a student. Often, any short essay was so because it was an excerpt. *Short Takes* was the result of my frustrations. This tenth edition still reflects the rhetorical framework of the first one, but it is flexible. You can even ignore it and use the thematic table of contents. But if you find the modes useful, you'll see them here.

This edition remains a collection of short, readable, interesting essays written by professionals and students, and the commentary continues to focus on reading and writing as interrelated activities. Much, however, is new:

- completely revised and shortened "Freeze Frame," the opening section that introduces students to critical reading and the writing process, including expanded explanations of how to get started, revise, edit, and proofread
- added annotated examples in "Freeze Frame" to illustrate how to read critically and how to revise
- completely revised and shortened chapter introductions that highlight the most important points and are therefore more accessible to students
- reorganized sequence of chapters to emphasize how they reinforce each other
- fresh topics and 20 new essays that engage students by analyzing subjects as varied as the effects of technology and the value of anger
- emphasis on subordinate modes so students can more clearly understand how various modes are used singly and together
- seven drawings—cartoons and comic strips—that comment on or add to several of the essays

- revised chapter on argument (Chapter 9) that includes both individual and paired essays
- two sets of three essays each that present differing perspectives on timely subjects so students can respond with their own analytical essays
- many writing assignments that include the use of the Internet, a ready resource for most students

At the same time, features that teachers particularly liked are still here. The text:

- provides chapter introductions directed to students that emphasize the writing process (as well as the kinds of choices and decisions all writers face)
- presents short, engaging, accessible essays and helpful introductions to each rhetorical pattern
- contains complete essays, not excerpts
- describes each author, context for the essay, and the essay's notable stylistic features
- includes questions on organization, ideas, technique, and style after each essay, engaging students to think critically about the readings
- for each selection, suggests a number of topics for writing journal entries and essays
- includes a variety of authors, styles, and subjects
- emphasizes how the rhetorical modes interact with invention and the entire writing process
- provides an alternate thematic table of contents
- comes with an *Instructor's Manual* that includes: key words and phrases for each essay; suggestions for group work; writing prompts keyed to the thematic table of contents; and additional suggestions for each rhetorical mode and for comparing two or more of the selections

Each chapter builds on the previous one and leads to the one that follows, culminating in argument—but argument with a difference. The chapter on argument is a basic introduction, an extension of the kind of emphasis on thesis and evidence that exists throughout the text. Within each chapter, the essays are presented in order of difficulty. All the supplementary information—the chapter introductions, background information, notes on style, questions on the essays, and suggestions for writing—balance process and product, working on the premise that the two, like reading and writing, are so closely interrelated that one cannot be considered without the other.

As always, I welcome responses from students and teachers to this new edition, along with suggestions for the future. You can e-mail me at epenfiel@uno.edu or in care of Longman's English Editor at PearsonLongman, 51 Madison Avenue, New York, NY 10010.

The Essays

This edition contains 50 essays, 20 of which are new. Because most of the papers assigned in composition courses fall into the 400- to 1000-word range, most of the essays are short—about 1000 words at most—and as such easily lend themselves to scrutiny and emulation. A few are longer and rely on the kind of research that students may be asked to carry out. Most illustrate the kind of prose expected from college students—analyzing and incorporating sources. And a few illustrate the problem–solution organization often found in argumentative pieces. All of the essays are complete pieces, not excerpts, illustrating the aims of discourse and rhetorical modes.

To write is to choose among alternatives, to select the most appropriate organization, persona, diction, and techniques for a given audience and purpose. Each of the essays included in this edition was chosen because it exemplifies each author's choices, and the apparatus emphasizes those choices and alternatives. The essays, therefore, serve as illustrative models of organization and stylistic techniques available to the writer. The essays were also chosen because their authors represent different genders, ages, and cultures. As a result, the subjects of the essays are accessible and their perspectives are lively, qualities that also allow them to serve as sources of invention, as jumping-off places for students to develop their own ideas in their own styles.

Rhetorical Modes and the Aims of Discourse

Anyone who has used a reader with essays arranged by mode has probably run into two problems: first, few essays are pure examples of a single mode; second, most collections of essays treat argument—an aim of writing—as though it were the equivalent of description, comparison/contrast, and so on. *Short Takes* addresses these inconsistencies by emphasizing the difference between mode—how an essay is organized—and purpose—how an essay is intended to affect the reader—and by pointing out how writing frequently blends two or more modes.

Because essays usually employ more than one mode, the essays here are grouped according to the *primary* rhetorical pattern that guides their organization; the questions that follow each essay point out the subordinate modes. As for the aims of discourse, the essays represent the various purposes for writing. The writers' self-expressive, informative, and persuasive purposes are underscored in the discussion questions. In addition, the apparatus connects academic writing and the kind of writing found outside the classroom.

Apparatus for Reading and Writing

The apparatus makes full use of the essays. Chapters 1 through 9 begin with a brief introduction to the student that depicts the mode or purpose under discussion, showing how it can be used in formal essays and in practical, everyday writing tasks. The introductions point out specifically how the modes can be shaped by considerations of audience, purpose, particular strategies, thesis, and organization, ending with advice on finding a subject, exploring a topic, and drafting a paper. This division of the writing process approximates the classic one of invention, arrangement, and style but is not intended to imply that these are separate stages.

To emphasize both what a text says and how it says it, each essay in Chapters 1 through 9 is preceded by background information on the author and the text and a brief discussion of a stylistic strategy. Two sets of questions—"Organization and Ideas" and "Technique and Style"—follow each essay, along with ideas for journal entries and essays. Throughout, process and product, as well as reading and writing, are interrelated, emphasizing the recursive nature of the act of writing. Writers constantly invent, organize, and revise; the lines that distinguish those activities are narrow, if not blurred.

"Suggestions for Writing" follow each essay and contain options for both journal entries and essays, all related by theme, organization, or ideas to the work that has just been read. The assignments allow a good deal of flexibility: Some lend themselves to general information or personal experience, some to research papers, many to group work (outlined in the *Instructor's Manual*), some to the classic technique of imitation.

Whether working alone or in groups, once students select their subjects, they will find flipping back to the chapter introductions helpful.

There, "Exploring the Topic" shapes questions so that no matter what type of paper they are writing, students can generate information. "Drafting the Paper" then helps organize the material and points out some of the pitfalls and advantages inherent in a particular mode or aim.

The index includes key terms as well as author names and essay titles, but the text is essentially a reader, not a handbook. That's a conscious decision. Discussions of usage and documentation are best left, I think, to the individual teacher.

The Instructor's Manual

An *Instructor's Manual* (ISBN 978-0-205-72546-5) includes additional writing assignments, key words and phrases, responses to the questions, and teaching suggestions for both the questions and the longer writing assignments. The manual also contains additional writing prompts at the end of each chapter for the mode or aim under discussion as well as for comparing and evaluating the essays. You'll also see an appendix that has writing prompts for the text's Thematic Guide.

Acknowledgments

I have many people to thank for their help in bringing this book to publication: Lynn Huddon, Rebecca Gilpin, and Sarah Burkhart for their good advice and encouragement; Danielle Urban for her expertise and patience; Hope Rajala, Leslie Taggart, Karen Helfrich, and Liza Rudneva for their able assistance with past editions; James Postema and Nancy Braun, for their help and that of their students; and Theodora Hill for her sound recommendations, patience, and help with the more mundane aspects of preparing a manuscript. The following reviewers all provided guidance and advice that improved the manuscript: Gordon Anderson, Delgado Community College; Susan Jaye Dauer, Valencia Community College; Marion G. Heyn, Los Angeles Valley College; Amy M. Hundley, Merced College; Melissa Manolas, Portland Community College; Brad Summerhill, Truckee Meadows Community College; Rebecca Whitus Longster, Purdue University; Sherida Yoder, Felician College.

ELIZABETH PENFIELD

Freeze Frame
Reading and Writing

This Book

In filmmaking, a "short take" is a brief scene filmed without interruption. Similarly, short essays, articles, and editorials—even cartoons and ads—move quickly to make their points. Those are the kinds of texts you will find in this book, short pieces that explain, argue, express the writer's opinions, or simply entertain.

Various kinds of writing carry out their purposes by drawing on various patterns of organization, patterns that can describe, tell a story, define a subject, provide examples, set up comparisons, or analyze a process or a cause and effect. These are the same strategies you will draw on when you write your own papers. These texts, then, can serve as models.

And just as the examples collected here are "short takes," this essay is a "freeze frame," as though you had stopped the film on one particular shot to get a better look at the details. So, too, this essay will stop and take a close-up look at what goes on when you read and when you write.

Reading Critically

A skilled reader interacts with the words on the page: reshaping, evaluating, selecting, analyzing. After all, you have your own world, one made up of everything you have experienced, from your first memory to your most recent thought—all of which you bring to what you read.

An essay analyzing why people are attracted to beaches, for example, will remind you of any beaches you know, and your associations will probably be pleasurable. As you begin to read the essay, you discover that the writer's associations are also pleasant ones, reinforcing yours. You read on, constantly reassessing your ideas about the essay as you add more and more information to your first impression. Now and then,

1

you may hit a sentence that at first doesn't make much sense, so you stop, perhaps to look up an unfamiliar word, perhaps to go back and review an earlier statement, then read on, again reevaluating your ideas about what the author is saying and what you think of it.

The result is analytical, critical reading—not critical in the sense of judging harshly but critical in the sense of questioning, weighing evidence, evaluating, comparing your world to the one the writer has created on the page.

The idea of revising and tinkering is usually associated with writing, less so with reading. Yet just as you tinker and wrestle with your own writing, you should do the same with what you read. You should:

- scribble
- underline
- question
- challenge
- analyze
- evaluate

Reading in this way, reading critically with pen or pencil in hand, will give you a fuller appreciation of what you read and a better understanding of the techniques the writer used to create the essay.

Identifying the Purpose   It helps to know what different kinds of writing have in common. Whether business letter, lab report, journal entry, news story, poem, or essay, all focus on a subject, address a reader, and have a point. And, too, all have a purpose and a style; they are written for specific reasons and in a certain way. You can explore how the writer uses these elements by using the familiar journalistic *who? what? where? when? how? why?*, questions perhaps more familiar when used to spark ideas for writing. Yet these questions can be equally useful for reading, and thinking about them will help you analyze what you read.

On page 220, you'll find Oliver Sacks' essay "When Music Heals Body and Soul," and its first six paragraphs are reprinted with comments on pages 5–7. Here, quoting from that introduction, is how the journalistic questions might apply:

- To whom is an essay addressed? Sacks' "all of us" suggests a general audience.
- What is the writer's main point? "I experienced a physical need for music."

- Where and when does the action take place? "When I became a patient"
- How is the piece organized? It moves from "I" (Sacks) to the general statement "Music can have the same effect on the neurologically impaired."
- Why is it structured that way? The organization allows Sacks to place his unique experience into a larger context that his readers can identify with—the power of music.

Many, many more inquiries can be spun off these seemingly simple questions, and they are useful tools for exploring an essay. Jotting down these questions and your answers to them in a notebook or journal can also sharpen your critical abilities and lead to a lively class discussion.

Looking for the Point   In much of the reading we do, we are looking for information. The election coverage reported in the newspaper, the syllabus for a course, and a set of directions all exemplify this kind of reading, but reading for information and reading for comprehension are as different as a vitamin pill and a five-course dinner. Understanding what a writer is saying and implying—as well as the choices involved—isn't easy.

The title of an essay is a good place to start because a title can:

- Announce a subject, as in Sacks' "When Music Heals Body and Soul"
- Imply the subject, the healing power of music
- Set the tone, the writer's attitude toward the subject, a serious one that suits the subject
- State or imply the thesis, the assertion the author is making about the subject

As for other essays, you don't need to turn to the essay titled "Sweatin' for Nothin'" to figure out it may be about exercising and that the author doesn't see much point to fitness fads. Some titles focus clearly on their subject, as in "Living on Tokyo Time." Still others tip you off to the author's tone—"A Fowl Trick" suggests a humorous narrative involving a bird.

Knowing or at least having a hint about the subject is the first step to discovering the thesis. The first paragraph or set of paragraphs that acts as an introduction will also help you deduce a tentative version. Sometimes the writer places the thesis in the first paragraph or introduction or even in the last paragraph, but sometimes a bare-bones version appears in the title: "Vote for X," "Support the Surge," "Spay Pets." If that's where it is, mark it.

If you don't spot a thesis in the title or first few paragraphs, you should still write down a tentative version of what it may be so that you focus on what follows, an idea against which you can test other ideas.

If the thesis isn't readily identifiable, you can discover it by identifying key sentences and then mentally composing a statement that covers those ideas, a process that often takes more than one reading but is made easier if you underline the important sentences. Even then, you may well find that someone else who reads the essay comes up with a different thesis statement. And you both may be right.

What's happening here? If you think about how slippery words are and the different experiences that different readers bring to an essay, you can begin to see why there's more than one "correct" thesis. If you were to give the same essay to ten critical readers, you would find that their versions of the thesis differ but overlap. But sometimes writers unwittingly set traps, making it easy to mistake a fact for a thesis. If you keep in mind that a thesis is both a sentence and an assertion—a value judgment—you can avoid these traps. "The average American watches a lot of TV" states a fact most readers would shrug off with a "So what?" On the other hand, "Television rots the minds of its viewers" takes a stand that will probably raise hackles and a "Hey, wait a minute!"

Recognizing Patterns of Development   Once you've nailed down a thesis, go a step further to examine how that thesis is developed. Writers depend on various patterns of thought or modes of thinking that are almost innate.

- To tell a joke is to narrate.
- To convey what friendships are like is to define, describe, and use examples.
- To decide which among many courses to take is to divide and classify.
- To figure out which car is better is to compare and contrast (and if you think of an old car as a peach or a lemon, you are drawing an analogy).
- To analyze the steps involved in researching a topic is to use process analysis.
- To analyze a baseball team's successful season is to weigh cause and effect.

Narration, description, example, division and classification, comparison and contrast, analogy, process, cause and effect, and definition are the natural modes of thinking upon which writers rely.

These patterns of thought provide the structure of an essay. A piece on the ethics of using prisoners to test new medicines might open with a brief narrative that sets the scene, go on to define what kinds of medicines are involved, and then explain the effects of such experiments on the prisoners, the development of new drugs, and society's concept of ethics. As you read, you should note each type of mode the writer uses so you can more fully understand how the thesis is developed and how the essay is organized. Though you may find an essay uses many types of modes, it's likely that one predominates.

Reading Oliver Sacks' "When Music Heals Body and Soul" To illustrate critical reading, here's an annotated example from the introduction to the essay that appears on page 220. There it's preceded by information about the author and publication, so you'd know Oliver Sacks is a physician and neurologist and that his essay appeared in *Parade,* a Sunday newspaper insert aimed at a general audience. Even so, you might suspect you'll encounter some difficulty because Sacks' experience differs from yours. His title gives you a general idea about his subject and suggests a causal relationship. You might think, "How can music heal the body? Soul, maybe, but body?" Then as you start to read the essay, you might make marginal notes similar to the following ones. The result would be an analysis of Sacks' introduction to the essay, giving you a good sense of direction for what follows.

Audience, general	1 (All) of (us) have all sorts of <u>personal experiences</u>
Effects of music, what it can do	with music. We find ourselves <u>calmed</u> by it, <u>excited</u> by it, <u>comforted</u> by it, <u>mystified</u> by it and often
Narrow to Sacks	<u>haunted</u> by it. It can <u>lift</u> us out of depression or move us to tears. (I) am no different. I need music
	to start the day and as company when I drive.
	I need it, <u>propulsively</u>, when I go for swims and
	runs. I need it, finally, to still my thoughts when
Move to narrative, explaining what happened	I retire, to <u>usher</u> me into the world of dreams.
	2 But it was only when I became a patient myself
	that I experienced a *physical* <u>need for music.</u>

Sets up identification between Sacks & readers
Main subject?

Look up. Why choose this word?

Good verb

Narrows subject

Cause ———— A <u>bad fall</u> while climbing a mountain in Norway had left me incapacitated by damage to the nerves

Effects ———— and muscles of one leg. After surgery to repair the torn tendons in my leg, I settled down to await some return of function in the torn nerves.

3   With the leg effectively paralyzed, I <u>lost all</u> ——— Effects <u>sense of its existence</u>—indeed, I seemed to <u>lose the very *idea* of moving it.</u> The leg stayed

Effects of paralysis & no music ——— nonfunctional for the longest 15 days of my life. These days were made longer and grimmer because there was <u>no music</u> in the hospital. ——— Back to music

Radio reception was bad. Finally, a friend brought me a tape recorder along with a tape   Sacks is losing me

Classical ———— of one of my favorite pieces: the <u>Mendelssohn</u> — here—don't know music *Violin Concerto.*

4   Playing this over and over <u>gave me great plea-</u>

Effects of ———— <u>sure</u> and a <u>general sense of being alive</u> and <u>well.</u> Concerto But the nerves in my damaged leg were still heal- ing. Two weeks later, I began to get small twitches

Look up ———— in the previously <u>flaccid</u> muscle and larger sudden, involuntary movements.

5   Strangely, however, I had no impulse to walk. I could barely remember how one would go about walking—until, unexpectedly, a day or two later, Cause. Music the *Violin Concerto* <u>played itself in my mind.</u> — in mind (soul) heals body. It seemed, suddenly, to lend me its own energy, and I recovered the lost rhythm of walking—like ——— Effects remembering a once-familiar but long-forgotten

Look up
Move from particular to general

Big claim. More than what doctors can do?

Rest of essay will give examples of effect of music on "neurologically impaired."

6

time. Only then did walking regain its natural, unconscious, <u>kinetic melody</u> and grace.

Music can have the same effect on the <u>neurologically impaired. It may have a power beyond anything else to restore them to themselves—at least in the precious few minutes that it lasts.</u>

Odd word to use but makes sense given the subject.

Thesis? Further narrowing of subject

Hedges the claim

Combine last two sentences for thesis.

From Reading to Writing

Essays can be deceptive. What you see on the printed page resembles the writer's work about as much as a portrait resembles the real person. What you don't see when you look at printed pages are all the beginnings and stops, the crumpled paper, the false starts, the notes, the discarded ideas, the changed words. Instead, you have a finished piece—the result of the writer's choices. Yet the process most writers go through to produce their essays is very like your own. The writer Andre Dubus puts it another way: "Anybody born physically able in the brain can sit down and begin to write something, and discover that there are depths in her soul or his soul that are untapped."

As a writer and a reader, you tap into those depths, depths that help make meaning of the world we live in. Stated concisely, this book reinforces a basic assumption: Reading and writing are highly individual processes that are active, powerful, and interrelated ways to discover meaning.

To write, then, is to create and structure a world; to read is to become part of someone else's. And just as reading makes a better writer, writing makes a better reader.

The Rough Draft: Getting Started

Whether you're working on an assigned topic or one of your own, a blank sheet of paper or an empty computer screen can be a terrifying thing, so how should you begin? Generating ideas isn't as hard as it may seem. You can try

using ideas from your journal
creating clusters of ideas

writing whatever comes to mind
asking questions
working with a list
discussing ideas with your classmates

Journal   Your journal provides a good place to comment on what
you read or discuss in class. An essay arguing that the minimum wage
should be raised might make you think about your own experience,
the jobs you've had in the past and now. But you need to go beyond
your own experience, so jot down some questions that put your experience into a larger context so that you don't focus only on yourself.
Flesh out answers to the questions, and you will have the makings of
an essay.

Clusters   On a blank sheet of paper, start by putting your topic in the
middle, for example "Raising the Minumum Wage." Then, scattered
around the page, write what you need to know and your ideas. The initial result may look like this:

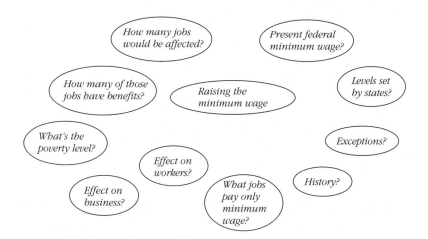

Analyzing what's on paper by linking like items, you find that many questions can be grouped under "facts" and a few under "speculation." Now
you need to do research. You can go to the Internet to gather answers
from sites such as the U.S. Department of Labor's www.dol.gov/
esa/minwage/america.htm. Armed with answers, you are in a position to

draw a tentative conclusion. Then you can come up with a working thesis and more questions to research.

Writing   Without stopping to think analytically, start writing about your subject. Some people find it helpful to set a timer for, say, five minutes. After that time, stop, read what you have written, and then in one sentence sum it up. Take that sentence as the lead for your next timed writing, and again, stop and sum up. Within an hour or so, you will have written your way into a working thesis and probably some topic sentences for paragraphs.

Asking Questions   Explore and develop your topic by using the standard journalistic questions: *who? what? where? when? how? why?*

> *Who* am I writing this for? *Who* is my audience?
> *What* is my main idea? *What* is my point?
> *Where* is the evidence for my point?
> *When* is that evidence sufficient?
> *How* is my thesis relevant?
> *Why* is what I say believable?

Or use the various patterns of development as strategies for expanding and generating ideas.

> How can minimum wage jobs be *described*? How many businesses/ workers fit the category?
> What *examples* work well?
> What are the key terms that need to be *defined*? How "minimum" is minimum?
> What kind of jobs are involved? How can they be *classified*?
> What would be the *effects* of raising the wage? On businesses? On workers? On the economy?
> How does the present minimum wage *compare* to those in the past in terms of buying power?
> What short *narrative* would work as an introduction?

These strategies can help you work out a thesis as well as come up with ideas that can be turned into lead sentences for paragraphs.

Listing   Experienced writers sometimes work from a list of their ideas, reworking it by numbering each one to organize and rank its importance.

No list is sacred, however, and often what was first most important may later give way to a more powerful point. Outlining is a variation of this strategy but some reject it as too restricting, too inflexible.

Discussing   This method is the most obvious, but it works best if some written record of the discussion is kept. If your class uses peer groups, then you can take turns keeping notes. Then with notes in hand, you can clarify ideas and add to them.

At this stage, you're brainstorming, coming up with ideas and bouncing them off each other so that you can figure out what you are trying to say. Figuring out how you want your reader to respond, shaping your ideas, organizing, and then polishing them can come later. Now you just want to end up with ideas that can be loosely organized into a rough draft.

Revising, Editing, and Proofreading

Revising, editing, and proofreading are three different stages of the writing process, but they don't necessarily occur as a set sequence. If you had a rough draft for an essay arguing for a federal speed limit, you would be revising if you moved paragraphs around or added examples or narrowed your thesis—all major changes. If your writing group suggested shifts or substitutions, that would be editing. And when your essay is ready to be turned in, then you would check it carefully for spelling and punctuation mistakes—proofreading. The process appears to be linear, but it's fluid: while revising, you might correct a misspelled word; while proofreading, you might add another example or change a sentence.

Major revision is often so messy that it's hard to reproduce as an example, but here's how an earlier draft of paragraph 4 on page 3 was revised:

1   *Original:* Knowing or at least having a hint

2   about the subject is the first step to discovering

3   an essay's thesis. The first paragraph or set of

4   paragraphs that acts as an introduction will also

deduce ——————————————————————————————— version

5   help you form a tentative thesis. Sometimes the

6   writer places the thesis in the first paragraph or

or even in the last ¶	7	introduction, but sometimes a bare-bones version
	8	~~of the thesis~~ appears in the title. If ~~you see it,~~ :
that's where it is,	9	~~you should~~ mark it. If you don't spot a thesis,
what it may be	10	you should still write down a ~~tentative version~~ of
	11	~~your own~~ so that you ~~have a~~ focus for ~~what is to~~
	12	follow, an idea against which you can test other
	13	ideas.

Margin notes: add examples — in the title or first few ¶s — working idea — on

Lines 3, 5, 8, 9, 10, and 11: unnecessary words cut
Line 5: more precise word substituted; wording changed to avoid repeating *thesis*
Line 7: idea of where thesis placed expanded, examples added, wording made more precise
Line 10: changed for greater clarity; "working idea" to avoid repetition
Line 11: emphasizes tentative version of thesis may change; noun replaced by verb for emphasis

If you are like most writers, your first draft won't look much like the finished work, so don't be afraid to be messy. Double space so you leave lots of room for scribbles. When you revise you're focusing on

Thesis
Ideas
Audience
Organization

Reread your draft, marking the main ideas and checking them to make sure they are related to and support your initial thesis. Then as you refine your thesis, check the main ideas again.

When you shift to proofreading, hone in on clarity, style, and matters of usage and punctuation. Read the paper out loud to check for repetition and sentence variety, and watch out for overusing "I." Make sure you check your spelling and reexamine your punctuation. You don't want your credibility as a writer questioned because of a misspelling or vagrant semicolon.

The Writing Process

Far from following a recipe, you will find that writing is like driving a car while at the same time trying to impress the passengers, talk on the cell phone, read a road map, recognize occasional familiar landmarks, follow scrawled and muttered directions, and watch for and listen to all the quirks of the car and other drivers. You know vaguely where you are going and how you want to get there, but the rest is risk and adventure. With work and a number of dry runs, you can smooth out the trip so that the passengers fully appreciate the pleasure of the drive and the satisfaction of reaching the destination. That is the challenge the writer faces, a challenge that demands critical reading as well as effective writing.

POINTERS FOR READING

1. **Settle in.** Gather up a good dictionary and whatever you like to write with, and then find a comfortable place to read.

2. **Think about the title.** What sort of expectations do you have about what will follow? Can you identify the subject? A thesis? Can you tell anything about the writer's tone?

3. **Look for a specific focus.** Where is the essay going? What appears to be its thesis? At what point does the introduction end and the body of the essay begin? What questions do you have about the essay so far?

4. **Think about the intended reader or readers.** Who is the intended audience? How would you describe it?

5. **Look for a predominant pattern of organization.** What are the most important ideas in the body of the essay? Note the patterns or modes the writer uses to develop those ideas.

6. **Identify the conclusion.** Where does the conclusion begin? How does it end the essay? What effect does it have on you?

7. **Evaluate the essay.** Did the essay answer the questions you had about it? How effective was the support for the main ideas? Did the writer's choice of words fit the audience? What effect did the essay have on you? Why?

POINTERS FOR WRITING AND REVISING

1. **Settle in.** Get hold of whatever you find comfortable to write with—computer, pen, pencil, legal pad, note paper, notebook—and settle into wherever you like to write. Start by jotting down words that represent a general idea of your subject. As words cross your mind, write them down so that at this point you have a vague focus.

2. **Focus.** Generate ideas by using your journal, clusters, timed writing, questions, strategies, listing, discussing—whatever works for you. Review your ideas and come up with a working thesis.

3. **Reread.** Go over what you've written, looking for sentences that state an opinion. Mark them in some way (a highlighter is useful). These sentences can become topic sentences that lead off paragraphs and therefore help organize the ideas. Work up those sentences and your tentative thesis into a rough draft.

4. **Organize what's there.** Go through the draft asking questions. What would make a good introduction? A good conclusion? What order best suits what's in between? What examples can you find? Where would they work best?

5. **Think about purpose.** As you reread, think about the kind of effect the paper should have on readers. Does it explain something to them? Argue a cause? Entertain? Some combination of purposes?

6. **Think about the readers.** What do they know about the subject? The answer to this question may help cut out some information; and what they don't know can be a guide to what needs to be included. Do they have a bias for or against the thesis? The answer will reveal whether those biases need to be accounted for and suggest how to do that.

7. **Revise.** You've probably been revising all along, but at this point you can revise more thoroughly and deeply. You know your purpose, audience, and thesis—all of which will help you organize your paper more effectively.

8. **Proofread.** Now look for surface errors, checking for spelling and punctuation. Run your text through the spelling checker, but pay attention to anything offered as a substitute because it

(Continued)

POINTERS FOR WRITING AND REVISING *(Continued)*

may be the wrong word. As for punctuation, if you have a grammar checker on your computer, try it. You may find it useful, but probably a handbook of grammar and usage will be much more helpful because the explanations are fuller and you'll find lots of examples. Just look up the key word in the handbook's index.

On Using Description

L ori Jakiela begins her essay "You'll Love the Way We Fly" by putting the reader in her shoes and space:

1   I'm in the galley, making coffee. I try to look busy, not in the mood to talk or help. This is the fourth leg of a six-leg day, and already I'm tired. I immerse myself in counting and recounting stacks of styrofoam cups, tightening the handles on metal coffee pots, scrubbing the steel galley counter until I can see my face, distorted and greenish in the plane's fluorescent light, eyes flecked with dried mascara.

2   I hear him coming before I can see him: the rustle of his nylon bag, brushing against seat backs and the heads of other passengers. He is old, thin. He plops the bag on the floor of the emergency exit row, right across from where I'm standing. I'm engrossed now in stocking Cokes into the beverage cart. I watch him from behind the galley wall, a talent all flight attendants learn, covert ways to size people up.

Immediately you know Jakiela is a flight attendant and passengers are boarding the plane, but that information is brought to life by details— the tasks she is carrying out, the way she looks, the passenger's progress down the aisle. And with her last sentence, she sets the focus for what is to follow, her sizing up.

Essays that rely on description recreate their subjects in such a way that they become alive again, so that the reader can see and understand them. While no essay relies solely on description, each of the essays that follow uses description as its primary pattern of organization. The essays' general subjects are familiar—a time of year, a place, a person—but by selecting details, each author tailors description uniquely.

How can you shape description for different purposes and readers? If, like Jakiela, you want to convey the impact of a chance meeting, you would be writing **exposition**[1] and your purpose would be

---

[1]Words printed in boldface are defined under "Useful Terms" at the end of each introductory section.

expository. When you read the rest of Jakiela's essay, you'll see her focus is clearly on her subject: She is the narrator, telling you about her subject, analyzing it, explaining it to you.

Jakiela writes for a general audience, one directly or indirectly familiar with commercial flights. In general, you address the same sort of audience in your own writing. You have a good idea about what your readers do and do not know. It also helps to know how your readers may feel about your subject and how you want them to feel.

How you want them to feel is a matter of **tone,** your attitude toward the subject and the audience. Many readers, for example, are understandably squeamish about the subject of war, and that creates a problem for the writer, particularly one who wants to describe a scene realistically and at the same time elicit sympathy. One solution is to pretty it up, but that does a disservice to reality; however, a description that is too realistic can be so revolting that no one would read it. Nor would anyone want to read a dry, objective account. Rudyard Kipling, whom many of us know through *The Jungle Book* and *The Second Jungle Book,* faced this problem when he wrote *The Irish Guards in the Great War,* a history of a military unit in World War I. His description of the German positions before the British attack on the Somme can be summarized objectively by removing most of the details to create an intentionally flat, dull tone:

> The Germans had been strengthening their defenses for two years. It was a defense in depth, exploiting the smooth slopes ascending to their high ground. They fortified forests and villages and dug deep underground shelters in the chalky soil. They protected their positions with copious wire, often arranged to force attackers into the fire of machine guns. (Fussell 172)

Now compare that prose with how Kipling solves the problem of tone by finding a middle yet realistic ground:

> Here the enemy had sat for two years, looking down upon France and daily strengthening himself. His trebled and quadrupled lines of defense, worked for him by his prisoners, ran below and along the flanks and on the tops of ranges of five-hundred-foot downs. Some of these were studded with close woods, deadlier even than the fortified villages between them; some cut with narrowing valleys that drew machine-gun fire as chimneys draw draughts; some opening into broad, seemingly smooth slopes, whose every haunch and hollow covered sunk forts, carefully placed mine-fields, machine-gun pits, gigantic quarries, enlarged in the chalk, connecting with systems of catacomb-like dug-outs and subterranean works at all depths, in which brigades could lie till the fitting

moment. Belt upon belt of fifty-yard-deep wire protected these points, either directly or at such angles as should herd and hold up attacking infantry to the fire of veiled guns. Nothing in the entire system had been neglected or unforeseen, except knowledge of the nature of the men who, in due time, should wear their red way through every yard of it.[2]

Kipling's description is essentially an explanation, but note the argumentative twist he puts in his last sentence, his reference to the men of the Irish Guards and their valiant attack and huge losses, the blood of their "red way." There's no question about whose side Kipling is on. And there's no question he wants to **persuade** his readers to sympathize with the Irish Guards.

How important are details? Details drive description. Note how many details are in the paragraph by Kipling, most of which are **concrete details.** The German defenses had not just been strengthened but "trebled and quadrupled." Nor is Kipling satisfied with **abstract words.** He tells us the quarries were "gigantic," an abstract word that has different meanings to different people, so he gives us a concrete sense of just how large those quarries are—they could hide whole brigades, groups of 1,500 to 3,300 soldiers. We get a visual idea of their size. Visual detail also helps us see the wire defenses. Kipling's prose was published shortly after the end of World War I, a time when tanks, missiles, and bombers as we know them were unheard of and the general particulars of trench warfare were still fresh in his readers' minds; they would know that the wire he refers to is barbed wire, but Kipling makes his audience (both then and now) see it by saying that it was "belt upon belt" of wire, "fifty-yard-deep" wire.

How can you make details effective? The words a writer chooses determine whether the description is more **objective** or **subjective,** whether its tone is factual or impressionistic. Although total objectivity is impossible, description that leans toward the objective is called for when the writer wants to focus on the subject as opposed to emotional effect, on what something is rather than how it felt.

The second paragraph of Jakiela's essay presents an objective account of the passenger: "I hear him coming before I can see him: the rustle of his nylon bag, brushing against seat backs and the heads of other passengers. He is old, thin. He plops the bag on the floor of

---

[2]Quoted in Paul Fussell's *The Great War and Modern Memory*. New York: Oxford UP, 1977.

the emergency exit row, right across from where I'm standing." But the next paragraph shifts:

> His hair is gray, and saliva has settled into the corners of his mouth. He holds a filthy handkerchief to his nose. He is coughing, a deep-lunged cough, the kind that fades into a feathery wheeze then begins again, a terrifying, endless loop. A pack of Marlboros is tucked into his left sock.

The more subjective description has an emotional effect.

What is the role of comparisons?   Take any object and try to describe what it looks, feels, smells, sounds, and tastes like, and you'll quickly find yourself shifting over to comparisons. Comparisons enrich description in that they can:

- produce an arresting image
- explain the unfamiliar
- make a connection with the reader's own experience
- reinforce the major point in the essay

Comparing the unfamiliar to the familiar makes what is being described more real. The term *World Wide Web* evokes an electronic spider web that encompasses the globe. The image is a metaphor, and often comparisons take the form of **metaphor, simile,** or **allusion.**

Simile and *metaphor* both draw a comparison between dissimilar things; the terms differ in that a simile uses a comparative word such as *like* or *as.* As a result, metaphor is often the more arresting because it is a direct equation. If you were writing and got stuck to the point where nothing worked—the classic writer's block—you might describe your state as "sinking in the quicksand of words."

Unfortunately, the first comparisons that often come to mind can be overworked ones known as **clichés**: *green as grass, hot as hell, mad as a hornet, red as a rose,* and the like. You can guard against them by being suspicious of any metaphor or simile that sounds familiar.

Analogy is another form of comparison. Think of it as a metaphor that is extended beyond a phrase into several sentences or a paragraph. You can understand how that can happen if you think of a metaphor for the way you write. Some may imagine a roller coaster; others might think of having to manage a busy switchboard; and for some it may be trying to build a house without having any blueprints or knowing what materials are needed. No matter which image, you can tell that it will take more than a sentence or two to develop the metaphor into an analogy.

How can you organize your essay? All the details, all the comparisons are organized so that they add up to a single dominant impression. In descriptive essays, this single dominant impression may be implicit or explicit, and it stands as the **thesis.** An explicit thesis jumps off the page and is usually stated openly in one or two easily identifiable sentences. An implicit thesis is more subtle. As reader, you can come to understand what the thesis is even though you can't identify any single sentence that states it. If that process of deduction seems mysterious, think of reading a description of the ultimate pizza, a description that alluringly recounts its aroma, taste, texture. After reading about that pizza you would probably think, Wow, that's a really good pizza. And that's an implied thesis.

Whether implicit or explicit, the thesis is what the writer builds the essay around. It's the main point. The writer must select the most important details, create sentences and paragraphs around them, and then sequence the paragraphs so that everything not only contributes to but also helps create the thesis. In description, paragraphs can be arranged by **patterns of organization,** such as process and definition, and according to spatial, temporal, or dramatic relationships. The writer can describe a scene so that the reader moves from one place to another, from one point in time to another, or according to a dramatic order. If this last idea seems vague, think of how a film or novel builds to a high point, one that usually occurs just before the end.

The building block for that high point and for the essay itself is the paragraph. And just as the essay has a controlling idea, an assertion that is its thesis, so, too, does the paragraph, usually in the form of a **topic sentence.** Like the thesis, the topic sentence can be explicit or implied, and it can be found in one sentence or deduced from the statements made in several. Because paragraphs frequently cluster around a central idea, particularly in a longer essay, one over 600 words or so, a topic sentence often covers more than one paragraph.

There's no magic number for how many words make up a paragraph and no magic number for how many paragraphs make up an essay, but it is safe to say that all essays have a beginning, middle, and end. The same is true of a paragraph or group of paragraphs that function under one topic sentence. As you read, ask yourself why a given paragraph ends where it does and how it connects to the one that follows. You may discover that sometimes paragraph breaks are not set in cement, that they could occur in several different places and still be "right."

Useful Terms

Abstract words Words that stand for something that cannot be easily visualized and, therefore, may hold different meanings for different people. A box of cereal labeled "large" may be your idea of "small."

Allusion An indirect reference to a real or fictitious person, place, or thing.

Analogy A point-by-point comparison to something seemingly unlike but more commonplace and less complex than the subject. An analogy is also an extended metaphor.

Cliché A comparison, direct or indirect, that has been used so often that it has worn out its novelty, such as *cool as a cucumber* or *ice cold*.

Concrete details Words that stand for something that can be easily visualized and have fixed meaning. If you replaced the "large" on the cereal box with "8 ounces" or "two servings for moderately hungry people," you would be replacing the abstract with more definite, concrete details.

Exposition Writing that explains; also called expository writing.

Metaphor An implied but direct comparison in which the primary term is made more vivid by associating it with a quite dissimilar term. "Life is a roller coaster" is a metaphor.

Objective prose Writing that is impersonal.

Patterns of organization Paragraphs and essays are usually organized according to the patterns illustrated in this book: description, narration, example, division and classification, comparison, process, cause and effect, and definition. Although more than one pattern may exist in a paragraph or essay, often one predominates.

Persuasion Writing that argues a point, that attempts to convince the reader to adopt the writer's stand.

Simile A comparison in which the primary term is linked to a dissimilar one by *like* or *as* to create a vivid image. "Life is like a roller coaster" is a simile. Remove the linking word and you have a metaphor.

Subjective prose Writing that is personal.

Thesis A one-sentence statement or summary of the basic arguable point of the essay.

Tone A writer's attitude toward the subject and the audience.

Topic sentence A statement of the topic of a paragraph containing an arguable point that is supported by the rest of the paragraph.

POINTERS FOR USING DESCRIPTION

Exploring the Topic

1. **What distinguishes your topic?** What characteristics, features, or actions stand out about your subject? Which are most important? Least important?
2. **To what senses can you appeal?** What can you emphasize about your subject that would appeal to sight? Smell? Touch? Taste? Motion?
3. **What concrete details can you use?** What abstract words do you associate with each of the features or events you want to emphasize? How can you make those abstractions concrete?
4. **How can you vary your narrative?** Where might you use quotations? Where might you use dialogue?
5. **What can your audience identify with?** What comparisons can you use? What similes, metaphors, or allusions come to mind?
6. **What order should you use?** Is your description best sequenced by time? Place? Dramatic order?
7. **What is your tentative thesis?** What is the dominant impression you want to create? Do you want it to be implicit? Explicit?
8. **What is your relationship to your subject?** Given your tentative thesis, how objective or subjective should you be? Do you want to be part of the action or removed from it? What personal pronoun should you use?

Drafting the Paper

1. **Know your reader.** If you are writing about a familiar subject, ask yourself what your reader might not know about it. If you are writing about an unfamiliar subject, ask yourself what your reader does know that you can use for comparison.
2. **Know your purpose.** If you are writing to inform, make sure you are presenting new information and offering enough detail to bring your subject to life. If you are writing to persuade, make sure your details add up so that the reader is moved to adopt your conviction. Keep in mind that your reader may not share your values and indeed may even hold opposite ones.

(Continued)

POINTERS FOR USING DESCRIPTION *(Continued)*

3. **Vary sensory details.** Emphasize important details by appealing to more than just one sense.
4. **Show, don't tell.** Avoid abstract terms such as *funny* or *beautiful.* Instead, use concrete details, quotations, and dialogue. Don't settle for vague adjectives such as *tall;* replace them with sharper details such as *6 feet 7 inches.*
5. **Use comparisons.** Make your description vivid with an occasional metaphor or simile. If you are writing about something quite unfamiliar, use literal comparison to make your description clear.
6. **Arrange your details to create a single dominant impression.** If you are writing descriptive paragraphs, check the order of your sentences to make sure they follow each other logically and support the impression you wish to create. If you are writing an essay that relies heavily on description, check for the same points from one paragraph to another. Is your topic sentence or thesis implicit or explicit? Reexamine your first paragraph. Does it establish the scene? The tone?

Summer Wind

Verlyn Klinkenborg

*Given his name, Verlyn Klinkenborg might more likely be the author of a
Scandinavian cookbook than a regular contributor to* The New York
Times *editorial pages. But the title of his column—"The Rural Life"—
accurately reflects his close relationship with nature.* Making Hay *(1986),
his first book, takes his readers to Iowa, Minnesota, and Montana, and
established him as a writer who lyrically depicts and admires the small
details of living and working on small family farms.* The Last Fine Time
*(1992) is very different and explores immigrant life in Buffalo, New York,
and its suburbs. Klinkenborg returns to nature in* The Rural Life *(2003),
a collection of his columns published in* The New York Times, *and in*
Timothy, Or Notes of an Abject Reptile *(2006) in which Klinkenborg
writes from the perspective of an eighteenth-century tortoise. He writes
from his own perspective in "Summer Wind," which the* Times *published
on July 18, 2008. His essays have also appeared in* The New Yorker,
Harper's Magazine, National Geographic, *and* Esquire.

What to Look For   Describing a summer wind may be a bit like trying
to explain a joke—you have to try to recreate it. As you read Klinkenborg's
essay, look for the ways he brings the wind to life.

1   For the past few hours, the wind has been rising and falling, the
precursor of a storm coming in from the west. When the wind
climbs, a kind of elation blows through the house—it's the hushing
sound of the leaves outside and the way the breeze sweeps
the floors and lifts the curtains and slams the doors. The dogs
snap to and look around when it gusts. And when the wind drops,
it seems to drop us—the dogs and me—into the trough of an
ordinary summer day.

2   I spent a humid morning recently in the barnyard with the farrier,
who was shoeing Remedy, my quarter horse. Remedy was dozing
the way a customer sometimes dozes in a barber's chair. First one
hoof, then another. Heel and toe trimmed and rasped and the shoe
nailed home, followed by more rasping. The other horses stood in
the corral, lower lips drooping in the heat. A twist of wind came
across the pasture, up from the highway, stirring the sumac along

the fenceline. The farrier stopped and stretched his back. Remedy shifted his feet and looked intently at the mares. I turned my face into the wind and recoiled the lead rope.

3   The breeze this afternoon is like respiration, in and out pretty steadily with a prolonged sigh now and then. In the pauses, when the wind is still, I can feel the expectation of a storm building. This isn't simply the quiet of an afternoon. It's the quiet in which something is about to happen.

4   I hope it's a good storm, a high wind, rain slanting across the pastures, geese splashing in the sudden puddles, chickens huddled inside their house trying to keep the wind from getting under their feathers. For a moment, the house I'm in seems to inflate, to fill with air that was just outside a few seconds ago. For a moment, it feels like a sail filling, lifting, as though this cranky old farmhouse might loose its mooring and reach toward the sea.

ORGANIZATION AND IDEAS

1. Trace how Klinkenborg uses time in his essay. What occurs when? Why might he have structured the essay as he did?
2. Think of the wind as a character in the essay. How does Klinkenborg portray it?
3. Klinkenborg mentions his dogs and horses. What do they add to the essay?
4. The essay begins and ends with the idea of the impending storm. How effectively does that frame his description?
5. Given how Klinkenborg portrays the wind and the coming storm, what do you find to be his thesis?

TECHNIQUE AND STYLE

1. What unusual words does Klinkenborg use? What reasons can you think of for those choices?
2. Klinkenborg compares his farm to a boat in paragraph 4. How effective is that comparison?
3. Paragraph 2 focuses on shoeing Remedy, a process you are probably not familiar with. How does Klinkenborg describe the scene so that you can see it?
4. Klinkenborg describes the dropping of the wind as "it seems to drop us—the dogs and me—into the trough of an ordinary summer day." Look up *trough* in a dictionary to explain how his choice of words works.
5. The words *farm* and *farmer* bring to mind certain images. To what extent do the farm and the Klinkenborg you meet in the essay conform to those images?

SUGGESTIONS FOR WRITING

Journal

1. Explain why you would or would not like to be part of the scene Klinkenborg describes.

2. Klinkenborg describes the feeling he has as the storm approaches as "the quiet in which something is about to happen." Describe one or two situations you have been in that had the same feeling.

Essay

1. Think of a force of nature that you have experienced. Write your own essay that describes the scene and how it affected you. Possible topics:

blizzard
flood
tornado
hurricane
riptide

2. Klinkenborg describes a quiet day in the life of his farm that he both enjoys and savors. Think about your own experiences and a quiet day that gave you pleasure. Choose a few key elements from that day to use in your own descriptive essay, making a point similar to Klinkenborg's.

The Bridge

Jason Holland

Almost everyone has a special place, either in the present or past, that represents any number of emotions, pleasure being first among them. For Jason Holland, that place was a bridge and the time was when he was in high school. At the time he wrote the essay, he was a student at Valley City State University in Valley City, North Dakota, having decided on attending VCSU because of the academic and athletic opportunities the university provided. When he began his first-semester composition course, he says that he was "somewhat skeptical of my writing skills, but began finding it was easy to write about memorable moments," particularly those spent with his friends in high school. He used "writing about these incidents as an outlet as well as a coping device" to accommodate himself to the difficulties of college life. One of the results is what he characterizes

*as "a short, descriptive essay," "The Bridge." Noreen Braun, his
instructor, reprinted the essay on a Web page devoted to what she
titled as "Some Fine Student Writing from Composition I, Fall
Semester, 1997."*

What to Look For   If you are having a difficult time giving your
reader a vivid picture of your scene, you might try writing down as
many adjectives and adverbs about various objects or people as you
associate with the place. After you have done this, then you can
choose the most appropriate ones. That is what Jason Holland did
when he was coming up with his descriptive essay about his adventures with his friends on a condemned bridge. As you read the essay
look specifically at the detail he uses to enhance his essay.

1   I can see it now. The four of us sitting out on the wood bridge
puffing on our cheap, Swisher cigars. The smoke rising above the
rusty, cast iron sides and filtering up to the full moon above. As
the moon reflects off the Goose River my friends and I sit and talk
about everything from girls to UFO theories. We sit without a
worry on our minds.

2   The bridge looks like it's something from a surreal movie with a
midnight atmosphere. Located two miles out of town, it's hidden on
a winding, gravel road that sometimes gets washed out if it rains
heavily. Because of the lack of maintenance the bridge has old oak
and maple trees leaning against it. The wood tiling on the bottom is
spaced far apart, almost to the point where our feet could fall
through.

3   When we were at the bridge we felt as though nothing could
go wrong. We thought that all our problems and fears would go
away if we stayed out there long enough. We felt as though our
parents, teachers, and coaches had no control over us. We could
talk about anything and anyone without even thinking about the
consequences. No one could touch us. We were like 1920 bootleg
gangsters that the law couldn't catch up with. We were almost in-
vincible as we smoked our cigars and talked about our dreams
and aspirations.

4   As we sat and smoked it felt as though we were the only people
on earth. The world revolved around us. It was like we could control the world while we were out at the bridge. It was a rickety, old

bridge, but it seemed to empower us to the point where we felt as though we could control our own destiny. My friend who didn't do well in school was a smarter and more insightful person when he was at the bridge. My friend who wasn't good at athletics felt like he was as good an athlete as any professional. My friend who didn't have a girlfriend seemed like he was a savvy, babe magnet. The bridge had the power to give us confidence.

5   The bridge was county property, but my friends and I felt like we were the owners. It was a mutual relationship. We owned the bridge, and the bridge owned us. On the long, cool summer nights we knew that the bridge needed company so we would get our cigars and take a ride down the long, windy road and leave our problems behind. We sat out at the bridge for hours basking in the sounds of an occasional swat of a mosquito, the cooing of an owl in the distance, the splashing of a fish in the river, with the cool yet comfortable, windless night.

6   I haven't yet found a place where I could be so much in my own world and in my own element as I could when I was at the bridge. Having my best friends and cheap cigars made me enjoy it even more.

ORGANIZATION AND IDEAS

1. Paragraph 1 tells you where the scene takes place and who is there. What else does it do?
2. Examine paragraphs 2–5 and in one or two words list a subject or main idea for each one. What progression do you find?
3. Considering the ideas you identified in question 2, what does the bridge represent to the writer?
4. State the thesis of the essay in your own words. Where in the essay does the writer place the thesis? How effective do you find that placement?
5. How important is it to have a place where you can "be in [your] own world and in [your] own element"?

TECHNIQUE AND STYLE

1. In a handbook of grammar and style, look up *sentence fragment* and then reexamine Holland's second and third sentences. What are they missing? Explain whether the two sentences are acceptable fragments.
2. If you vary the length of your sentences, you'll find that your prose moves more smoothly and is apt to be of greater interest to the reader. What evidence can you find that Holland uses this technique?
3. Reread paragraph 2. Which sentence functions as a topic sentence? What words in the other sentences are related to it?

4. Repetition can be effective or ineffective. Explain how you judge Holland's similar sentence beginnings in paragraph 3.

5. Reread paragraph 5, looking for details that appeal to the senses. What are they?

SUGGESTIONS FOR WRITING

Journal

1. Imagine that you are the narrator of "The Bridge." What "problems and fears" would you be leaving behind?

2. Holland describes the bridge as looking like "something from a surreal movie with a midnight atmosphere." Think about places you know about that match that description and describe one of them.

Essay

1. Almost everyone has at least one "special place" that represents a particular mood or feeling, either positive or negative. To write an essay about such a place that holds meaning for you, think first about an emotion and then about the place you associate with it. Here's a list of emotions to consider, but others will probably occur to you as well:

comfort
fear
happiness
excitement
curiosity

Once you've decided on a topic, then you can start accumulating details that will make your scene and the way you feel about it come alive for the reader.

2. Holland's essay deals with two strong human bonds—to place and to a sense of community. Choose one of the two and analyze its importance to you. Try to distance yourself from your subject by limiting your use of the first person *I* so that what you write is a general thought piece rather than a narrative or personal essay.

Tommy

Kelly Ruth Winter

*A recent graduate of the University of Iowa, where she majored in
English as well as Journalism and Mass Communication, Kelly Ruth
Winter is already on her way to a career in writing literary nonfic-
tion. While at Iowa, her honors thesis earned her the university's
Anderson Prize for Undergraduate Expository Writing. She is now in
graduate school at the university, working on an MAT in English
Education. Her work has appeared in* upstreet, *a literary anthology
published annually, and in* Brevity, *a journal devoted to short essays
by emerging and established writers. Winter's "Tommy" appeared in*
Brevity's *twenty-fifth issue, published in the fall of 2007.*

What to Look For   When you read Winter's essay, note how she uses
present tense and short paragraphs to recreate the different times within
her narrative. Also, pause after each group of short paragraphs to think
about how they function as a unit.

1   Tommy Schmidt does not drink milk. He is scrawny and freckled and eight years old to my five. We are in love.

2   His mom pays my mom to watch him after school. I watch him
from the kitchen as he sits Indian-style on the brown shag carpet in
front of our T.V.

3   Later, in the entryway of our house, Tommy and I tap our feet on
the linoleum, imitating the patterns of speech.

4   Tap, ta—p, tap, says the dirty sole of his white tennis shoe.

5   "I love you?" I guess.

6   He grins.

7   The next day, I draw a picture of us getting married, crisscross-
ing the pencil over my face for the veil. I include a baby. My mom
says I shouldn't have my baby at my wedding. Her eyebrows say
I shouldn't marry Tommy.

8   A year later, I sit in the middle of the school bus while Tommy
sits in back with the older kids. I lean into the aisle, pretend to look
out the back window, but really look at him.

9   He's a bad boy now. I can tell from his ripped jeans and the number of times the bus driver makes him sit up front. His eyes meet mine, and he hands me a half-dollar-sized piece of leather covered in turquoise beads.

10   "Want it?" he asks.

11   "Sure. Thanks." I face the front and bite my smile. At home, I tuck the trinket in my pink plastic jewelry box, next to the beaded Indian figurine from my family's South Dakota vacation.

12   The summer after second grade, my family moves seven miles, from one tiny Iowa town to another, so I don't have to ride the bus anymore. My dad gives Tommy's dad our old record player—a big wooden box with a heavy hinged lid.

13   I miss listening to the Oakridge Boys and hopping until the record skips and I am told to settle down.

14   My dad and Tommy's dad used to ride motorcycles out to Wyoming and Washington, sleeping in a tent along the way. I imagine our fathers each rolling a t-shirt to fit in the pouches on the backrests of their bikes.

15   If our fathers rolled their t-shirts, kept them in the leather pouches of motorcycles, if they listen to the same music on the very same record player, what made me good and Tommy bad?

16   When Tommy is in sixth grade and I am in third, he lights his house on fire and tries to kill himself with a pair of scissors.

17   During art class, I stare at a blue vein that snakes from my palm, then run the edge my scissors over it. A faint white line appears, then vanishes.

18   My mom says Tommy's in a mental institution.

19   Tommy's freckled mug smiles from his first-grade picture as my dad and I page through my photo book.

20   "You should probably rip that up and throw it away," he tells me. I am ten, struggling through multiplication tables, but taking straight A's in everything else. My dad wants me to stay away from the bad kids.

21   I tear up the picture, but feel guilty as I stare at the pieces of Tommy's face in my pink garbage can.

22   Later, I am relieved to find his second-grade picture farther back in the book.

23   When I'm in high school and Tommy has long since dropped out, he comes in the town hardware store where I work, dusting shelves and helping customers find pop rivets and three-eighths-sized bolts.

24   He's been in and out of boys' homes and jail, has long, frayed rust-colored hair, and is missing his front right tooth—but I still recognize him.

25   "Shotgun shells," he says, voice low.

26   I bite my lip and try not to look at him as I stride to the case. I want him to recognize me, to tell me that I grew up pretty. But he just follows me, stares at the floor.

27   Fumbling with the keys, I wonder if I should sell him shotgun shells at all—but there's no background check for ammunition. When I count back the change, my fingertips graze his palm. He just grabs his shells and saunters out the door.

28   After I graduate, I go to college with my scholarships and hand-me-down T.V.

29   Tommy dies alone at his parents' house in the country. Suicide, but I'll never know how. Sitting alone in my apartment, I find his obituary online, only five lines long.

ORGANIZATION AND IDEAS

1. The short paragraphs form seven distinct times in Winter's life. How old is Winter in each one?

2. In paragraph 17, what does the "white line" suggest about the relationship between Winter and Tommy?

3. The essay deals with scenes from different times of Winter's life, but those times also correspond to different stages of maturity. What are those stages?

4. What does Winter think about and feel toward Tommy? What can you infer that Tommy thinks and feels toward Winter?

5. Winter never states her thesis but instead describes Tommy and how she feels about him. What thesis can you deduce from what she says?

TECHNIQUE AND STYLE

1. In paragraph 9, Tommy gives Winter a "half-dollar-sized piece of leather covered in turquoise beads." What might it symbolize or represent? What is Winter's reaction?

2. Reread the essay looking for contrasts. What do you find and what meaning do they carry?

3. Winter poses a question in paragraph 15. What answers does the essay suggest?

4. Take a look at the last sentence in the essay. What impact does it have?

5. Throughout the essay, Winter manages to imply a great deal in only a few simple words as in her opening sentence: "Tommy Schmidt does not drink milk." Where else in the essay does she use this technique? How effective is it?

SUGGESTIONS FOR WRITING

Journal

1. What other titles can you think of for the essay? Which do you prefer and why?
2. Use your journal to describe your own encounter with a "bad boy" or "bad girl."

Essay

1. Winter describes various stages in her relationship with Tommy, starting with when she was five and ending with her going to college. Write your own essay in which you compare a "then" and a "now." If, like Winter, you want to spell out the stages in between, fine; but if you just want to focus on the contrast, that's fine too. Possible topics:
   friendship
   political view
   change of mind
   taste in music
   event
2. Readers may respond to Winter's essay in different ways, but most will agree it makes quite an impact. Reread the essay noting the various ways Winter creates that impact, and write an essay that analyzes her techniques. You will find that you need to quote from the essay, but remember that when you do you also need to comment on the quotation.

You'll Love the Way We Fly

Lori Jakiela

The title of Lori Jakiela's essay was for years the popular advertising slogan for Delta Airlines, a time when Jakiela worked for Delta as a flight attendant. She recounts some of her experiences in her memoir Miss New York Has Everything *(2006). One of those experiences forms the basis of the essay that follows. Jakiela now directs the writing program at the University of Pittsburgh at Greensburg and is an established writer whose work has been published in a number of journals,* Double Take, Creative Nonfiction, The Chicago Review, *and* Slipstream *among them. You would enjoy her Web site, http://www.lorijakiela.com/bio.aspx, where she points out that her name rhymes with tequila and that her hometown is known as "the birthplace of the chocolate-covered pickle." And if you click on "Favorite Links," you find a list of various "magazines, publishers, books, and wonderful writers and writers' organizations." The essay below appeared in* Creative Nonfiction, *issue 27, in 2005.*

What to Look For   As you read Jakiela's essay, you'll see how closely related description is to narration. What happens in the essay supplies the narrative, but the descriptions bring it alive.

1   **I'**m in the galley, making coffee. I try to look busy, not in the mood to talk or help. This is the fourth leg of a six-leg day, and already I'm tired. I immerse myself in counting and recounting stacks of Styrofoam cups, tightening the handles on metal coffee pots, scrubbing the steel galley counter until I can see my face, distorted and greenish in the plane's fluorescent light, eyes flecked with dried mascara.

2   I hear him coming before I can see him: the rustle of his nylon bag, brushing against seat backs and the heads of other passengers. He is old, thin. He plops the bag on the floor of the emergency exit row, right across from where I'm standing. I'm engrossed now in stocking Cokes into the beverage cart. I watch him from behind the galley wall, a talent all flight attendants learn, covert ways to size people up.

3   His hair is gray, and saliva has settled into the corners of his mouth. He holds a filthy handkerchief to his nose. He is coughing, a deep-lunged cough, the kind that fades into a feathery wheeze then begins again, a terrifying, endless loop. A pack of Marlboros is tucked into his left sock.

4   I am afraid to go near him, afraid of what I might catch. When you make your living on an airplane, there are things you become afraid of, like germs and crashes and how cold the ocean is off LaGuardia in winter.

5   "They're not supposed to let them on like this," says my friend, who's working with me.

6   They're not supposed to let them on drunk, either, but this is how it is. That's what I think, but I don't say anything.

7   The man coughs, then follows with his wet-rattled breaths.

8   I think: This is serious, maybe not contagious, but serious. I call to him from the galley. "Sir, would you like water?"

9   He wheezes, coughs, shakes his head. I look at my friend, who's busy alphabetizing magazines and stacking pillows in the overhead bins.

10   "Excuse me, sir?" I say. "Can I get you something?

11   He coughs, points. Coffee.

12   "Cream and sugar?"

13   He nods, and so I bring him what he wants, along with some water.

14   "Thank you," he says and grabs hold of my hand. I feel myself pull back. His hand is damp and cold; the fingers are all bone. "Thank you, I—" he coughs again, and I don't get the rest, so I have to lean closer, "—really appreciate."

15   Later, he tries to give me a tip: two quarters wrapped in a wet dollar and held together with a rubber band. I say, "No, no," but he presses it into my palm, gasping, "You take it for taking care. I appreciate."

16   The effort of breathing has made him sound foreign. He's American, I'm sure, a New Yorker, though disease has taken the hardness out of his eyes. They are brown and damp, the whites yellowing like old paper. Still, he thinks small kindnesses are things you have to pay for.

17   I haven't really been kind. I've just done my job, against what I wanted, despite my own disgust. I am paid to smile, to talk to strangers about the latest issue of *People,* to bring coffee and water, to make people comfortable.

18   I take the money.

19   "What is it you say?" he's asking, but I don't understand. "What is it you say on TV?"

20   "You'll love the way we fly," my friend sing-songs from the galley.

21   The man nods gravely, repeats it.

22   I laugh now. I don't know what else to do. He's dying, I'm sure. Emphysema or lung cancer, probably, like my father.

23   The flight is only an hour, D.C. to New York. When the man gets up to leave, I keep my head down, eyes focused on my hand, checking off items on a list. What we need: tea bags, stir sticks, Band-Aids, first-aid cream, two bags of peanuts. I try not to think, but I can't help it.

24   Who will be there in the airport to meet him? What is his home like? Who brings him coffee the way he likes it? Who is not afraid to touch him?

Organization and Ideas

1. In what ways does the essay relate to the slogan that provides the title?

2. Describe what the essay reveals about Jakiela. How would you characterize her?

3. In paragraph 2, Jakiela watches the passenger "from behind the galley wall, a talent all flight attendants learn, covert ways to size people up." How accurate is her initial impression?

4. The similar actions and details from paragraph 1 are repeated in paragraph 23. How effective is that framing device?

5. The essay is a good example of an implied thesis. Given what you now know about the situation, the passenger, and Jakiela, what thesis do you draw out?

TECHNIQUE AND STYLE

1. Reread the essay noting Jakiela's use of appeals to the senses. What do you find? Which ones stand out? What reasons can you find for that choice?

2. The essay incorporates a fair amount of dialogue. What does it add? How realistic do you find it?

3. What does the incident with the tip suggest? What does it add to the essay?

4. Given the essay as a whole, what do you learn about Jakiela? Do you find anything that is unnecessary, and if so, how so?

5. The essay ends with a string of questions. What answers, if any, are implied? How effective is the ending?

SUGGESTIONS FOR WRITING

Journal

1. Like Jakiela, you have probably had to do something you didn't want to do but felt obliged to do it. Select one example and describe it in your journal.

2. Reread the essay's last paragraph and supply your own answers, explaining them.

Essay

1. In a way, Jakiela's essay is about living up to what's expected of her as a flight attendant. That sort of pressure applies to many different situations. Consider your own experience from that perspective, one of having to meet expectations. Possible topics:

    as a parent, son, or daughter
    in a job
    as a student
    as an owner of an animal
    as a citizen

2. Doing one's job can be demanding. Think about the jobs you have had and their demands. What were they? What effect did they have? How did you respond to those demands? What did you learn or conclude from your experience? Choose one experience and describe it so that your reader understands your position and your conclusions.

El Hoyo

Mario Suárez

Son of immigrants and the oldest of five children, Mario Suárez grew up in Tucson, Arizona, in the neighborhood known as "El Hoyo." Shortly after graduating from high school, Suárez joined the Navy and served his tour of duty during World War II. When he returned home, he enrolled at the University of Arizona and found himself taking freshman English. The essay that follows was written for that class and so impressed his teacher, Ruth Keenan, that she not only encouraged him to take other writing courses but also to submit "El Hoyo" to the Arizona Quarterly, where it was published. That was a long time ago (1947), but it started Suárez on a successful writing career; it rare for any anthology of Chicano literature to not include at least one of Suárez's works. Hailed as a "key figure in the foundation of Chicano literature," Suárez's stories have recently been collected and reissued as Chicano Sketches, published by the University of Arizona Press in 2004.

What to Look For   Like many writers, Suárez faces the problem of explaining the unfamiliar, but for Suárez the problem is compounded. Many of his readers do not know the meaning of *barrio,* nor are they familiar with Latino culture. Some of those who do know the terms may have negative associations with them. As you read his essay, note the techniques he uses to combat these problems. Also note how Suárez uses repetition effectively to lend emphasis to his description. Read Suárez's second paragraph out loud so you can hear the repetition more clearly.

1   From the center of downtown Tucson the ground slopes gently away to Main Street, drops a few feet, and then rolls to the banks of the Santa Cruz River. Here lies the section of the city known as El Hoyo. Why it is called El Hoyo is not very clear. In no sense is it a hole as its name would imply; it is simply the river's immediate valley. Its inhabitants are chicanos who raise hell on Saturday night and listen to Padre Estanislao on Sunday morning. While the term chicano is the short way of saying Mexicano, it is not restricted to the paisanos who came from old Mexico with the territory or the last famine to work for the railroad,

labor, sing, and go on relief. Chicano is the easy way of referring to everybody. Pablo Gutíerrez married the Chinese grocer's daughter and now runs a meat department; his sons are chicanos. So are the sons of Killer Jones who threw a fight in Harlem and fled to El Hoyo to marry Cristina Mendez. And so are all of them. However, it is doubtful that all these spiritual sons of Mexico live in El Hoyo because they love each other—many fight and bicker constantly. It is doubtful they live in El Hoyo because of its scenic beauty—it is everything but beautiful. Its houses are simple affairs of unplastered adobe, wood, and abandoned car parts. Its narrow streets are mostly clearings which have, in time, acquired names. Except for some tall trees which nobody has ever cared to identify, nurse, or destroy, the main things known to grow in the general area are weeds, garbage piles, dark-eyed chavalos, and dogs. And it is doubtful that the chicanos live in El Hoyo because it is safe—many times the Santa Cruz has risen and inundated the area.

2   In other respects living in El Hoyo has its advantages. If one is born with weakness for acquiring bills, El Hoyo is where the collectors are less likely to find you. If one has acquired the habit of listening to Octavio Perea's Mexican Hour in the wee hours of the morning with the radio on at full blast, El Hoyo is where you are less likely to be reported to the authorities. Besides, Perea is very popular and sooner or later to everyone "Smoke in the Eyes" is dedicated between the pinto beans and white flour commercials. If one, for any reason what-ever, comes on an extended period of hard times, where, if not in El Hoyo, are the neighbors more willing to offer solace? When Teofila Malacara's house burned to the ground with all her belongings and two children, a benevolent gentleman carried through the gesture that made tolerable her burden. He made a list of 500 names and solicited from each a dollar. At the end of a month he turned over to the tearful but grateful señora $100 in cold cash and then accompanied her on a short vacation. When the new manager of a local store decided that no more chicanas were to work behind the counters, it was the chicanos of El Hoyo who, on taking their individually small but collectively great buying power elsewhere, drove the manager out and the girls returned to their jobs. When the Mexican Army was en route to Baja California and the chicanos found out that the enlisted men ate only at infrequent intervals, it was El Hoyo's chicanos who crusaded across town with pots of beans and trays of tortillas to meet the train. When someone gets married, celebrating is not restricted to the immediate friends of the couple. Everybody is invited. Anything calls for a celebration and a celebration calls for anything. On Memorial Day there are no less than half a dozen good fights at the Riverside Dance Hall. On Mexican

Independence Day more than one flag is sworn allegiance to amid cheers for the queen.

3   And El Hoyo is something more. It is this something more which brought Felipe Suárez back from the wars after having killed a score of Japanese with his body resembling a patchwork quilt to marry Julia Armijo. It brought Joe Zepeda, a gunner,…back to compose boleros. He has a metal plate for a skull. Perhaps El Hoyo is proof that those people exist, and perhaps exist best, who have as yet failed to observe the more popular modes of human conduct. Perhaps the humble appearance of El Hoyo justifies the indifferent shrug of those made aware of its existence. Perhaps El Hoyo's simplicity motivates an occasional chicano to move away from its narrow streets, babbling comadres and shrieking children to deny the bloodwell from which he springs and to claim the blood of a conquistador while his hair is straight and his face beardless. Yet El Hoyo is not an outpost of a few families against the world. It fights for no causes except those which soothe its immediate angers. It laughs and cries with the same amount of passion in times of plenty and of want.

4   Perhaps El Hoyo, its inhabitants, and its essence can best be explained by telling a bit about a dish called capirotada. Its origin is uncertain. But, according to the time and the circumstance, it is made of old, new or hard bread. It is softened with water and then cooked with peanuts, raisins, onions, cheese, and panocha. It is fired with sherry wine. Then it is served hot, cold, or just "on the weather" as they say in El Hoyo. The Sermeños like it one way, the Garcias another, and the Ortegas still another. While it might differ greatly from one home to another, nevertheless it is still capirotada. And so it is with El Hoyo's chicanos. While being divided from within and from without, like the capirotada, they remain chicanos.

ORGANIZATION AND IDEAS

1. Examine the essay using the standard journalistic questions. Which paragraph describes *where* El Hoyo is? What paragraphs describe *who* lives there? What paragraph or paragraphs describe *how* they live? *Why* they live there?

2. All of the questions above lead to a larger one: *What* is El Hoyo? Given the people and place, and how and why they live there, what statement is the author making about El Hoyo?

3. The essay ends with an analogy, and toward the end of paragraph 4, Suárez spells out some details of the analogy. What other characteristics of *capirotada* correspond to those of *chicanos*? Where in the essay do you find evidence for your opinion?

4. How would you describe the movement in the essay? Does it move from the general to the particular? From the particular to the general? What reasons can you give for the author's choice of direction?

5. It's obvious that Suárez likes and appreciates El Hoyo, but to what extent, if any, does he gloss over its negative qualities?

TECHNIQUE AND STYLE

1. The introductory paragraph achieves coherence and cohesion through the author's use of subtle unifying phrases. Trace Suárez's use of "it is doubtful." How often does the phrase occur? Rewrite the sentences to avoid using the phrase. What is lost? Gained?

2. What key words are repeated in paragraph 2? What is the effect of the repetition?

3. Paragraph 2 gives many examples of the advantages of living in El Hoyo. List the examples in the order in which they appear. The first two can be grouped together under the idea of El Hoyo as a sanctuary, a place where people aren't bothered. What other groupings does the list of examples suggest? What principle appears to have guided the ordering of the examples?

4. Why might the author have chosen not to use either first or second person? What is gained by using "one"?

SUGGESTIONS FOR WRITING

Journal

1. Write a journal entry explaining why you would or would not like to live in El Hoyo. Use examples from the essay to flesh out your reasons.

2. Suárez compares the dish capirotada to El Hoyo, developing it as a metaphor. Think of a metaphor that would work for your neighborhood or for one of your classes. Write a paragraph or two developing your comparison and you will probably discover that using metaphor may also make you see the familiar in a new way.

Essay

1. If you live in an ethnic neighborhood, you can use the essay as a close model. If you do not, you can still use the essay as a general model by choosing a topic that combines people and place. Suggestions:
    family ritual at Christmas, Hanukkah, or Ramadan
    family ritual at Thanksgiving
    dinner at a neighborhood restaurant
    busy time at the university student center

2. Write an essay analyzing and explaining why you would or would not like to live in El Hoyo. Use examples from the essay to flesh out your reasons.

On Using Narration

2

1   There was a peahen in the garage one day last week. It stayed four hours and left. A peahen, of course, is a female peacock, and the way you tell a peahen from a peacock is that a peahen is less ornamental and a peacock doesn't lay eggs.

2   The one in my garage was a sort of dull green—at least it would have been dull for a peacock, but being a peahen, I supposed it was about average. It was standing in front of the trash compactor, staring at a small red light that stays on while the compactor is in its "extra-pack" mode.

3   I saw the peahen as I came into the garage on my tractor, and while no exotic bird had ever wandered into my garage before, I was not in the frame of mind to appreciate it. While I'd been cutting the grass, the tractor had begun making horrible noises. I am close to my tractor; I depend on it emotionally. And until the day this happened, the tractor itself had always been so loud that I'd been unable to hear anything else while I was riding it. Or, now that I think about it, for a couple of hours afterward.

4   It seemed to me this was big trouble.

So begins Pete Dexter's narrative "A Fowl Trick to Play on a Lawn Tractor." As an introduction to his essay, it sets the scene, names the characters— Dexter, the peahen, and the tractor—hints at the conflict, and establishes a humorous tone. Reading it, you may note he draws on some of the same skills used in description:

- keen observation
- careful selection of details
- coherent sequencing

But to turn description into **narration,** you have to add two other elements:

- conflict
- resolution

The conflict in Dexter's essay appears to be man versus tractor.

All the essays in this chapter rely on narration for their primary structure. All present conflicts, build to a point, and spring from personal experience—from the something that happened. But narrative can also play a supporting role. In other chapters in this book, you'll see how writers use narrative to introduce or to conclude an essay or perhaps to do both, thus building a narrative framework. Narrative is also an effective way to emphasize a particular point.

How can questions generate ideas? *Who? What? Where? When? How? Why?*—all are standard questions used in journalism, and they can help you write narration. *What happened?* That's the essential question for narrative, and you'll probably find that the greater part of your essay supplies the answer. *How* and *why* will probably figure in as well, and *who* is obviously essential. But it's easy to neglect *where* and *when*.

If you think of both *where* and *when* as the **setting,** as ways to set the scene, you can remember them more easily and perhaps put them to good use. Dexter's setting is obviously rural, the kind of place that might well forge a bond between man and tractor and where a peahen may be out of place but not amazingly so. The tractor's home (and perhaps the peahen's too) is the garage, and that's also where the compactor sits. Tractor, peahen, and compactor supply a setting that builds the readers' interest in what will happen next, the meat of the essay.

How can you shape narration for your readers? Dexter uses his personal experience and the fight with his tractor to entertain. And since most of his reader know little about tractors and may have never seen a peahen, he has a lot of explaining to do, relying on details and description to fill the gaps. You'll find other essays in this chapter that address the problem of the distance between what the writer and what the reader knows: Meg Gifford writes about taking a "gap year"; Flavius Stan tells of a Christmas in Romania; Magdoline Asfahani writes about her heritage; Anchee Min analyzes the clash between two cultures. All depend on description, details, and comparisons to explain the unfamiliar. What you have learned about description in the previous chapter will help your reader see the scene, while details will make your narrative vivid.

What is the role of conflict? Narratives are structured around a **conflict.** In its simplest form, conflict is x versus y, Superman versus the Penguin, the Roadrunner versus Wile E. Coyote. But rarely does conflict exist in such a clear-cut way. Put real people in place of any of those names, and you begin to understand that what seemed so simple is not;

the defense versus the prosecution, a Republican candidate versus a Democrat—these conflicts are complex. The issues become even more complex when you substitute ideas, such as reality versus illusion, a distinction that even a postcard can blur (how many of us have been disappointed when a scene didn't live up to its photograph?). Even distinguishing good from evil isn't always clear, as the debates over capital punishment and abortion constantly remind us. When a writer explores the complexity involved in a conflict, the essay gains depth and substance, making the reader think. That exploration can be direct, such as naming the opposing forces, or indirect, implying them.

On the surface, Dexter's conflict is **external,** man versus machine. But he also has a love/hate relationship with that tractor, an **internal** battle. When you read the entire essay, you'll discover other conflicts as well.

How do you choose a point of view?   A not-so-obvious question about any narrative you're about to write is "Who tells it?" This question identifies the **point of view,** the perspective from which the narrative is related. Probably the first pronoun that comes to mind is *I,* first-person singular, and that's a good choice if you want your readers to identify with you and your angle on the narrative you're relating. When a reader sees first person, an automatic psychological identification takes place; you see Dexter's "big trouble" through his eyes. That sort of identification is strongest if you, like Dexter, are part of the action. Obviously, there's a huge difference between "I was there" and "I heard about it."

But using first person can be a hazard, and that's why at some point in some classroom, you have probably been warned off using *I.* There are at least three reasons: it's easy to overuse the pronoun; it can modify your purpose in a way you hadn't intended; and it can lead to an overly informal tone. If you were to take a look at your first draft for an essay you wrote using *I,* odds are you used it too frequently. The result is apt to be short, choppy sentences that are similar in structure—subject (*I*) followed by a verb and its complement (the word or words that complete the sense of the verb). That's fine for a first draft, and you can revise your way out of the problem. You *need* to revise because too many *I*'s can shift the aim of your essay away from exposition or argument to self-expression; what then becomes important is you, not your subject. Your tone may also change, becoming more informal than the assignment calls for, which is why you don't see many research papers that use first person.

Choosing to relate the narrative from the position of *he* or *she* (rarely *they*) puts more distance between the subject and the reader. Think of the difference between "I fell out of the window" and "He fell out of the window." The former enlists the reader's sympathy immediately, but the latter a bit less so. That's not the case with the second person, *you*. *You* is direct and that's what makes it a somewhat slippery choice. If you're going to use a second-person point of view, make sure the reader understands exactly who is meant by *you*. Many a teacher has been stopped short when reading an essay that has a sentence such as "When you graduate, you'll start looking for a job that can turn into a career." One way around that problem is to specify the audience in your paper. "All of us who are now in college worry about jobs" tells the reader just who the audience is, and the teacher then reads the essay from the perspective of a college student.

Where might you place the thesis and how should you lead up to it? Look again at Dexter's opening and you'll see that he begins with the setting, which is the context for the conflict, then establishes the nature of the conflict, and moves toward its resolution. That kind of introduction is typical of narratives, and setting, conflict, and resolution all reinforce the essay's thesis, one that can be explicit or implicit. If the thesis is explicit, it's apt to occur in the introduction; sometimes, however, the writer will reserve it for the conclusion. That kind of placement demands that everything in the essay builds to the conclusion. If the organization isn't tight, the reader wonders where the story is going; with a delayed thesis, the reader needs to have the feeling that the story is going somewhere, even though the final destination isn't apparent till the very end.

With narrative essays, as with short stories, the thesis is often implied and the reader must deduce it. If you opt for an implied thesis, make sure that the reader can easily identify your subject and then, without too much effort, move on to infer your thesis. The question that the reader needs to ask is "What is the writer saying about the subject?" The answer, phrased as a complete sentence, is the thesis.

You can control what the reader infers by working with the narrative's chronology. The sequence of events can be shaped to emphasize different elements. It may help to list the most important incidents in the narrative on a scrap of paper; then you can review them to check that each one is essential and to figure out the best order in which to present them. Writers often disrupt exact chronology, opting for dramatic placement over actual time sequence. The **flashback** is a technique that allows the writer to drop from the present into the past and bring in an event that occurred prior to the narrative's action. You may be most familiar with this device from seeing it in films, the moment when the camera fades out of a scene and then fades into a past event.

Useful Terms

Conflict An element essential to narrative. Conflict involves pitting one force, a force that may be represented by a person or a physical object or an abstract concept, against another.

External conflict Conflict that is outside of a person in the narrative though it may involve that person, as in St. George versus the Dragon.

Internal conflict Conflict that takes place within a person, as in "Should I or should I not?"

Flashback A break in the narrative that takes the reader to a scene or event that occurred earlier.

Narration Narration tells a story, emphasizing what happened.

Point of view In essays, point of view usually refers to the writer's use of personal pronouns. These pronouns control the perspective flow from which the work is written. For example, if the writer uses *I* or *we* (first-person pronouns), the essay will have a somewhat subjective tone because the reader will tend to identify with the writer. If the writer depends primarily on *he, she, it,* or *they* (third-person pronouns), the essay will have a somewhat objective tone because the reader will be distanced from the writer. Opting for *you* (second person) can be a bit tricky in that *you* can mean you the reader, quite particular, or you a member of a larger group, fairly general. In both cases, *you* brings the reader into the text.

Setting The *where* and *when* in the narrative, its physical context.

POINTERS FOR USING NARRATION

Exploring the Topic

1. **What point do you want to make?** What is the subject of your narrative? What assertion do you want your narrative to make about the subject? Is your primary purpose to inform, to persuade, or to entertain?

2. **What happened?** What are the events involved in the narrative? When does the action start? Stop? Which events are crucial?

3. **Why and how did it happen?** What caused the events? How did it cause them?

4. **Who or what was involved?** What does the reader need to know about the characters? What do the characters look like? Talk like? How do they think? How do others respond to them?

5. **What is the setting for your story?** What does the reader need to know about the setting? What features are particularly noteworthy? How can they best be described?

6. **When did the story occur?** What tense will be most effective in relating the narrative?

7. **What was the sequence of events?** What happened when? Within that chronology, what is most important: time, place, attitude?

8. **What conflicts were involved?** What levels of conflict exist? Is there any internal conflict?

9. **What is the relationship between the narrator and the action?** Is the narrator a participant or an observer? What is the attitude of the narrator toward the story? What feelings should the narrator evoke from the reader? What should be the attitude of the reader toward the narrative? What can be gained by using first person? Second person? Third person?

Drafting the Paper

1. **Know your reader.** Try to second-guess your reader's initial attitude toward your narrative so that if it is not what you want it to be, you can choose your details to elicit the desired reaction. A reader can be easily bored, so keep your details to the point and your action moving. Play on similar experiences your reader may have had or on information you can assume is widely known.

2. **Know your purpose.** If you are writing to inform, make sure you provide enough information to carry your point. If you are writing to persuade, work on how you present yourself and your thesis so that the reader will be favorably inclined to adopt your viewpoint. If you are writing to entertain, keep your tone in mind. A humorous piece, for instance, can and probably will vary from chuckle to guffaw to belly laugh. Make sure you're getting the right kind of laugh in the right place.

3. **Establish the setting and time of the action.** Use descriptive details to make the setting vivid and concrete. Keep in mind the

(Continued)

---

reaction you want to get from your reader, and choose your details accordingly. If, for instance, you are writing a narrative that depicts your first experience with fear, describe the setting in such a way that you prepare the reader for that emotion. If the time the story took place is important, bring it out early.

4. **Set out the characters.** When you introduce a character, immediately identify the person with a short phrase, such as "Anne, my sister." If a character doesn't enter the narrative until midpoint or so, make sure the reader is prepared for the entrance so that the person doesn't appear to be merely plopped in. If characterization is important to the narrative, use a variety of techniques to portray the character, but make sure whatever you use is consistent with the impression you want to create. You can depict a person directly—through appearance, dialogue, and actions—as well as indirectly—through what others say and think and how they act toward the person.

5. **Clarify the action.** Narration is set within strict time limits. Make sure the time frame of your story is set out clearly. Within that time limit, much more action occurred than you will want to use in your narrative. Pick only the high points so that every action directly supports your thesis. Feel free to tinker with the action, sacrificing a bit of reality for the sake of your point.

6. **Sharpen the plot.** Conflict is essential to narration, so be sure your lines of conflict are clearly drawn. Keeping conflict in mind, review the action you have decided to include so that the plot and action support each other.

7. **Determine the principle behind the sequence of events.** Given the action and plot you have worked out, determine what principle should guide the reader through the events. Perhaps time is the element you want to stress, perhaps place, perhaps gradual change. No matter what you choose, make sure that the sequence has dramatic tension so that it builds to the point you want to make.

8. **Choose an appropriate point of view.** Your choice of grammatical point of view depends on what attitude you wish to take toward your narrative and your audience. If you can make your point more effectively by distancing yourself from the

story, you will want to use *he, she,* or *they.* On the other hand, if you can make your point most effectively by being in the story, use first person and then decide whether you want to be *I* the narrator only or *I* the narrator who is also directly involved in the story.

9. **Make a point.** The action of the narrative should lead to a conclusion, an implicit or explicit point that serves as the thesis of the piece. If explicit, the thesis can appear in a single sentence or it can be inferred from several sentences, in either the introduction or conclusion of the essay. Ask yourself if everything in the narrative ties into the thesis.

A Fowl Trick to Play on a Lawn Tractor

Pete Dexter

You may be familiar with Pete Dexter's Paris Trout *(1988), which won the National Book Award for fiction in 1988 and in 1991 was made into a movie starring Dennis Hopper. Or perhaps you have seen the HBO series* Deadwood, *based on Dexter's novel of the same name (1986). He has also written four other novels and numerous screen plays, including the television drama* Mulholland Falls *and the films* Rush *and* Michael *(the latter coauthored). If you do know his work, you know it's given to violence and fits the genre of noir films. The essay included here, however, is quite different, closer to the writing Dexter has done for various newspapers: the* Philadelphia Daily News, Sacramento Bee, *and* Seattle Post-Intelligencer. *"A Fowl Trick" is one of a number of his essays published in newspapers and magazines and collected in* Paper Trails: True Stories of Confusion, Mindless Violence, and Forbidden Desires, a Surprising Number of Which Are Not About Marriage *(2007).*

> **What to Look For**   The pun in Dexter's title suggests his essay will take a humorous view, but humor comes in many guises. As you read his essay, mark each spot where he uses humor and then decide what sort of humor it is.

1   There was a peahen in the garage one day last week. It stayed four hours and left. A peahen, of course, is a female peacock, and the way you tell a peahen from a peacock is that a peahen is less ornamental and a peacock doesn't lay eggs.

2   The one in my garage was a sort of dull green—at least it would have been dull for a peacock, but being a peahen, I supposed it was about average. It was standing in front of the trash compactor, staring at a small red light that stays on while the compactor is in its "extra-pack" mode.

3   I saw the peahen as I came into the garage on my tractor, and while no exotic bird had ever wandered into my garage before, I was not in the frame of mind to appreciate it. While I'd been cutting the

grass, the tractor had begun making horrible noises. I am close to my tractor; I depend on it emotionally. And until the day this happened, the tractor itself had always been so loud that I'd been unable to hear anything else while I was riding it. Or, now that I think about it, for a couple of hours afterward.

4   It seemed to me this was big trouble.

5   And not just for the noise. The tractor is an Allis-Chalmers, a company that went into bankruptcy immediately following my purchase of the machine, and whose closest authorized dealer, as far as I know, is in downstate Illinois.

6   Worse still, I do not live in downstate Illinois. I live on an island in the Puget Sound, and 2,000 miles is a long way to push a tractor to get it fixed. Not that anybody in Illinois could fix it anyway. The engine is a 920 diesel Lombardini, made in Italy, a country famous for—and proud of—its heritage as the manufacturer of the most temperamental engines and transmissions in the world.

7   I suspected the problem was either in the engine or the transmission, because the noise—an unearthly scream, something that perhaps would sound healthy to your Rolfing therapist—occurred half a dozen times just as I was climbing the steepest hill on the property.

8   And after the sixth time it happened, I drove my Chapter 11 tractor with the Italian background into the garage, to think for awhile about why I couldn't have just bought a John Deere like everybody else, and then maybe to burn myself touching some stuff under the hood.

9   And there, standing in the dark, was the peahen.

10   If she was bothered by the noise of the tractor—it had stopped screaming now that it wasn't climbing hills—she kept it to herself. She stared at me a minute; I stared at her. When I killed the engine—with a Lombardini 920 diesel, by the way, you do not just turn a key, you pull a lever that strangles it—she went back to watching the trash compactor.

11   I walked over to see what she thought she was doing in my garage, and while you couldn't call her friendly—there are no friendly birds—she did sidle over a step or two to make room so I could watch the light on the trash compactor too.

12   And so we stood there awhile, the peahen and me, enjoying the "extra-pack" light, and when I began to imagine us as a married couple watching the sunset, I realized it was time to go back and look at the tractor.

13   The peahen stayed where she was. I guess she knew what she liked when she saw it.

14   I lifted the lid off the engine, got the metric wrenches, and began, as they say, at the beginning.

15   Meaning, I started with Mussolini and worked my way forward to the Sawyer Brothers Allis-Chalmers dealership in Maryland, where I bought this thing. I used terrible language, so bad that at one point I stopped and went into the house and called my old friend Mickey Rosati in Philadelphia to apologize for what I'd been saying about Italians.

16   Mick accepted the apology in the name of Italians everywhere, and hearing my description of the scream, he suggested the problem might be in the tension of the belts. I went back outside to check.

17   The bird didn't even stir as I walked past. She was completely involved in the compactor light.

18   I reached underneath the tractor and fingered the belt that connects the engine to the lawn mower. It seemed all right—it gave about as much as a brassiere when you pull the strap in back—but still, it was hard to say for sure. I couldn't really get at it, which, going back thirty years or so, was always a problem with brassieres too.

19   I have never been good with these things. In the end, some of us are Italians and some of us aren't.

20   Anyway, I thought it over a long time, then reached for the wrenches, dropped the lawn-mowing deck off the tractor, and then slid it out from underneath.

21   It weighs about a hundred pounds, and I distinctly remembered one of the Sawyer brothers telling me how easy this thing was going to be to take off for sharpening. A couple of bolts, a couple of linch-pins, and it's done. In fairness, I am not sure he said anything about putting it back together.

22   Three hours later, sweating, arms shaking, I finally got one of those pins back in place and was able from there to reassemble my lawn mower. I had found nothing wrong with it, but I had dropped the mower deck on the same hand twice, and to even the casual observer it was clear that this hand would never unhook a brassiere again.

23   I got up off the floor and noticed the peahen still standing in front of the compactor, staring at the red light.

24   "Show's over," I said as I went past and switched the button to "regular-pack," and a moment later the red light went off.

25   The bird stared at me as if she couldn't believe what I'd done, and then, as I headed up the stairs to the house to call Mickey again and report it was not the belts, she opened her mouth, and in a moment the walls seemed to shatter, and I understood in that moment that the noise had not come from the tractor.

ORGANIZATION AND IDEAS

1. The peahen enters the scene in paragraph 3 but is more fully described in paragraphs 10 through 13. How is she portrayed?
2. Dexter is both the narrator and main character in the essay. How would you describe him? How does he characterize his tractor?
3. How many different conflicts can you find in the essay? What are they?
4. To what extent does the last paragraph resolve the essay's conflict? How successful a resolution is it?
5. If the narrative were in the form of a fable, what would the moral be?

TECHNIQUE AND STYLE

1. Read the essay looking for examples of Dexter's humor. What do you find? How would you describe it?
2. Go through the essay again to work out all the cause-and-effect relationships, real and imagined. What are they? Considering all of them together, how would you rate them in terms of complexity?
3. Dexter compares the tractor's belt to a brassiere in paragraph 18 and then refers to a brassiere again in paragraph 22. What does the comparison add? In what way might it be considered sexist?
4. Reread paragraphs 12, 15, and 25. Given the conflict and the way the narrative builds, what do they add?
5. Dexter uses the exact names of the company that made the tractor and its engine as well as Rolfing (paragraph 7) and Chapter 11 (paragraph 8). What do these details add to the essay?

SUGGESTIONS FOR WRITING

Journal

1. Write an entry in which you describe your own battle with a machine.
2. Put yourself in the position of the peahen or the tractor and retell the story in your journal from that perspective.

Essay

1. Think of a time when you expected one thing but got another. Perhaps you expected a good outcome and got a bad one or vice versa. The difference between expectation and reality can become the central conflict for your own narrative essay. Possible topics:
   a test you were dreading
   a party you were looking forward to
   a film or concert you were dragged to
   a friend who let you down or an "enemy" who didn't

2. If you responded to the first suggestion for a journal entry, you have a rough draft of an essay. Given the mechanical and technological world we live in, it's likely that you have been frustrated by one of its products. Turn that frustration into an essay, either a nonfictional narrative similar to Dexter's or a straightforward one that relates and analyzes the situation.

Learning, then College

Meg Gifford

When Meg Gifford was considering taking a year off before college, her peers and high school guidance counselor opposed the idea, but she had her parents' support. Her mother even suggested she write the essay that follows and send it in to her local newspaper, the Baltimore Sun. *Not only did the* Sun *publish it, but it was reprinted in the* New Orleans Times-Picayune *on April 10, 2002. After taking her year off, Gifford enrolled at the University of Maryland, majoring in family studies and spending one semester at the University of Edinburgh in Scotland. By the time you read this note, she will probably have finished graduate school, earning a master's degree in public health. She reports, "I received several emails thanking me for speaking up on the issue—one from as far away as Mexico."*

What to Look For   A major flaw in some narratives that use first person is the failure to generalize about an individual experience. As you read Meg Gifford's essay, notice how often she uses *I* and how she broadens her experience so that it connects with the experience of others.

1   As my younger friends receive their college acceptance letters this time of year, I think about my senior year at Western High School in Baltimore City and the decision I made that changed my life forever: taking time off before college.

2   In Britain, it's called a gap year—the sabbatical that most students take between high school and college.

3   This is a time for young people to discover themselves before their devotion to another four years of intensive schoolwork. Not a

bad idea, considering that a good number of college freshmen flunk out because of the overwhelming temptations of extracurricular college life.

4   Most gap year students take a job or an internship to get a better grasp on the real world and pick up some life skills along the way. Some students understand that they are just not ready for college.

5   I chose to take a gap year for this very reason. I knew I wasn't ready to settle down and work. And because college is so expensive, I wanted to be sure that I would take that investment seriously.

6   I acknowledge that postponing college is not easy. Few people supported my decision, telling me that once I stopped my education I'd never get back on track. My classmates were especially doubtful, thinking that my time off was just an excuse for being lazy. It was infuriating to think that people could and would not associate my travels or internship as an extension of my education.

7   I learned more in my gap year than I have in two years of college. I discovered life skills that continue to help me through the hardest of times. I found independence and a new self-esteem. I learned the value of a dollar, and then I learned the value of not having a dollar. I learned that eggs are cheap and easy to cook.

8   Being 18 is wonderful. There's a whole world waiting to be discovered with a lifetime to do it. The average person doesn't retire until he is well into his 60s, and he probably has been working since he graduated from college. As I see my friends now settling down with careers and families, many of them express regrets at not having seen the world before taking on such unyielding responsibilities.

9   My advice to high school seniors is this: Now is your chance to explore. Do it before you have devoted your life to something else.

10   By the age of 20, I delivered three babies as part of my midwifery internship in Hyden, Ky., and learned how to cook a fine Kentucky rattlesnake. After teaching a 90-year-old-man the alphabet, he showed me how to make furniture.

11   I also have attended two years of college so far, making the dean's list every semester. What story will you be able to tell?

Organization and Ideas

  1. In what ways does paragraph 1 prepare you for what follows in the rest of the essay?
  2. Work out a timeline for the essay, noting when each paragraph takes place. What happens when?
  3. How effective is Gifford's use of time?

4. Consider the pros and cons Gifford outlines and summarize them in one sentence. What is her thesis?
5. To what extent does Gifford persuade you that a gap year is a good idea?

TECHNIQUE AND STYLE

1. Reread the essay, paying particular attention to Gifford's audience. Who is it? What reasons do you have for your choice?
2. Consider the tone of the essay, the author's attitude toward her audience and subject. Is she earnest? Supercilious? Know-it-all? Caring? What?
3. To what extent is Gifford someone you would like to know? Why?
4. In paragraph 7, Gifford uses a lot of repetition. How effective is it?
5. Paragraph 10 summarizes Gifford's experience by presenting the highlights of her year off. How effective are her examples?

SUGGESTIONS FOR WRITING

Journal

1. Did you consider taking a year off before entering college? Use your journal to explore why or why not.
2. Paragraph 7 summarizes what Gifford learned during her gap year. To what extent do you believe her and why?

Essay

1. One way to view Gifford's essay is to think of it as describing the kind of learning that is vital yet can take place out of the classroom. Consider what Gifford learned that she states in paragraph 7. Where have you gained knowledge that you value? Narrow down your choice to one example and write an essay in which you explore what you learned, where, and why. Suggestions:
   working part-time
   working full-time
   participating in a sport
   participating in an extracurricular activity
   being responsible for someone
2. Gifford cites the "overwhelming temptations of extracurricular college life" as a reason some students flunk out. Flunking out aside, consider the various "temptations" you face in college and write an essay in which you analyze the most hazardous one and how you dealt with it.

The Night of Oranges

Flavius Stan

Flavius Stan was 17 years old when this piece was published on Christmas Eve day, 1995, in The New York Times. *At the time, he was an exchange student at the Fieldston School in the Bronx, one of New York City's five boroughs. The time and place he writes about, however, is Christmas Eve in the city of Timisoara in the Romania of 1989, when the country was emerging from Communist rule. It had been an incredible month. On December 16, government forces opened fire on antigovernment demonstrators in Timisoara, killing hundreds. The president, Nicolae Ceausescu, immediately declared a state of emergency, but that did not stop antigovernment protests in other cities. Finally, on December 22, army units also rebelled, the president was overthrown, and civil war raged. The new government quickly won out, and Ceausescu was tried and found guilty of genocide. He was executed on December 25.*

What to Look For Few of us reading this essay have had firsthand experience of a revolution, nor have many of us lived under Communism or a dictatorship, much less a government whose leader was not only overthrown but also executed. But all of us know oranges. What is familiar to us was strange to Stan, and what is strange to us was his everyday world. The resulting gap between Stan's society and ours is huge, yet in this essay he is able to bring his readers into the cold, postrevolution world of a city in Romania and make us see our familiar orange in a new way. Read the essay once for pleasure and then read it again, looking for the ways in which he makes the unfamiliar familiar and vice versa.

1 It is Christmas Eve in 1989 in Timisoara and the ice is still dirty from the boots of the Romanian revolution. The dictator Nicolae Ceausescu had been deposed a few days before, and on Christmas Day he would be executed by firing squad. I am in the center of the city with my friends, empty now of the crowds that prayed outside the cathedral during the worst of the fighting. My friends and I

still hear shots here and there. Our cold hands are gray like the sky above us, and we want to see a movie.

2   There is a rumor that there will be oranges for sale tonight. Hundreds of people are already waiting in line. We were used to such lines under the former Communist Government—lines for bread, lines for meat, lines for everything. Families would wait much of the day for rationed items. As children, we would take turns for an hour or more, holding our family's place in line.

3   But this line is different. There are children in Romania who don't know what an orange looks like. It is a special treat. Having the chance to eat a single orange will keep a child happy for a week. It will also make him a hero in the eyes of his friends. For the first time, someone is selling oranges by the kilo.

4   Suddenly I want to do something important: I want to give my brother a big surprise. He is only 8 years old, and I want him to celebrate Christmas with lots of oranges at the table. I also want my parents to be proud of me.

5   So I call home and tell my parents that I'm going to be late. I forget about going to the movie, leave my friends and join the line.

6   People aren't silent, upset, frustrated, as they were before the revolution; they are talking to one another about life, politics and the new situation in the country.

7   The oranges are sold out of the back doorway of a food shop. The clerk has gone from anonymity to unexpected importance. As he handles the oranges, he acts like a movie star in front of his fans.

8   He moves his arms in an exaggerated manner as he tells the other workers where to go and what to do. All I can do is stare at the stack of cardboard boxes, piled higher than me. I have never seen so many oranges in my life.

9   Finally, it is my turn. It is 8 o'clock, and I have been waiting for six hours. It doesn't seem like a long time because my mind has been flying from the oranges in front of me to my brother and then back to the oranges. I hand over the money I was going to spend on the movie and watch each orange being thrown into my bag. I try to count them, but I lose their number.

10   I am drunk with the idea of oranges. I put the bag inside my coat as if I want to absorb their warmth. They aren't heavy at all, and I feel that it is going to be the best Christmas of my life. I begin thinking of how I am going to present my gift.

11   I get home and my father opens the door. He is amazed when he sees the oranges, and we decide to hide them until dinner. At dessert that night, I give my brother the present. Everyone is silent. They can't believe it.

12   My brother doesn't touch them. He is afraid even to look at them. Maybe they aren't real. Maybe they are an illusion, like everything else these days. We have to tell him he can eat them before he has the courage to touch one of the oranges.

13   I stare at my brother eating the oranges. They are my oranges. My parents are proud of me.

ORGANIZATION AND IDEAS

1. Paragraphs 1–3 introduce the essay. Explain how they do or do not fit the journalistic questions establishing *who, what, where, why, when, how.*

2. The central part of the essay takes the reader from the time Stan decides to buy the oranges to his presenting them to his brother. What is the effect of presenting the narrative chronologically?

3. The last paragraph functions as the essay's one-paragraph conclusion, a conclusion presented in three short sentences. Explain whether you find the ending effective.

4. On the surface, Stan's essay has a simple thesis—that finding the rare and perfect gift for his brother fills him with pride, pride also reflected by his family. If you dig a bit, however, you may also discover other less obvious theses. What, for instance, might Stan be implying about Christmas? About Romania's future?

5. How would you characterize the conflict or conflicts in this essay?

TECHNIQUE AND STYLE

1. Although the essay was written in 1995, it is set at an earlier time, 1989. Many writers would, therefore, opt for the past tense, but Stan relates his narrative in the present. What does he gain by this choice?

2. Trace the number of contrasts Stan has in his essay. What do you discover? How do they relate to the thesis?

3. Paragraphs 7 and 8 describe the clerk in charge of selling the oranges in some detail. What does this description add to the essay?

4. Why is it important that the money Stan spends on the oranges is the money he was going to spend on the movies?

5. Reread the first paragraph, one that sets not only the scene but also the atmosphere, the emotional impression arising from the scene. In your own words, describe that atmosphere.

Suggestions for Writing

Journal

1. Choose a common object and describe it as though you were seeing it for the first time.

2. In a sense, Stan's essay is written from the perspective of an 11-year-old, the age he was at the time of the narrative. Leaf through your journal to find a short narrative and then try rewriting it from the perspective of a much younger person.

Essay

1. Sift through your memory to find several times when you felt proud. Choose one to turn into a narrative essay. Perhaps, like Stan, you may want to retell the event in the present tense, placing yourself in the position of reliving it. If you do, check your draft to see if you have an implied thesis that is larger than the apparent one, because you want your essay to have some depth to it. For ideas of what might have made you feel proud, consider something you

   did
   didn't do
   saw
   owned
   said

2. For a more generalized essay, consider the times you felt pride and list them. What were the occasions? What do they have in common? In what ways are those examples similar? Different? Write an essay in which you define *pride,* using your experiences as examples and keeping first person to a minimum so that you emphasize the subject, not yourself.

Time to Look and Listen

Magdoline Asfahani

> Newsweek *runs a regular column called "My Turn," one that you can check out by going to www.newsweek.com. There, just under the blank for a search, you'll see "Voices." Click on it and then scroll down till you see "My Turn," and you'll find a list of columns that have been published earlier. Magdoline Asfahani's piece was published on December 2, 1996, when Asfahani was a student at the University of Texas at El Paso. Then, she was trying to balance her identity in ways that honored her parents' Syrian and Lebanese cultures while embracing her American-born values. It wasn't easy. Reflecting on what she wrote, Asfahani now finds "the piece is probably more meaningful now than it was when I wrote it." See if you agree.*

What to Look For   If you have ever written about a painful experience, you know that it's hard to keep your emotions under control. Anger, resentment, pain can break through and overwhelm what you are trying to portray in a cool, rational manner. As you read Asfahani's essay, look for the ways she keeps her emotions from engulfing her ideas.

1   I love my country as many who have been here for generations cannot. Perhaps that's because I'm the child of immigrants, raised with a conscious respect for America that many people take for granted. My parents chose this country because it offered them a new life, freedom and possibilities. But I learned at a young age that the country we loved so much did not feel the same way about us.

2   Discrimination is not unique to America. It occurs in any country that allows immigration. Anyone who is unlike the majority is looked at a little suspiciously, dealt with a little differently. I knew that I was an Arab and a Muslim. This meant nothing to me. At school I stood up to say the Pledge of Allegiance every day. These things did not seem incompatible at all. Then everything changed for me, suddenly and permanently, in 1985. I was only in seventh grade, but that was the beginning of my political education.

3   That year a TWA plane originating in Athens was diverted to Beirut. Two years earlier the U.S. Marine barracks in Beirut had been bombed. That seemed to start a chain of events that would forever link Arabs with terrorism. After the hijacking, I faced classmates who taunted me with cruel names, attacking my heritage and my religion. I became an outcast and had to apologize for myself constantly.

4   After a while, I tried to forget my heritage. No matter what race, religion or ethnicity, a child who is attacked often retreats. I was the only Arab I knew of in my class, so I had no one in my peer group as an ally. No matter what my parents tried to tell me about my proud cultural history, I would ignore it. My classmates told me I came from an uncivilized, brutal place, that Arabs were by nature anti-American, and I believed them. They did not know the hours my parents spent studying, working, trying to preserve part of their old lives while embracing, willingly, the new.

5   I tried to forget the Arabic I knew, because if I didn't I'd be forever linked to murderers. I stopped inviting friends over for dinner, because I thought the food we ate was "weird." I lied about where my parents had come from. Their accents (although they spoke English perfectly) humiliated me. Though Islam is a major monotheistic religion with many similarities to Judaism and Christianity, there were no holidays near Chanukah or Christmas, nothing to tie me to the "Judeo-Christian" tradition. I felt more excluded. I slowly began to turn into someone without a past.

6   Civil war was raging in Lebanon, and all that Americans saw of that country was destruction and violence. Every other movie seemed to feature Arab terrorists. The most common questions I was asked were if I had ever ridden a camel or if my family lived in tents. I felt burdened with responsibility. Why should an adolescent be asked questions like "Is it true you hate Jews and you want Israel destroyed?" I didn't hate anybody. My parents had never said anything even alluding to such sentiments. I was confused and hurt.

7   As I grew older and began to form my own opinions, my embarrassment lessened and my anger grew. The turning point came in high school. My grandmother had become very ill, and it was necessary for me to leave school a few days before Christmas vacation. My chemistry teacher was very sympathetic until I said I was going to the Middle East. "Don't come back in a body bag," he said cheerfully. The class laughed. Suddenly, those years of watching movies that mocked me and listening to others who knew nothing about

Arabs and Muslims except what they saw on television seemed like a bad dream. I knew then that I would never be silent again.

8   I've tried to reclaim those lost years. I realize now that I come from a culture that has a rich history. The Arab world is a medley of people of different religions; not every Arab is a Muslim, and vice versa. The Arabs brought tremendous advances in the sciences and mathematics, as well as creating a literary tradition that has never been surpassed. The language itself is flexible and beautiful, with nuances and shades of meaning unparalleled in any language. Though many find it hard to believe, Islam has made progress in women's rights. There is a specific provision in the Koran that permits women to own property and ensures that their inheritance is protected—although recent events have shown that interpretation of these laws can vary.

9   My youngest brother, who is 12, is now at the crossroads I faced. When initial reports of the Oklahoma City bombing pointed to "Arab-looking individuals" as the culprits, he came home from school crying. "Mom, why do Muslims kill people? Why are the Arabs so bad?" She was angry and brokenhearted, but tried to handle the situation in the best way possible through education. She went to his class, armed with Arabic music, pictures, traditional dress and cookies. She brought a chapter of the social-studies book to life and the children asked intelligent, thoughtful questions, even after the class was over. Some even asked if she was coming back. When my brother came home, he was excited and proud instead of ashamed.

10   I only recently told my mother about my past experience. Maybe if I had told her then, I would have been better equipped to deal with the thoughtless teasing. But, fortunately, the world is changing. Although discrimination and stereotyping still exist, many people are trying to lessen and end it. Teachers, schools and the media are showing greater sensitivity to cultural issues. However, there is still much that needs to be done, not for the sake of any particular ethnic or cultural groups but for the sake of our country.

11   The America that I love is one that values freedom and the differences of its people. Education is the key to understanding. As Americans we need to take a little time to look and listen carefully to what is around us and not rush to judgment without knowing the facts. And we must never be ashamed of our pasts. It is our collective differences that unite and make us unique as a nation. It's what determines our present and our future.

ORGANIZATION AND IDEAS

1. In paragraphs 3–6, Asfahani recreates her experiences as a seventh-grader. How well does she do it?
2. It's possible to find a number of subjects in Asfahani's essay: discrimination, education, American values, stereotyping. Which is the most important? What evidence can you find to support your opinion?
3. What statement is Asfahani making about that subject?
4. How would you characterize the essay's aim: Is Asfahani trying to persuade the reader? Explain her position? Let off steam? If some combination, which dominates?
5. The essay was published in 1996 just after Thanksgiving. To what extent, if any, is it dated?

TECHNIQUE AND STYLE

1. Asfahani describes her "political education" (paragraphs 2–9). Which example is the most telling and why?
2. In paragraph 8, Asfahani asserts that she comes "from a culture that has a rich history." How well does she back up that claim?
3. Asfahani never told her parents what she was going through when she was in the seventh grade, keeping it to herself. How realistic is that reaction?
4. According to Asfahani, "Education is the key to understanding" (paragraph 11). What evidence does she present to back up that idea?
5. What examples can you find of Asfahani appealing to the reader's emotions? To reason? Which predominates?

SUGGESTIONS FOR WRITING

Journal

1. Use your journal to record the time you first recognized or experienced discrimination.
2. Think of how culture is expressed through language, food, celebrations, dress, gestures, relationships, and the like. Write a brief entry in which you tell of a time when you first experienced a culture different from your own.

Essay

1. "Know thyself" was a basic belief of the ancient Greeks, and it is as difficult to do today as it was then. You can define yourself, for example, in any number of ways by associating yourself with a group

or belief or heritage, to name just a few. Think about the various ways in which you define yourself and write an essay in which you explain who you are. To generate some ideas, try thinking about who you are in relation to

family
ethnic heritage
friends
religion
political beliefs

Choose one of these ideas, or any other, and consider the conflicts you encountered in becoming who you are. The danger here is taking on too much so that you have the first chapter of your autobiography instead of an essay, so be sure you narrow down your topic.

2. Asfahani says that in high school, she reached a "turning point" and "would never be silent again" (paragraph 7). Think of such turning points in your own life and select one to explore in an essay. Like Asfahani, you should try to distance yourself from the time so that you can balance the emotional and the rational.

Footprints on the Flag

Anchee Min

Anchee Min's narrative will tell you about her earlier life under the rule of Mao Zedong, China's Chairman Mao. China provides the main focus for her books, where she explores life—her own and that of historical figures. Red Azalea *(1994) is a memoir in which she describes her experiences under the Maoist regime. Min's first novel was* Katherine *(1995), followed by* Wild Ginger *(2002) and* Empress Orchid *(2004), the latter a fictionalized account of the life of Tzu Hsi that Min continues in* The Last Empress *(2007). Her most successful novel is* Becoming Madame Mao *(2000), based not only on personal experience but also on more than five years' worth of research. Madame Mao was known in China as "White-bone-demon," a name that gives you a good idea about her character. The following essay was first published in the October 15, 2001, issue of* The New Yorker, *and revised by Min in 2007.*

What to Look For   The time frame for Min's essay extends from September 1984 to 2000. As you read her narrative, be thinking of how she covers that amount of time and how she compresses it.

1   I arrived in America in 1984 and attended The School of the Art Institute of Chicago. I worked as a gallery attendant. During the 1987 art exhibition, one of the pieces was an American flag laid flat on the floor. About three feet above, mounted from the wall, was the artist's diary. I noticed that the viewers had to step on the flag in order to read the diary. As a result, the flag started to have footprints on it. I thought that I had neglected my duty, so each time after a viewer left I would take off my jacket and wipe the flag clean. I kept thinking if someone did this to our national flag in China, he would have been prosecuted.

2   I became sick of cleaning the flag. Eventually when a viewer came I would go up to him or her and would say politely, "Please do not step on the flag."

3   Weeks later the artist came. He was displeased that there were not enough footprints on the flag. He explained that it was his intention to have people step on the flag.

4   What offended me more was that the artist planned to burn the flag in public when the show ended. I understood that I had no right to stop him. I was emotional because if it were not for America I would not have been alive today. America took me in after I denounced the Communist China.

5   When the artist's admirers told me to get my English straight so that I could have the "right understanding of this evil country," I wished that I could sound out the words that were boiling inside my head. "Twenty years earlier I had done exactly what you are doing now!" As a child, I was taught to hate Americans. "Long Live Chairman Mao" was the first phrase I learned to write before my own name. I not only burnt American flags, but also denounced my beloved teacher as an American spy in order to demonstrate my loyalty toward the Communist Party. As a teen, I was given a gun with a knife to practice stabbing a straw dummy wearing a U.S. soldier's uniform. My schoolmates and I watched propaganda films, where American soldiers were shown scooping out the eyes of a young Viet Cong, a girl of my own age.

6   I was ready to die for my country if Americans dared to set their foot on the soil of China. I couldn't wait to be sent to Vietnam to

become a martyr. I wanted to model myself after the hero who tied grenades on his back and jumped into a group of U.S. Marines, blowing them up as well as himself. I dreamed of my remains being shipped back to the homeland wrapped in the Communist red flag—my family and friends sad, but proud.

7   The American artist protested that he lacked freedom. In my view, he had too much. He took America for granted. If he had been in China twenty years ago, I would have taught him a good lesson.

ORGANIZATION AND IDEAS

1. The first paragraph sets out the scene but also depicts Min's words and actions. What do they tell you about her?
2. The most dramatic conflict is between Min and the artist. What other conflicts does the narrative present or imply?
3. Of those conflicts, which is the most important and why?
4. In the last paragraph, Min states what she has learned about freedom. What else did she learn from her overall experience? How can you turn what she learned into the essay's thesis?
5. In paragraphs 4 and 5, Min describes the intentions behind the artist's work. Explain whether you find that part of her narrative realistic, exaggerated, or some place in between?

TECHNIQUE AND STYLE

1. Reread paragraph 5, Min's account of her life in China. How would you characterize her description? On a scale from objective to subjective, where would you put it and why?
2. Min's life under the Maoist regime was cruel, hard, unjust, unfree. To what extent do you think she feels sorry for herself?
3. Reexamine the details Min chooses to use in paragraphs 5 and 6. Explain whether you find them effective. What emotions do they arouse?
4. On a scale of one to ten, how would you rate Min's anger and why? To what extent does it add or detract from the essay's effectiveness?
5. Reread the essay looking for comparisons. What do you find? What do they contribute to the essay's organization? To its thesis?

SUGGESTIONS FOR WRITING

Journal

1. Use your journal to record the emotions you felt when you read Min's narrative. What were they? What in the essay triggered them?
2. Look up *patriotism* in an unabridged dictionary. Use your journal to explore how the term might apply to Min.

Essay

1. The artist Min encountered saw the American flag as a symbol of all he thought wrong about the country, and indeed the flag is a potent symbol. Think about other objects that have symbolic value within our culture and write a narrative in which you relate an experience you had with one. To find a suitable subject, consider anything that can be thought of as absolutely American:

   the hamburger
   the hot dog
   baseball caps
   blue jeans
   fast food

2. When Min saw Andy Warhol's Mao series, she reacted: "I couldn't understand why a professor would project slides of Mao in an American classroom, when more than a billion Chinese were finally taking Mao buttons off their jackets, Mao portraits off their walls, and Mao quotations out of their speeches." The Art Institute of Chicago owns the series and operates a Web site called "Art Access." Use it to learn more about the work at http://www.artic.edu/artaccess/AA_Modern/pages/MOD_9.shtml. Given that information and anything else you turn up in your research, write an essay that analyzes the impact of Warhol's series.

The Flag

Ann Telnaes

A syndicated editorial cartoonist, Ann Telnaes is unusual for a number of reasons. Born in Sweden, educated at the California Institute of the Arts, winner of a Pulitzer Prize for Editorial Cartooning (2001) as well as numerous other awards, she is one of few women who has pursued a career as an editorial cartoonist. You can see her work in newspapers such as The New York Times, Chicago Tribune, Washington Post, *and* USA Today. *A collection of her work was exhibited at the Library of Congress and then published as* Humor's Edge *(2004). She now lives in Washington, D.C., a good place for anyone in her line of work.*

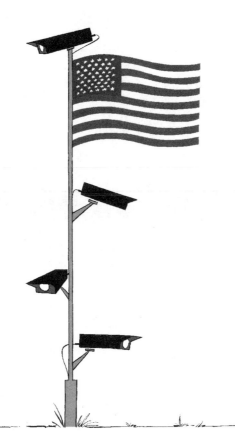

FOR DISCUSSION

1. Telnaes depicts the American flag atop a flagpole that has four cameras attached to it. What is her point?
2. Why might Telnaes have chosen not to include any people?
3. Telnaes tries to draw attention to the flag by indicating it is waving while everything else is still. What does she imply by that choice?
4. What connections do you find between Min's essay and Telnaes' cartoon?
5. What connections do you find between Asfahani's essay and Telnaes' cartoon?

SUGGESTIONS FOR WRITING

Journal

Take another look at Telnaes' cartoon and think about what it is saying. What possible subjects might she be addressing? Which one do you think is the most important and why?

Essay

Cameras are now fairly commonplace in stores, and some cities have installed them to catch speeders and people who run traffic lights. Cities such as London use them in areas where crowds congregate as a measure to thwart terrorists. Are such uses legitimate? Necessary? An infringement on personal freedom? What? Pick one of these questions or one of your own choosing and then use the Web to research it. Write an essay that either reports on the topic or takes a stand.

On Using Example

1   I heard that Reba McEntire's new album, "Read My Mind," shot to No. 5
     on the Billboard chart the first weekend of its release.
2   Well, she got my $11.95.
3   I'm a 40-something black woman who spent her youth in Washington,
     lip-syncing to the Supremes and slow dancing to the Temptations. Now I
     often come home to my Manhattan apartment and put on Vince Gill,
     Randy Travis or Reba. Consider me a fan of country music. So there. Deal
     with it.

Lena Williams titles her essay "A Black Fan of Country Music Finally
Tells All," suggesting a confessional and humorous tone. The three paragraphs that follow give the reader a lot of information but also work more
subtly to hint at her thesis and set up the essay's structure. From that point
on, you expect lots of **examples** and a sharp look at tastes in music.
Examples also

- develop
- illustrate
- clarify
- support
- emphasize

a main point. The most basic building block of all, examples pin down
generalizations, supporting them with specifics.

What types of examples are there?   Examples generally fall into two
categories: extended and multiple. An essay that rests its assertion on
only one example is relatively rare, but you will run across one now and
then. When you do, the example often takes the form of a narrative in
support of the author's thesis. To show that a minimum-wage job can be
a fulfilling one (or a demeaning one—take your pick), you might support
your thesis by telling about a typical day on the job. While you are relying on only one example, you will have developed it in considerable
depth, and you probably will have included a sentence or two to indicate

that other experiences may contradict yours, so your readers will accept your extended example as valid.

Far more frequent, however, are multiple examples—the kind you see in Williams' first paragraphs. They add clarity, support, and emphasis. Sometimes the examples will be drawn from your own experience and the experiences of others, but often you will find you want more generalized sources, so you consult books, magazines, the Internet, interviews, reports, and so on. You may well find that examples drawn from outside sources give your essay a more objective, reasoned **tone.** If you think of that term as similar to tone of voice, you will realize that it means the writer's attitude toward the subject and audience. Examples drawn from personal experience are apt to create an informal, conversational tone; those drawn from outside sources often provide a cooler, more formal tone. No matter where you find your examples, however, you can present them with some variety, summarizing some, quoting others.

How do you find examples?   The first place to start is with your own experience, but don't stop there. You need to connect with readers who may have little in common with you. Use the Internet to find other examples that will fit your topic. Perhaps you're a NASCAR fan and want to find out more about its appeal. Try searching "NASCAR fan" and you'll turn up close to two million hits. You'll also discover photographs and videos that may help with your topic by providing visual information: what the fans look like, the size of the crowds, the excitement a race can generate. After you've looked at a few sites, you'll be able to form a working thesis that you can then refine and illustrate through examples drawn both from your own experience and that of others.

How do you structure your essay?   In your first draft, you may want to state your thesis in one sentence and in an obvious place, such as the end of your introduction. When you revise, however, you may want to play with the placement of the thesis, delaying it until the conclusion. If that's where you decide you want it, check to make sure that everything that precedes the conclusion leads up to it and that along the way the reader has a clear focus on your subject.

Delaying your thesis or weaving it into your introduction is a subtle way of treating your major assertion, but if you are worried these techniques are too subtle, consider getting some mileage out of a title. An imaginative title can arouse the reader's curiosity, set the tone, highlight the subject, reveal the essay's organization, pave the way for the thesis. That's what Lena Williams does with "A Black Fan of Country Music Finally Tells All."

Examples not only illustrate generalizations; they also expand and develop them. After you have written a draft of an essay, you may find it useful to double-check each of your examples by asking several questions: How does the example support the generalization? Is the source of the example clear? How does it connect to the readers' experiences? If the example is an extended one, is it sufficiently developed so that it can support the thesis by itself? Then you might think about the examples as a whole: Do they draw on a variety of sources? Do they incorporate both summary and quotation?

When examples structure an essay, they are usually in chronological or dramatic order, moving from what came first and ending with what came last, or beginning with the least dramatic and finishing with the most dramatic. To decide which example is the most dramatic, all you need to do is ask some obvious questions: Which is the most important? Which is most likely to affect the reader? Which carries the most impact? You'll probably come up with the same answer for each question. That's the example you should use to cap your essay.

How do you link your examples? After you have found good examples and sequenced them logically, you should check your **transitions** to avoid overusing terms such as "for example." It's possible to group transitions by their functions:

- addition: *and, also, again, besides, moreover, next,* or *finally*
- for a turn or concession: *but, yet, however, instead, in contrast, of course, certainly,* or *granted*
- for a result or summary: *therefore, thus, as a result, so, finally, in conclusion, hence,* or *in brief*

Less obvious and, therefore, apt to be more effective are transitions that don't call attention to themselves, such as the repetition of a key word from the previous sentence or the use of a personal or demonstrative pronoun. If you use pronouns, however, make sure that what they refer to is clear. The demonstrative pronoun *this,* for instance, should usually be followed by a noun, as in *this sentence* or *this idea.* A *this* standing by itself may force your reader to go back to the previous sentence to understand exactly what it refers to.

Although all the essays in this chapter have a thesis developed by examples, the examples themselves often cross over into other categories. You will discover that is also the case with your own writing. You may well find yourself using an example that is also description, or, to put it more precisely, a description that functions as an example. A description of a crowd watching the Daytona 500 can serve as an example of car racing's popularity. Other patterns of organization, such as narrative, causal relationships, comparison, definition, or analysis of a process, can also serve as examples. The function—to support and develop an assertion—is more important than the label.

Useful Terms

Example An illustration that supports a generalization, usually an assertion, by providing evidence that develops or clarifies it.

Tone A writer's attitude toward the subject and the audience. An author's tone can be contemplative, intense, tongue-in-cheek, aloof, matter of fact—as many kinds as there are tones of voice.

Transition A word, phrase, sentence, or paragraph that carries the reader smoothly from point A to point B. Some transitions, such as time markers (*first, next,* and the like) are obvious; others are more subtle, such as a repeated word or phrase or a synonym for a key term.

POINTERS FOR USING EXAMPLE

Exploring the Topic

1. **What examples can you think of to illustrate your topic?** Are all of them from your own experience? What examples can you find from other sources?
2. **Are your examples pertinent and representative?** Do they fit? Do they illustrate?
3. **Are your examples of equal weight?** Which are relatively unimportant?
4. **How familiar is your audience with each of your examples?**
5. **Which examples best lend themselves to your topic?** In what order would they best be presented?
6. **What point do you want to make?** Do your examples all support that point? Do they lead the reader to your major assertion?
7. **What is your purpose behind your point?** Is your primary aim to inform, persuade, or entertain?

Drafting the Paper

1. **Know your reader.** It may be that your audience knows little about your subject or that the reader simply hasn't thought much about it; on the other hand, maybe the reader knows a great deal and holds a definite opinion. Once you have made an informed guess about your audience's attitude toward your topic and thesis, reexamine your examples in light of that information. Some may have to be explained in greater detail than others, and the more familiar ones will need to be presented in a new or different light. Use the techniques you would employ in writing descriptive papers.

2. **Know your purpose.** Personal experience papers are often difficult to write because you are so tied to your own experience. If you are writing with this aim in mind, try making yourself conscious of the personality you project as a writer. Jot down the characteristics you wish to convey about yourself and refer to this list as you revise your paper. While this is a highly self-conscious way to revise, when it is done well, the result appears natural. Also double-check your examples, making sure that you present them in sufficient detail to communicate fully to your audience. That warning serves as well for informative and persuasive papers. Again, use description to make your examples effective: Use sensory detail, compare the unfamiliar to the familiar, be concrete. If you are writing a persuasive paper, use these techniques to appeal to emotions.

3. **Consider extended example.** If an essay rests on one example, choose and develop that illustration with great care. Make sure your example represents its category and that you provide all relevant information. Make as many connections as you can between your example and the category it represents. During revision, you may eliminate some of these references, but at first it's best to have too many.

4. **Consider multiple examples.** Most essays rely on multiple examples to support their points; nevertheless, some examples will be more developed than others. Figure out which examples are particularly striking and develop them, reserving the others for mere mention. To lend breadth and credibility to your point,

(Continued)

POINTERS FOR USING EXAMPLE *(Continued)*

consider citing statistics, quotations, authorities, and the experience of others. Comment on what you take from other sources in order to make it more your own.

5. **Arrange your examples effectively.** Most essays move from the less dramatic, less important to the most, but examples can also be arranged chronologically or in terms of frequency (from least to most frequent). Like the essay itself, each paragraph should be developed around a central assertion, either stated or implied. In longer papers, groups of paragraphs will support a unifying statement.

6. **Check your transitions.** Take a hard look at what links one example and paragraph to another. The transitions should perform the appropriate function, so you might also check them against the list on page 71.

7. **Make a point.** Examples so obviously need to lead up to something that it's not hard to make a point. But your point may not be an assertion. Test your thesis by asking whether your point carries any information. If it does, it's an assertion. Say you come up with, "We live in a world of time-saving technology." You can think of lots of examples and even narrow down the "we" to "anyone who cooks today." The setting is obviously the kitchen, but is the revised thesis an assertion? Given the information test, it fails. Your audience knows what you are supposedly informing them about. But if you revise and come up with "Electronic gizmos have turned the kitchen into a laboratory," you've given the topic a fresher look, one that does contain information.

Sweatin' for Nothin'

Michael Barlow

Unlike many students at the University of New Orleans, Michael Barlow went straight on to college after graduating from high school. As his essay implies, he is not a fitness freak, although he is engaged in a number of college activities. An education major who concentrated on teaching English at the secondary level, he graduated and tried the other side of the desk. No matter what he chooses to do, he will try not to emulate Mimi.

What to Look For   Starting and ending an essay are often the most difficult parts of writing. One technique that works well is the one Barlow uses. You'll see that he sets up a framework by first setting out the image of the hamster in the cage and then, in his conclusion, returning to it. The effect is a sense of closure. You can use the same technique by ending your essay with a reference to an idea you bring out in your introduction.

1   During spring break, I visited my family in Fort Worth. It was a pleasant visit, but my, how things have changed. My mother has purchased a Stairmaster and joined a fitness club. My father now jogs at 6:00 every morning, and my sister is contemplating aerobics as one of her first electives when she goes off to college this August. This was not the group of people I last saw in January. These were not the laid-back complacent folks I've known so well. This was not *my* family.

2   One night around 2 a.m., after partying with some friends from high school, I was lying in bed watching Mimi, my pet hamster, crank out revolutions on an exercise wheel. I should have gone to sleep but I was captivated. The creaking of the wheel made me think of the strenuous exercise that seems to have plagued everyone at 301 Lake Country Drive. What was it? What was going on? So I asked myself whether or not Mimi knew that sprinting in a metal cylinder wouldn't get her out of the cage. She probably didn't know—her brain is smaller than a kernel of corn.

3   But what about humans? What about my family? I see millions of Americans, like my family, in Spandex outfits and gel-cushioned shoes trying to get out of their cages. Something is wrong with the fitness mania that has swept the Western World, and from watching Mimi I know what it is. Entropy.

4   Entropy is the measure of the amount of energy unavailable for useful work in a system—metaphorically speaking, it is a measure of waste. In our throwaway society, we waste energy at a maddening pace. Coal is lit to make a fire, which produces a lot of carbon dioxide, while heating a small amount of water to make steam, which produces electricity, which lights an incandescent bulb in a room in a house where nobody's home. Basic waste.

5   Exercise mania has crippled our culture. It is no coincidence that we are running out of cheap and available energy while at the same time polluting the air, land, and sea with our waste. According to the laws of physics, entropy diminishes in a closed system, meaning that eventually everything will be reduced to an amorphous, undifferentiated blob. The universe is a closed system. There are some parallels to a hamster cage, and Mimi creates entropy at a noisy rate.

6   What did we do for exercise in those past centuries when people did not act like captive hamsters? If a person chopped down wood or ran a long way, it was because he or she needed fuel or wanted to get somewhere. Now we do such things to fit into new pants or to develop our biceps. We have treadmills, rowing machines, Stairmasters, stationary bikes, NordicTracks, butt busters, and wall climbers, and we labor at them while going nowhere. Absolutely nowhere! We do work that is beyond useless; we do work that takes energy and casts it to the wind like lint. And we don't even enjoy the work. Look at people in a health club. See anybody smiling?

7   There is nothing magical about fitness machines. We can get the exact same result by climbing up stairs in our homes or offices. Take a look at any set of stairs in any building. Anybody in Spandex headed up or down? No. People ride elevators all day, then drive to their fitness centers where they pay to walk up steps.

8   When I was looking at Mimi, I was thinking of Richard Simmons, the King of Entropy, who wants everybody to exercise all the time and has made insane amounts of money saying so. Simmons says that he has raised his metabolism so high that he can eat more without gaining weight. Working out to pig out—an entropy double whammy.

9   I have a solution for such gratuitous narcissism and I think Simmons might find a tearful video in it. Let people on the machines

create useable energy as they burn off their flabby thighs and excess baggage. Hook up engines and cams and drive shafts that will rotate turbines and generate electricity. Let exercisers light the health club itself. Let them air condition it. Let the clubs store excess energy and sell it to nearby shop owners at low rates.

10   Better yet, create health clubs whose sole purpose is the generation of energy. Pipe the energy into housing projects. Have energy nights where singles get together to pedal, chat, and swap phone numbers. Build a giant pony wheel that operates a flour mill, a rock crusher, a draw bridge, a BMW repair shop. Have the poles protrude from the wheel with spots for a couple hundred joggers to push the wheel around. Install magazine racks on the poles. Have calorie collections and wattage wars. Make it "cool" to sweat for the betterment of mankind, not just for yourself.

11   We cannot afford much more entropy. If we forget that, we might as well be rodents in cages, running into the night. Just like Mimi.

ORGANIZATION AND IDEAS

1. The essay has a problem–solution structure. In your own words, what does Barlow describe as the problem?
2. Paragraphs 5–7 give examples of kinds of exercise. What distinctions does Barlow draw among them?
3. The solution appears in paragraphs 9–10 and is a humorous one. Summarize it.
4. What do you find to be the main subject of the essay? Exercise? Fads? Waste? Entropy? American culture? What reasons can you find for your choice?
5. To what extent, if any, do you agree with Barlow's thesis?

TECHNIQUE AND STYLE

1. Look up *analogy* in an unabridged dictionary. What analogy does Barlow draw? What does the analogy contribute to the essay?
2. Paragraph 4 defines *entropy*. How necessary is that definition? What does it add to the essay?
3. What does the essay gain with the example of Richard Simmons?
4. Imagine you are one of the people filling up the fitness club. Would you be offended by this essay? Why or why not?
5. The person behind the words always comes through in an essay, sometimes more clearly than others. Explain why you would or would not want Michael Barlow as a classmate or friend.

SUGGESTIONS FOR WRITING

Journal

1. Take a few minutes to write down what you think about the exercise craze or to record your reaction to a television commercial advertising an exercise product.

2. How does exercise make you feel? Write about why you do or do not enjoy exercising.

Essay

1. Try your own hand at a problem–solution essay, giving detailed examples of both the problem and the solution. Like Barlow, you may want your tone to be humorous, sugarcoating a serious point. As for the problem, you're apt to be surrounded with choices:

getting enough hours into the day
scraping tuition together
keeping up with schoolwork
deciding which pleasure to indulge
sorting out family loyalties

Illustrate the problem by using examples. You may find examples for the solution harder to come by, in which case, like Barlow, you may want to propose something fantastic.

2. If you responded to the first suggestion for a journal entry, then you are already on your way to a rough draft. Think of all the ways people participate in America's fitness craze. What do they do? How do they do it? What do they get out of it? What are its hazards? Benefits? To what extent are you involved? Write an essay in which you explore what you think about the subject, providing examples to support your thesis.

Have Fun

Allison Silverman

If you have watched The Daily Show with Jon Stewart *or* The Colbert
Report, *you have met Allison Silverman without knowing it. As one of
the writers for* The Daily Show, *she won not only an Emmy but also a
coveted Peabody Award, the latter given "for excellence in radio and
television broadcasting." A graduate of Yale University, where she
majored in molecular biology, Silverman sharpened her sense of
comedy and timing in Chicago doing improvisational skits before
joining first* The Daily Show, *then* Late Night with Conan O'Brien,
and now The Colbert Report, *where she is the head writer and executive producer. You'll see some of that wacky humor in "Have Fun,"
her essay that appeared in* The New York Times Magazine *on April 8,
2007, as one of the magazine's "True-Life Tales."*

What to Look For   Although Silverman's essay has an informal tone,
she has organized the essay very carefully. As you read, mark the various places she echoes or ties events together. The result is a sense of
seamlessness, coherence.

1   There's a particular tone of voice that mothers use when they
watch their kids at the pool—a queasy combination of "have fun"
and "don't die." It's how my mother sounded when I was leaving the
country last year.

2   "Be safe," she said as I was packing. "Remember what happened
to Jill Carroll." I did remember. Jill Carroll is the journalist held for
82 days by masked gunmen who ambushed her car in a notoriously
dangerous district of Baghdad. I, on the other hand, was going to a
friend's wedding on the Italian Riviera.

3   Like all mothers, mine worries. When I got my driver's license,
she explained how to get wherever I wanted without taking a single left turn. When I said I might not have children, she expressed
a disarming readiness to "harvest" my eggs against my will. There
are times when my mother warns me of so many dangers that
I find them irresistible. A few years ago, I had friends take my picture in "hazardous" situations. In one, I am standing on a boulder

by the sea, pointing to a road sign that reads: "Caution: Extremely Dangerous—People Have Been Swept From the Rocks and Drowned." The idea was to send them to my mother, but I never could bring myself to do it.

4   Before the wedding, I took a train to Trieste, which was empty except for the teenagers on the pier and the women in housecoats who fed chicken livers to stray cats. There, I caught a bus for Ljubljana, and then four trains and a taxi back west to the town of Lerici, where the wedding was held. After several nights of limoncello and rides home with new friends, I headed to Florence, all by myself.

5   My last morning there, I walked to the train station and checked the board that listed arrivals and departures. My train was 30 minutes late. When I checked again, it was 80 minutes late. Each time the numbers on the board fluttered, my train magically receded farther from the Florence station. It didn't make sense. Weren't the Florentines the first to master perspective?

6   I bought some Peanut M&M's and tried not to be annoyed. When I turned around, there was a woman walking toward me, a beggar. She had legs the color of butternut squash and a look that made you wonder if she'd ever baked children into pies. Her swinging bag hit a man square in the face—a tourist in a floppy hat who had been sitting on the platform—and she didn't even stop. My hands started to sweat; the Peanut M&M's slid around in my fist. Perhaps the worst time to be approached by a beggar is while you're eating Peanut M&M's. The way they tumble carelessly from their golden wrapper. Playful. Abundant. Incriminating.

7   She had set her sights specifically on me—a young woman alone, an easy mark. So when she asked for money, I said no.

8   She got louder. She talked faster.

9   I said no again.

10   She pulled out an empty baby bottle and waved it in my face, yelling.

11   But, I thought, this woman was in her 60s. She was no needy young mother. Instead, I suddenly felt she was an angry, older mother confronting an ungrateful child: me. I didn't understand what she was saying, but I got the unnerving sense that she was scolding me for taking last-minute trips in foreign countries, for hiking through forests alone, for hanging out at Internet cafes in the middle of the night, for making all those unnecessary left turns. How could I possibly do that to my mother?

12   And then she hit me. A hard, backhanded slap on the shoulder from a woman I had never met. I took a step back, and the postcard rack behind me teetered. She stared. I stared.

13   Then I hit her back. The tourist in the floppy hat applauded.

14   The woman shoved the baby bottle back in her bag. "Tu sei cattiva," she said. You are wicked. She pulled down the lower lid of her right eye. I was cursed. The train finally arrived. It took me to a bus, which took me to an airport terminal, where I was supposed to catch a shuttle to my hotel to sleep before an early-morning flight. But there was no shuttle. The terminal was empty except for a man in a business suit.

15   I waited. No one came. I showed the man in the business suit the address of my hotel. My Italian was too thin to explain much else. He left, and I sat in the terminal alone. Half an hour later, he reappeared, said nothing, picked up my bag and led me to his car.

16   I got in, trying not to think about Jill Carroll and being cursed. When curses are directed at other people, I absolutely know for a fact that they are complete hogwash. But I'm considerably more open-minded when it comes to curses directed at me.

17   Neither of us talked. We didn't even make eye contact. When we reached the hotel, he took my bag to the front desk and I kissed him on the cheek. By the time I found my room, I was in tears. I'd had fun. I didn't die. I wondered if I'd ever tell my mother.

ORGANIZATION AND IDEAS

1. Paragraphs 1–3 introduce the essay. What do they tell you about the mother? Silverman?

2. What kind of example does what happened to Jill Carroll illustrate?

3. How would you characterize Silverman? Her mother? Their relationship?

4. Silverman uses description and narration to illustrate two events—one in the train station and the other in the airport. In what ways are those two events examples? What do they illustrate?

5. Considering your responses to questions 1–4, what thesis does Silverman imply?

TECHNIQUE AND STYLE

1. Consider all the negative details and the positive ones. Which group predominates? Why might Silverman have wanted that choice?

2. How would you describe the atmosphere Silverman creates in paragraphs 4 and 14–16?

3. Reread the essay paying particular attention to tone. What different kinds of humor do you find? What effect do they achieve?

4. Silverman describes the incident with the old woman in considerable detail. Trace your emotional responses to each of paragraphs 4–14. How do your responses change and why?

5. Silverman's essay deals with personal experience centered on events that would be foreign to many readers. How does she try to link her experience to that of her readers? How well does she succeed?

SUGGESTIONS FOR WRITING

Journal

1. Reread paragraphs 4–14. To what extent are Silverman's reactions justified? Those of the old lady?

2. At the end of the essay, Silverman comments on her adventures, "I wondered if I'd ever tell my mother." Write up the version she might tell.

Essay

1. Think about the times you had an unexpected encounter. Where were you? What caused it? How did it affect you? Why? If nothing comes to mind, consider one of these suggestions:

seeing an old friend
visiting a once-familiar place
confronting an unfamiliar food
discovering a cultural difference
meeting up with a poisonous snake or wild animal

Use your ideas to write an essay in which you depend on examples to support your main point.

2. Think about your answers to question 3 in Technique and Style and use what you discovered to write an essay discussing Silverman's kind of humor. You may find it helpful to read about her work writing for Jon Stewart and Stephen Colbert, accounts that are readily available on the Web.

Stop Ordering Me Around

Stacey Wilkins

Like many students, Stacey Wilkins worked in a restaurant waiting on tables, a job that helped her pay off a student loan but also extracted its own price, as her essay points out. The essay appeared in the January 4, 1993, issue of Newsweek *in a regular feature, the "My Turn" column. Wilkins took the $1,000 she made writing the article to buy a one-way ticket to Hong Kong, where she landed a reporting job with CNN's international affiliate. She has not waited on a table since. Her career later included postings in Singapore, Australia, Alaska, Atlanta, and New York City. Wilkins left the news business in 2005 to attend Yale University, where she completed her teaching certification. She is currently an English and journalism teacher at Darien High School in Darien, Connecticut. Ironically, she works just a few miles from the very restaurant that inspired her to write the essay.*

What to Look For   The narrative that opens Wilkins' essay serves as the primary example in the essay, and one that sets the essay's tone as well. As you read the essay, try to hear it so that you can identify her tone more exactly. At times, the tone may strike you as angry, hurt, bitter, sarcastic, and any number of other variations. How would you characterize it?

1   I had just sat an extra hour and a half waiting for some country-club tennis buddies to finish a pizza. They came in 15 minutes after the restaurant closed—they hadn't wanted to cut short their tennis match. The owner complied and agreed to turn the oven back on and make them a pizza. The cook had long since gone home.

2   The customers had no problem demanding service after I explained that the restaurant had closed. They had no problem sitting there until well after 11 o'clock to recount the highlights of their tennis game (the restaurant closed at 9:30 p.m.). And, most important, they had no problem making me the brunt of their cruel little post-tennis match. What fun it was to harass the pathetic little waitress. "Oh, it's just so nice sitting here like this," one man said. After getting no response, he

continued: "Boy, I guess you want us to leave." I was ready to explode in anger. "I am not going to respond to your comments," I said, and walked away.

3   He was geared up for a fight. The red flag had been waved. The man approached me and asked about dessert. A regular customer, he had never made a practice of ordering dessert before. You know, the '90s low-fat thing. But that night he enjoyed the power. He felt strong, I felt violated.

4   Three dollars and 20 cents later, I went home. Their tip was my payment for this emotional rape. As I drove, tears streamed down my face. Why was I crying? I had been harassed before. Ten years of waitressing should have inured me to this all-too-common situation. But this was a watershed: the culmination of a decade of abuse.

5   I am now at the breaking point. I can't take being the public's punching bag. People seem to think abuse is included in the price of an entree. All sense of decency and manners is checked with their coats at the door. They see themselves in a position far superior to mine. They are the kings. I am the peasant.

6   I would like them to be the peasants. I am a strong advocate of compulsory restaurant service in the United States. What a great comeuppance it would be for the oppressors to have to work a double shift—slinging drinks, cleaning up after kids and getting pissed off that a party of 10 tied up one of their tables for three hours and left a bad tip. Best of all, I would like to see that rude man with tomato sauce on his tennis shorts.

7   Eating in a restaurant is about more than eating food. It is an opportunity to take your frustrations out on the waiter. It is a chance to feel better than the person serving your food. People think there is nothing wrong with rudeness or sexual harassment if it is inflicted on a waiter.

8   Customers have no problem with ignoring the wait staff when they go to take an order. Or they won't answer when the waiter comes to the table laden with hot plates asking who gets what meal. My personal pet peeve is when they make a waiter take a separate trip for each item. "Oh, I'll take another Coke." The waiter asks, "Would anyone else like one?" No response. Inevitably when he comes back to the table someone will say, "I'll have a Coke, too." And so on and so on.

9   I find it odd because no matter what an insolent cad someone might be, they generally make an effort to cover it up in public. The majority of people practice common etiquette. Most individuals won't

openly cut in line or talk throughout a movie. People are cognizant of acceptable behavior and adhere to the strictures it demands. That common code of decency does not apply while eating out.

10 Food-service positions are the last bastion of accepted prejudice. People go into a restaurant and openly torment the waiter, leave a small tip and don't think twice about it. Friends allow companions to be rude and don't say a word. The friends of this man did not once tell him to stop taunting me. They remained silent.

11 It doesn't cross their minds that someone has just been rotten to another human being. I have yet to hear someone stick up for the waitress, to insist a person stop being so cruel. This is because people don't think anything wrong has occurred.

12 However, if this man had shouted obscenities at another patron about her ethnicity, say, it would have rightly been deemed unacceptable. Why don't people understand that bad manners are just as unacceptable in a restaurant? Why do they think they have license to mistreat restaurant personnel?

13 I believe it is because food-service workers are relegated to such a low position on the social stratum. Customers have the power. Food-service employees have none. Thus we are easy targets for any angry person's pent-up frustrations. What better sparring partner than one who can't fight back? Most waiters won't respond for fear of losing their jobs. Consequently, we are the designated gripe-catchers of society, along with similar service workers.

14 If people stepped down from their spurious pedestals, they might see how wrong they are. We have dreams and aspirations just like everyone else. Our wages finance those dreams. Even an insulting 10 percent tip helps us to move toward a goal, pay the rent, feed the kids.

15 I'm using my earnings to pay off an encumbering graduate-school debt. Our bus girl is financing her education at the University of Pennsylvania. My manager is saving for her first baby. Another waitress is living on her earnings while she pursues an acting career. The dishwasher sends his pay back to his children in Ecuador.

16 Our dreams are no less valid than those of someone who holds a prestigious job at a large corporation. A restaurant's flexible working hours appeal to many people who dislike the regimen of a 9-to-5 day. Our employment doesn't give someone the right to treat us as non-entities. I deserve respect whether I remain a waitress or move on to a different career. And so do the thousands of waiters and waitresses who make your dining experience a pleasant one.

ORGANIZATION AND IDEAS

1. How does the opening narrative set the scene? Where else in the essay do you find references to that narrative? Do they unify the essay or distract you? Why?
2. At what point in the essay does the author move from the particular to the general? Which gets the most emphasis?
3. Reexamine the essay as one that poses a problem and a solution. What is the problem? The solution?
4. To what extent does Wilkins' experience coincide with your own? That of your friends?
5. Where do you find Wilkins' thesis? Explain whether you find that placement effective.

TECHNIQUE AND STYLE

1. How would you characterize the author's tone?
2. Does the opening narrative enlist your sympathies? Why or why not?
3. Some readers may find the essay's aim is more expressive than expository or persuasive, that the author is more concerned with venting her feelings than explaining the problem or persuading her readers to resolve it. Make a case for your interpretation of the author's aim.
4. In paragraph 2, Wilkins repeats variations on "they had no problem." Explain whether you find the repetition effective.
5. At various times in the essay, Wilkins uses words that suggest she is really writing about issues of power and class, as in her use of "peasant" (paragraphs 5 and 6) and "low position on the social stratum" (paragraph 13). What other examples can you find? Would the essay be stronger or weaker if these issues were discussed more openly?

SUGGESTIONS FOR WRITING

Journal

1. We live in a service society, yet as Wilkins points out, sometimes we demand too much of those who provide the services. Record a few examples of rudeness that you have observed.
2. Write an entry recording your reaction to Wilkins' essay. Do you think her complaints are justified?

Essay

1. More than likely you have or have had a job similar to Wilkins', if not waiting on tables then some other low-paying job that is also low on the totem pole of status. Like Wilkins, you may have found you were (or are) not treated with respect. On the other hand, your experience

may be quite the opposite. Write an essay in which you use examples from your own experience or the experiences of others to explain how you were (or are) treated on your job. You will want to narrow your subject so that you can cover it thoroughly in three to five pages, so you might focus on a specific category of people:

customers

co-workers

supervisor(s)

2. Wilkins raises the issues of power and class in her essay (see paragraphs 5, 6, and 13), but as Americans we like to think we live in a classless society. Think about the idea of class and write an essay in which you test the validity of the claim of classlessness. Make sure you define what you mean by class, and use examples from the news and any other sources to support your thesis.

A Black Fan of Country Music Finally Tells All

Lena Williams

Lena Williams started her career in journalism as a reporter for a radio station while she was a student at Howard University. After earning her BA at Howard, she entered the Columbia University Graduate School of Journalism, from which she received an MSc. She worked as a reporter while she was an intern at the Washington Post, *then as an associate editor at* Black Sports Magazine, *and has been on the staff of* The New York Times *since 1974, first as a clerk, then trainee, and now senior writer. She has written on civil rights, lifestyles, metropolitan news, and sports, winning various publishing awards along the way. An article she originally wrote for the* Times *in 1997 is now a book,* It's the Little Things: The Everyday Interactions That Get under the Skin of Blacks and Whites (2000). *Since 1998, she has moved from being a lifestyles writer to sports. The essay that follows appeared on Sunday, June 19, 1994, in the* Times' *"Arts and Leisure" section's coverage of "Pop Music." The column was titled "Pop View."*

What to Look For   At times, you may find yourself writing an essay on a subject that you're somewhat embarrassed about, which is the position Lena Williams found herself in when she wrote the essay that follows. In that case, you'll need to make a decision about your tone, the attitude you take toward your subject and your audience. Williams, as you will see, takes an unapologetic stance, almost daring her readers to challenge her. Yet the overall tone of the essay is not antagonistic because she takes the edge off of her "challenge" with humor and personal narrative, techniques that you can incorporate into your own writing.

1   I heard that Reba McEntire's new album, "Read My Mind," shot to No. 5 on the Billboard chart the first weekend of its release.

2   Well, she got my $11.95.

3   I'm a 40-something black woman who spent her youth in Washington, lip-syncing to the Supremes and slow dancing to the Temptations. Now I often come home to my Manhattan apartment and put on Vince Gill, Randy Travis or Reba. Consider me a fan of country music. So there. Deal with it.

4   For most of my adult life, I was a closet country music fan. I'd hide my Waylon Jennings and Willie Nelson albums between the dusty, psychedelic rock. I'd listen to Dolly Parton on my earphones, singing along softly, afraid my neighbors might mistake my imitation twang for a cry for help. I'd enter a music store, looking over my shoulder in search of familiar faces and flip through the rhythm-and-blues section for about five minutes before sneaking off to the country aisle where I'd surreptitiously grab a Travis Tritt tape off the rack and make a bee-line for the shortest cashier's line.

5   Just when I'd reached for my American Express card, I'd spot a tall, dark, handsome type in an Armani suit standing behind me with a puzzled look. What's he going to think? "The sister seems down, but what's she doing with that Dwight Yoakum CD?"

6   So now I'm publicly coming out of the closet and proclaiming my affection for country perennials like Ms. McEntire.

7   When I told a friend I was preparing this confessional, he offered a word of caution: "No self-respecting black person would ever admit to that in public."

8   I thought about his comment. As a child growing up in the 1950's, in a predominantly black community, I wasn't allowed to play country-and-western music in my house. Blacks weren't supposed to like country—or classical for that matter—but that's another story. Blacks'

contribution to American music was in jazz, blues and funk. Country music was dismissed as poor white folks' blues and associated with regions of the nation that symbolized prejudice and racial bigotry. Even mainstream white America viewed country as lower class and less desirable, often poking fun at its twangy chords and bellyaching sentiments.

9   But I was always a cowgirl at heart. I liked country's wild side; its down-home, aw-shucks musicians with the yodel in their voices and the angst in their lyrics. I saw an honesty in country and its universal tales of love lost and found. Besides, the South didn't have a monopoly on racial hatred, and country artists, like everybody else, were stealing black music, so why should I hold it against country?

10   And while snickering at country, white America also demonstrated a similar cultural backwardness toward black music, be it gospel, ragtime or the blues. So I allowed country to enter my heart and my mind, in spite of its faults. Indeed, when prodded, some blacks who rejected country conceded that there was a spirituality that resounded in the music and that in its heartfelt sentiment, country was a lot like blues. Yet they could never bring themselves to spend hard-earned dollars on Hank Williams Jr.

11   The 1980's saw country (western was dropped, much to my chagrin) become mainstream. Suddenly there was country at the Copa and at Town Hall. WYNY-FM radio in New York now claims the largest audience of any country station, with more than one million listeners. Dolly Parton and Kenny Rogers became movie stars. Garth Brooks became an American phenomenon.

12   Wall Street investment bankers bought cowboy boots and hats and learned to do the two-step. And black and white artists like Patti LaBelle and Lyle Lovett and Natalie Cole and Ms. McEntire now sing duets and clearly admire one another's music.

13   Perhaps the nation's acceptance of country has something to do with an evolutionary change in the music. Country has got edge. It has acquired an attitude. Womens' voices have been given strength. Oh, the hardship and misery is still there. But the stuff about "standing by your man" has changed to a more assertive posture.

14   In "I Won't Stand in Line," a song on Ms. McEntire's new album, she makes it clear to a skirt-chasing lover that "I'd do almost anything just to make you mine, but I won't stand in line." That line alone makes me think of Aretha Franklin's "Respect."

15   One other thing: I don't like sad songs. I've cried enough for a lifetime. Country makes me laugh, always has. Maybe because it never

took itself so seriously. Think about it. "Drop-Kick Me, Jesus, Through the Goal Posts of Life." "A Boy Named Sue."

16   Ms. McEntire serves up a humorous touch in "Why Haven't I Heard From You." "That thing they call the telephone/ Now there's one on every corner, in the back of every bar/ You can get one in your briefcase, on a plane or in your car/ So tell me why haven't I heard from you, darlin', honey, what is your excuse?" Call it Everywoman's lament.

17   Well it's off my chest; and it feels good.

18   I will no longer make excuses for my musical tastes. Not when millions are being made by performers exhorting listeners to "put your hands in the air and wave 'em like you just don't care."

19   Compare that with the haunting refrain of Ms. McEntire's "I Think His Name Was John," a song about a woman, a one-night stand and AIDS: "She lays all alone and cries herself to sleep/ 'Cause she let a stranger kill her hopes and her dreams/ And in the end when she was barely hanging on/ All she could say is she thinks his name was John."

ORGANIZATION AND IDEAS

1. What paragraph or paragraphs introduce the essay?

2. Paragraphs 4 and 5 detail a short narrative. What is Williams' point?

3. Paragraphs 8–12 sketch the evolution of country-and-western music. Trace the chronology and the changes in attitude toward the genre.

4. The essay ends with a comparison in paragraphs 18 and 19, one that Williams doesn't spell out. What is it? How does it relate to her thesis?

5. Williams maintains that since the 1980s, country music has "become mainstream" (paragraph 11). How accurate is that assertion?

TECHNIQUE AND STYLE

1. Paragraphs 2 and 17 consist of one sentence each. What effect does Williams achieve with a one-sentence paragraph?

2. Is the essay addressed primarily to a black or white audience or both? What evidence can you find to support your view?

3. Although the essay expresses Williams' personal opinion and is subjective, she achieves a balance between the personal and the general. How does she do that?

4. Williams supports her thesis with examples from popular music, both country-western and black. Explain whether you find her examples sufficient evidence for her thesis.

5. Analyze the effectiveness of the essay's title. What other titles can you think of? Which is the more effective and why?

SUGGESTIONS FOR WRITING

Journal

1. Taste in music, as in most everything else, is apt to be idiosyncratic. Think of a band or song or type of music that represents your particular taste and explain why you like it, using examples to support your ideas.
2. Make a list of the names and titles Williams uses as examples. What examples can you provide to update that list?

Essay

1. If you look back on your tastes, you will probably find that they change over time. Perhaps a type of music that you liked some years ago you would now have a hard time listening to. Or perhaps you were disappointed in a film you recently saw again or a book that you reread, one that had impressed you in the past and belonged to a particular genre such as horror films or adventure stories. You might start by drawing up two columns—*Then* and *Now*—and jotting down examples representing your earlier tastes and your present ones. Like Williams, you may want to write about how your taste has evolved or explain why you like what you like. For a general category, you might think about

   music
   food
   films
   books
   heroes
   sports

2. Williams' essay is an assertive defense of her taste in music. Write an essay in which you evaluate the essay's effectiveness. You might start by asking yourself questions such as, "Does she present enough evidence?" "Are her examples apt?" "Does she provide enough background for her explanations?"

Bananas for Rent

Michiko Kakutani

Anyone who reads the book reviews in The New York Times *is famil-iar with Michiko Kakutani's byline, for she's the lead reviewer for the newspaper, covering both fiction and nonfiction, bestowing both praise and punches. As you might suspect, that sort of extensive analytical reading makes her an astute critic of the contemporary scene, so it was only fitting that she also contributed to the column "Culture Zone" in* The New York Times Magazine, *a column in which Ms. Kakutani takes a tough view of popular culture. Her wide range of interests is reflected in her book* Poet at the Piano: Portraits of Writers, Filmmakers, and Other Artists at Work *(1988). In 1998, Ms. Kakutani was awarded the Pulitzer Prize for Criticism. Her essay "Bananas for Rent" was a "Culture Zone" piece published on November 9, 1997.*

What to Look For If you are writing about the contemporary scene and using examples to back up your points, you may find that some of your readers may not be familiar with the examples you use. One way out of that bind is to use lots. That is what Kakutani does in her essay, so be on the lookout for multiple examples as you read. It's easiest to think of multiple examples when you are making notes for an essay. If you were writing about blue jeans, for instance, you might be tempted to just name Levi's, but at that point, it's also easy to think of other brand names as well—Guess, Gap, Gloria Vanderbilt, and the like.

1   They are as pervasive as roaches, as persuasive as the weather, as popular as Princess Diana. They adorn our clothes, our luggage, our sneakers and our hats. They are ubiquitous on television, unavoidable in magazines and inevitable on the Internet. The average American, it is estimated, is pelted by some 3,000 advertising messages a day, some 38,000 TV commercials a year.

2   Not so long ago, it was only race cars, tennis stars and sports stadiums that were lacquered head-to-toe with ads. Nowadays, school buses and trucks rent out advertising space by the foot.

There are entire towns that have signed exclusive deals with Coke or Pepsi. The dead, including Marilyn Monroe (Chanel No. 5), Gene Kelly (Gap khakis) and Fred Astaire (Dirt Devil vacuum cleaners), have been hired as pitchmen, and so have New Delhi paraplegics, who now hawk Coca-Cola under bright red-and-white umbrellas. Even bananas have been colonized as billboard space, with stickers promoting the video release of "Space Jam" and the "Got Milk?" campaign turning up on the fruit.

3   As the scholar James Twitchell observes, advertising has become "our cultural literacy—it's what we know." Twitchell, author of a book called *Adcult USA* and a professor at the University of Florida, says his students share no common culture of books or history; what they share is a knowledge of commercials. When he questions them at random about concepts from "The Dictionary of Cultural Literacy," he says he is likely to draw a blank. When, however, he recites a commercial jingle, his students "instantaneously know it, and they're exultant," he says. "They actually think Benetton ads are profound. To them, advertising is high culture."

4   Schoolchildren around the country avidly collect Absolut ads, and college students decorate their walls with poster-size reproductions of ads that are available from a four-year-old company called Beyond the Wall. Forget Monet and Van Gogh. Think Nike, BMW and Calvin Klein. As Brian Gordon, one of the company's founders, sees it, kids regard ads as "a form of self-expression." In today's "short-attention society," he reasons, ads are something people can relate to: they provide "insights into current culture," and they provide them in 30 seconds or less.

5   No doubt this is why entire "Seinfeld" episodes have been built around products like Pez and Junior Mints. The popularity of Nick at Nite's vintage commercials, Rosie O'Donnell's peppy renditions of old jingles, the almost nightly commercial spoofs by Letterman and Leno—all are testaments to the prominent role advertising has assumed in our lives. A whole school of fiction known as Kmart realism has grown up around the use of brand names, while a host of well-known songs (from Nirvana's "Smells Like Teen Spirit" to Oasis' "Shakermaker") satirize old commercials. It used to be that advertisers would appropriate a hit song (like the Beatles' "Revolution") to promote a product; nowadays, the advertising clout of a company like Volkswagen has the power to turn a song (even an old song like "Da Da Da," by the now defunct German band Trio) into a hit.

6   So what does advertising's takeover of American culture mean? It's not just that the world has increasingly come to resemble the Home Shopping Network. It's that advertising's ethos of spin—which makes selling a means *and* an end—has thoroughly infected everything from politics (think of Clinton's "permanent campaign") to TV shows like "Entertainment Tonight" that try to pass off publicity as information. It's that advertising's attention-grabbing hype has become, in our information-glutted age, the modus operandi of the world at large. "Advertising is the most pervasive form of propaganda in human history," says the scholar Mark Crispin Miller. "It's reflected in every esthetic form today."

7   Miller points out that just as commercials have appropriated techniques that once belonged to avant-garde film—cross-cutting, jump cuts, hand-held camera shots—so have mainstream movies and TV shows begun to ape the look and shape of ads, replacing character and story with razzle-dazzle special effects. For that matter, more and more film makers, including Howard Zieff, Michael Bay, Adrian Lyne and Simon West, got their starts in advertising.

8   Advertising has a more insidious effect as well. Advertisers scouting TV shows and magazines are inclined to select those vehicles likely to provide a congenial (and therefore accessible or upbeat) backdrop for their products, while a public that has grown up in a petri dish of ads has grown impatient with any art that defies the easy-access, quick-study esthetic of commercials—that is, anything that's difficult or ambiguous. "People have become less capable of tolerating any kind of darkness or sadness," Miller says. "I think it ultimately has to do with advertising, with a vision of life as a shopping trip."

9   There are occasional signs of a backlash against advertising—the Vancouver-based Media Foundation uses ad parodies to fight rampant consumerism—but advertising implacably forges ahead like one of those indestructible sci-fi monsters, nonchalantly co-opting the very techniques used against it. Just as it has co-opted rock-and-roll, alienation (a Pontiac commercial features an animated version of Munch's painting "The Scream") and Dadaist jokes (an ad campaign for Kohler featured interpretations of bidets and faucets by contemporary artists), so it has now co-opted irony, parody and satire.

10   The end result of advertising's ability to disguise itself as entertainment and entertainment's willingness to adopt the hard-sell methods of advertising is a blurring of the lines between art and commerce. Even as this makes us increasingly oblivious to advertising's agenda

(to sell us stuff), it also makes us increasingly cynical about everything else—ready to dismiss it, unthinkingly, as junk or fluff or spin, just another pitch lobbed out by that gigantic machine called contemporary culture.

ORGANIZATION AND IDEAS

1. Kakutani's opening sentence announces qualities that unify the essay that follows. What paragraph or paragraphs focus on ads as "pervasive"? As "persuasive"? As "popular"?
2. Which paragraphs emphasize the effect of ads? What effect do they have?
3. Reread the first and last paragraphs. What is the thesis of the essay? What evidence can you cite to back up your opinion?
4. To what extent do you agree with Kakutani's thesis?
5. Kakutani maintains that advertising "disguise[s] itself as entertainment" (paragraph 10). How accurate do you find that assertion?

TECHNIQUE AND STYLE

1. Kakutani violates a principle of usage in her first paragraph in that the pronoun "they" has no antecedent. What effect does she achieve by not initially specifying to whom the "they" refers?
2. Ads and the culture within which they exist come in for much negative criticism in this essay. How would you characterize Kakutani's tone— negative, reasoned, thoughtful, strident, what?
3. Describe what you perceive to be Kakutani's persona. What evidence can you find to support your view?
4. In a handbook of grammar and usage, look up the uses of the dash. You'll note that Kakutani uses dashes frequently, as in paragraphs 3, and 5–10. What other punctuation could she have used? What reasons can you think of for her choice of the dash?
5. Kakutani uses three similes in her first sentence. Choose one of them and make up three or four of your own. Which do you prefer and why?

SUGGESTIONS FOR WRITING

Journal

1. Anyone who watches television learns to hate certain ads. Take a minute to write down the ads you dislike the most and then, for each, put down the reasons. You'll end up with the working notes for an essay.
2. Kakutani states that thanks to ads we are becoming "increasingly cynical about everything else—ready to dismiss it, unthinkingly, as junk or fluff

or spin, just another pitch lobbed out by that gigantic machine called contemporary culture" (paragraph 10). Write an entry in which you agree or disagree with Kakutani's statement, citing examples to support your views.

Essay

1. Whether or not you agree with Kakutani, there's no arguing about the prevalence of advertisements. To test Kakutani's points or simply to analyze advertisements on your own, flip through a popular magazine noting various categories of advertisements—cars, liquor, clothes, perfumes, and the like. Choosing a group of ads for a type of product, examine it as though it were a window into our culture. What do you see? What does it say about our concerns? Fears? Attention span? Tastes? Use your notes to write an essay that illustrates its points through multiple examples. If advertising doesn't seem to be a worthwhile subject, then choose another topic that you can use as a way to examine popular culture. Here are some suggestions:
   television shows
   films
   books
   styles
   fads
   franchises

2. What television ads do you remember and like? Make a short list (it only needs to make sense to you), and then select one to explain why you like it.

On Using Definition

Before even naming her subject, Diane Ackerman begins her essay with a question: "What food do you crave?" She then announces her subject—chocolate—and follows with a scattershot of short definitions:

> A wooer's gift. A child's reward. A jilted lover's solace. A cozy mug of slumber. Halloween manna. A gimme-more that tantalizes young and old alike. Almost every candy bar. Chocolate.

The subject is very familiar, one readers both know and have opinions about. Ackerman's task, then, is to define her subject in a way that gets her audience interested enough to keep reading. To do that she explores the central term's **connotations,** the word's associative or emotional meanings. A dictionary will provide the word's explicit meaning, its **denotation**—the different ways in which the word can be used, and also its etymology. But none of that will convey the rich layers of meaning the word has accumulated through the years, nor will it connect with the experiences of the reader.

How do you find a subject? Find a word that interests you. Perhaps it's an abstract one such as *freedom* or *honesty*. Think about some basic questions, such as "Whose freedom?" If it's your freedom you are writing about, who or what sets limits on your freedom? The law? The church? Parents? Family responsibilities? Ask yourself how the concept of freedom touches your life. The more specific your examples, the more concrete your definition can be, and the less the danger of slipping into clichés, images so familiar that they have lost any power they might have had, as in "free as a bird."

Perhaps it's a concrete word or term you want to write about, such as *hot dog* or *T-shirt*. Like Ackerman, you might begin with what your reader may associate with it and then move on to its history, leading up to its current use. The T-shirt, for instance, has progressed from undershirt to personal billboard. Throughout your essay, you'd want to include examples drawn from your own experience and from outside sources. And like Ackerman, perhaps you have a personal narrative you could include.

What does your reader know?   Unless the word you are defining is quite unusual, most readers will be familiar with its dictionary definition; your own definition and your speculations on the word's connotations are of much greater interest. Jot down what you can assume your reader knows about your subject and then consider what effect you want to have. Are you explaining, persuading, entertaining, expressing your feelings to make a larger point? In the example quoted on page 97, for example, Ackerman uses positive images to express her own equally positive feelings, interest her readers, and persuade them to read on. The rest of the essay explains the lure of chocolate.

How do you explore your subject?   You can start by using various patterns of thought, jotting down your ideas and questions. If you were thinking of the general topic "college students," you might be struck by how they are portrayed in popular culture and how different that is from the reality. To write an essay that defines real college students, you might think of

Example What films or TV shows portray college students?
Description How can you describe them? What senses can you appeal to?
Narration What are those students involved in? What conflicts do they face?
Comparison and contrast How do these depictions differ from reality?
Division and classification Who are the real college students? What types or categories can they be grouped into?
Process How can you find out factual information? What steps are involved?
Cause and effect What are the negative effects of the popular impression of "the college student"? Are there any positive ones?
Analogy What metaphor might contrast the popular against the real?

When questions such as these are tailored to the particular word or concept under scrutiny, they will help you develop your ideas and generate a rough draft.

If you don't find those probes useful or need to supplement them, you can draw on any number of outside sources. Check out Google and other Web search engines to find out more information. For the preceding topic, a quick search will turn up a huge selection of movies that are set on college campuses. Checking out the plots of several recent ones will give you many examples of how college students are portrayed—probably more than you can use. And sites such as the National Center for Educational Statistics (http://nces.ed.gov/) will give you a very different view, one based on reality, revealing facts such as that the average age of a college student is 25 and one-fourth of the college-age population is over 30. Research such as this has the additional advantage of broadening the base of your information and adding to your credibility, your **persona**—the image of yourself that you create and then present through the prose in your essay.

What's your thesis and where do you put it?   Several of the essays in this chapter deal with the idea of identity: how one defines oneself or is defined by others. Thinking through the topic on your own, you might discover many ways one's identity can be defined: by age, race, nationality, religion, beliefs, and so on. Perhaps your thinking ends up as a question: What does it mean to be a _____? You can fill in the blank with anything that interests you—first-generation American, single father/mother, Lakers fan. No matter what your topic, your answer could be developed into a draft of a definition essay, with your working thesis as a one-sentence assertion. You can tinker with the wording to make it as effective as possible, but no matter what your thesis, you probably want to lead up to it and then place it at the end of your introduction. If you want to try a more unusual choice, place the thesis at the end of your essay and then check to make sure that everything that comes before it leads logically to that statement.

How do you organize the content?   You may want to use a roughly chronological pattern of organization, starting at one point in time and moving forward to another. Structuring an essay so that it moves from the least to the most important point is another obvious pattern, one used by several of the writers in this chapter. You might also consider organizing your paper by question/answer, the introduction posing a question and the body of the essay answering it. A variation on that pattern is one in which one part of the essay poses a problem that is then discussed and analyzed in terms of possible solutions. Or perhaps you'd prefer a more subtle structure that moves from the particular to the general. For that essay defining "college student," for example, you might start with the particular—the popular stereotype you find in movies and television—and then discuss the general, the broader view you've discovered through your research—one perhaps far removed from carefree party days.

Useful Terms

Connotation The associations suggested by a word that add to its literal meaning. *Home* and *domicile* have similar dictionary meanings, but they differ radically in their connotation.

Denotation The literal meaning of a word, its dictionary definition.

Persona The character of the writer that comes through from the prose.

POINTERS FOR USING DEFINITION

Exploring the Topic

1. **What are the denotations of your term?** You should consult an unabridged dictionary and perhaps a more complete or specialized one, such as the *Oxford English Dictionary* or a dictionary of slang.

2. **What are the connotations of your term?** What emotional reactions or associations does it elicit from people? What situations evoke what responses and why?

3. **What other words can be used for your term?** Which are similar?

4. **What are the characteristics, qualities, or components of your term?** Which are most important? Are some not worth mentioning?

5. **What other modes are appropriate?** What modes can you draw on to help support your definition and the organization of the essay? Where can you use description? Narration? What examples can you use to illustrate your term?

6. **Has your word been used or misused?** If so, might that misuse be turned into an introductory narrative? A closing one?

Drafting the Paper

1. **Know your reader.** Review your lists of denotations and connotations together with the characteristics related to your term to
   see how familiar they are to your reader. Check to see if your
   reader may have particular associations that you need to redirect
   or change. Or if your reader is directly affected by your topic,
   make sure your definition does not offend.
2. **Know your purpose.** Unless your term is unusual, one of your
   biggest problems is to tell the reader something new about it.
   Work on your first paragraph so that it will engage the reader
   from the start. From that point on, keep your primary purpose in
   mind. If you are writing a paper that is basically self-expressive or
   persuasive, make sure you have an audience other than yourself.
   If your aim is informative, consider narration, example, cause and
   effect, and analogy as possible ways of presenting familiar material in a fresh light.
3. **Use evidence.** Provide examples as evidence to illustrate what
   your key term means. Also consider using negative examples
   and setting out distinctions between the meaning of your word
   and other, similar words.
4. **Draw on a variety of sources.** Define your term from several
   perspectives. Perhaps a brief history of the word would be
   helpful, or maybe some statistical information is in order. See if
   a brief narrative might provide additional meaning for the term.
5. **Make a point.** Don't mistake your definition for your thesis.
   The two are certainly related, but one is an assertion; the other
   is not. Perhaps your definition is a jumping-off place for a larger
   point you wish to make or a key part of that point. Or perhaps
   your term evokes a single dominant impression you want to
   convey. Whatever purpose your definition serves, it needs to
   support your thesis.

Chocolate Equals Love

Diane Ackerman

As an undergraduate at Boston University and then Pennsylvania State University, Diane Ackerman studied both science and literature, twin interests she would pursue as a writer while earning an MFA and PhD. A staff writer for The New Yorker, *Ackerman often writes on a wide variety of subjects.* The Moon by Whale Light *(1991) examines the threats to endangered animals. Another nonfiction book,* A Slender Thread *(1997), grew out of her volunteer work as a counselor at a suicide prevention and crisis center. Three of her books are* Natural Histor[ies]...of The Senses *(1990), of* Love *(1995), and of* My Garden *(2001). One of her more recent nonfiction works has the descriptive title* An Alchemy of Mind: The Marvel and Mystery of the Brain *(2004). Ackerman has also written* The Zookeeper's Wife: A War Story *(2007), a moving account of the director of the Warsaw Zoo and his wife who sheltered over 300 Jews and members of the resistance during the Nazi occupation of Poland in World War II. That's a long way from chocolate, the subject of her essay that follows, published in* Parade Magazine *on February 9, 2003. Reading it, you will be able to tell why Ackerman is also a well-published and respected poet, for in "Chocolate Equals Love" she manages to combine the vivid detail and compression characteristic of poetry with the precise detail and keen observation associated with science.*

What to Look For Good writers have a way of listening to words so that they are aware of a word's sound as well as sense. If you read Ackerman's second paragraph out loud, for instance, you'll hear a lot of *s* sounds that help make the prose flow smoothly. Reading your own work out loud will help you develop your own ear for the sound of good writing.

1 What food do you crave? Add a hint of mischief to your desire, and the answer is bound to be chocolate, Dark, divine, sense-bludgeoning chocolate. A wooer's gift. A child's reward. A jilted lover's solace. A cozy mug of slumber. Halloween manna. A gimmemore that tantalizes young and old alike. Almost every candy bar. Chocolate.

2 We can thank the Indians of Central and South America for chocolate's bewitching lusciousness. As the Spanish explorer Hernán Cortés

found, the Aztecs worshiped chocolate (which they named *cacahuatl*) as a gift from their wise god Quetzalcoatl. Aztec soldiers and male members of court drank as many as 2000 pitchers of chocolate every day. They spiked their drink with vanilla beans and spices, then drank it bubbly thick from golden cups. Adding chili peppers gave it bite. The Aztec leader Montezuma required a chocolate ice, made by pouring syrup over snow that runners brought to him from the nearest mountain.

3   Invigorating and dangerously sublime, chocolate dominated every facet of Aztec life, from sexuality to economy. Cocoa beans even served as currency: You could buy a rabbit for 10 beans, a slave for 100 beans.

4   At first, Cortés hated chocolate's shocking taste, which mingled bitter, spicy, pungent, silky, dank and dusty flavors. But in time its magic seduced him, and it is said that he introduced it to Spain, flavoring it with sugar instead of hot chili peppers.

5   By the 17th century, chocolate was thrilling Europeans with its sensory jolt—less devilish than liquor but still stimulating, luxurious and pleasantly addictive. Those who could afford it drank it thick and hot, as the Indians did, sometimes adding orange, vanilla or spices. Society ladies sipped several cups a day and even insisted on drinking it during church services. Doctors prescribed chocolate as a flesh-and-bone rejuvenator that could lift the spirits, hasten healing and raise a flagging libido.

6   Forget Viagra. Think bonbons.

7   Casanova, it is said, swore by chocolate and ate it as a prelude to lovemaking. The French King Louis XV's principal mistress Madame du Barry, served exquisitely refined but essentially drug-level chocolate to her various suitors. Unknowingly, they were following the custom of Montezuma, who was believed to have consumed extra chocolate before visiting his harem.

8   A liquid treasure until the 19th century, chocolate suddenly changed shape and personality when a Dutch chemist discovered how to separate cocoa butter, leaving powdered cocoa. The public clamored for portable, ever-ready chocolate, and confectioners obliged with pyramids of chocolate bars. Joining the chocolamania, the Cadbury brothers introduced chocolate in heart-shaped boxes in 1868. Milk chocolate appeared in Switzerland in 1875, thanks to Peter Daniel and Henri Nestlé. Then American mass-production provided cheap chocolates for the multitudes, thanks to the foresight of Milton Hershey. And the rest is history.

9   Is chocolate a health food? Chocolate is chemically active—a mind-altering drug that's good for you in moderation. The higher the cocoa content, the more antioxidants and other nutritious bonuses. Cocoa powder contains the most antioxidants, followed by dark chocolate and milk chocolate.

10   What delivers the chocolate buzz? Chocolate contains more than 300 chemicals, including tiny amounts of anandamide, which mimics the active ingredient in marijuana, plus such stimulants as theobromine and phenylethylamine. A 1.4-ounce bar of chocolate also can provide 20 milligrams of caffeine. That's jitters away from the 140 milligrams of an average cup of coffee, not to mention a thimbleful of espresso. But it's rousing enough, combined with the rest of chocolate's chemical bag of tricks. And the full sensory and nostalgic saga of eating chocolate— the mouth feel, the aroma, the taste, the memories—can calm the brain or lighten one's thoughts, for a while anyway.

11   If we luxuriate in a memory framed by the heaven of chocolate— say, eating s'mores around a campfire with a giggling Girl Scout troop or receiving a box of chocolates from a sappy beau and then sampling them with him—a small constellation of pleasure will attach itself to the idea of chocolate lifelong. That happens early on to nearly everyone.

12   For example, when I was a child, each year my mother and I would choose a colossal chocolate Easter rabbit with pink candy dot eyes. Together, we would sit on the floor in the aptly named "den" and devour most of the hollow rabbit—always start- ing with the ears and working our way down—until we went way beyond sated and started to feel a little sick. We would laugh with shared delight as we gobbled and afterward lounged about in a chocolate haze.

13   It was a cherished bonding ritual more visceral than verbal, reminding me how much we adore our senses. They're our house- guests, our explorers, our pets—and we love to give them treats. So how do you reward the sense of taste? For ages, the delicacy of choice has been rich, sensuously inviting chocolate.

ORGANIZATION AND IDEAS

1. Paragraph 1 announces the subject and describes it with quick images, all to interest the reader. How well does it succeed?
2. Ackerman chooses to begin the body of the essay (paragraphs 2–8) with a brief history of chocolate. How does that history help define it?

3. Paragraphs 9 and 10 provide a scientific view of chocolate. What information surprises you and why?
4. Think of the ideas Ackerman presents in paragraphs 2–10 and how chocolate can cause an emotional attachment, as described in paragraphs 11–13. State her thesis in one sentence.
5. To what extent does Ackerman's account of and appreciation for chocolate mesh with your own?

TECHNIQUE AND STYLE

1. Consult a handbook of grammar and usage for what it says about a sentence fragment, and then take another look at paragraph 1. To what extent, if any, are those fragments effective?
2. You are probably used to paragraphs as units that extend an idea, but Ackerman's sixth paragraph is quite different. What is its function?
3. In the last paragraph, Ackerman uses several metaphors for our senses. Which do you prefer and why?
4. In paragraphs 1, 9, 10, and 13, Ackerman uses questions. What purpose do they serve?
5. Most of the essay can be categorized as expository and objective, but in paragraphs 12 and 13, Ackerman switches to the personal. Why might she have chosen to do that and what effect does it have?

SUGGESTIONS FOR WRITING

Journal

1. Use your journal to explore how the senses can be viewed as pets.
2. Write a description that defines the kind of chocolate you like or dislike the most.

Essay

1. Think of the senses as possible topics for an essay that explains and defines the one you depend on the most: sight, smell, hearing, touch, or taste. Like Ackerman, you will want to include some scientific information, so you should do some research to be able to explain how that sense functions (a medical encyclopedia or medical Web page would be a good source). And, of course, use your own experience to explain why that sense is important to you.
2. Think about a kind of snack or food that you like a great deal, and write an essay that defines it. Like Ackerman, you can point out its history, how it is produced, the various forms it comes in, and your experiences with it. No matter what your topic, you can find a great deal of information about it from the Web by using a search engine.

I Was a Member of the Kung Fu Crew

Henry Han Xi Lau

New York City is still in many ways a city of neighborhoods, many of which are ethnic ones. The Chinatown that Henry Han Xi Lau writes about is one of the oldest, and it's where you can still walk down the street and not hear a word of English. To Lau, it's also home, even though he and his family had moved to Brooklyn, which, like Manhattan, is one of the city's five boroughs or districts. A sophomore at Yale University at the time he wrote this essay, Lau describes the people and places of Chinatown, defining it as "ghetto." Lau went on to graduate with distinctions in history and international studies and to earn a law degree from the University of California at Berkeley. He is now an associate in the law firm of Debevoise and Plimpton, working in Hong Kong. His essay was published in The New York Times Magazine *on October 19, 1997. After it came out, Lau objected to the way it had been edited, and in a later piece he wrote for* Discourses, *an undergraduate journal at Yale, he called it a "warped presentation." If you'd like to read his critique, you can find it by typing his name into a search engine; it was reprinted in* Macrocosm, *a Web journal published by Rice University. What's missing in the* Times *version that follows, according to Lau, is the "resourcefulness and hard-working side of ghettoness." See if you agree.*

What to Look For   Lau relies heavily on definition to convey what it's like to be a member of the Kung Fu Crew and to be "ghetto." Many of the techniques he uses are ones that can carry over to your own writing, so be on the lookout for the details that define the Crew's physical prowess, hair, pants, attitudes, accessories, and language, all of which add up to being "cool."

1   Chinatown is ghetto, my friends are ghetto, I am ghetto. I went away to college last year, but I still have a long strand of hair that reaches past my chin. I need it when I go back home to hang with the K.F.C.—for Kung Fu Crew, not Kentucky Fried Chicken. We all

met in a Northern Shaolin kung fu class years ago. Our *si-fu* was Rocky. He told us: "In the early 1900's in China, your grand master was walking in the streets when a foreigner riding on a horse disrespected him. So then he felt the belly of the horse with his palms and left. Shortly thereafter, the horse buckled and died because our grand master had used *qi-gong* to mess up the horse's internal organs." Everyone said, "Cool, I would like to do that." Rocky emphasized, "You've got to practice really hard for a long time to reach that level."

2   By the time my friends and I were in the eighth grade, we were able to do 20-plus pushups on our knuckles and fingers. When we practiced our crescent, roundhouse and tornado kicks, we had 10-pound weights strapped to our legs. Someone once remarked, "Goddamn—that's a freaking mountain!" when he saw my thigh muscles in gym class.

3   Most Chinatown kids fall into a few general categories. There are pale-faced nerds who study all the time to get into the Ivies. There are the recent immigrants with uncombed hair and crooked teeth who sing karaoke in bars. There are the punks with highlighted hair who cut school, and the gangsters, whom everyone else avoids.

4   Then there is the K.F.C. We work hard like the nerds, but we identify with the punks. Now we are reunited, and just as in the old days we amble onto Canal Street, where we stick out above the older folks, elderly women bearing leaden bags of bok choy and oranges. As an opposing crew nears us, I assess them to determine whether to grill them or not. Grilling is the fine art of staring others down and trying to emerge victorious.

5   How the hair is worn is important in determining one's order on the streets. In the 80's, the dominant style was the mushroom cut, combed neatly or left wild in the front so that a person can appear menacing as he peers through his bangs. To gain an edge in grilling now, some kids have asymmetrical cuts, with long random strands sprouting in the front, sides or back. Some dye their hair blue or green, while blood red is usually reserved for gang members.

6   Only a few years ago, examination of the hair was sufficient. But now there is a second step: assessing pants. A couple of years ago, wide legs first appeared in New York City, and my friends and I switched from baggy pants. In the good old days, Merry-Go-Round in the Village sold wide legs for only $15 a pair. When Merry-Go-Round

went bankrupt, Chinatown kids despaired. Wide-leg prices at other stores increased drastically as they became more popular. There are different ways of wearing wide legs. Some fold their pant legs inward and staple them at the hem. Some clip the back ends of their pants to their shoes with safety pins. Others simply cut the bottoms so that fuzzy strings hang out.

7   We grill the opposing punks. I untuck my long strand of hair so that it swings in front of my face. Nel used to have a strand, but he chewed it off one day in class by accident. Chu and Tom cut their strands off because it scared people at college. Jack has a patch of blond hair, while Tone's head is a ball of orange flame. Chi has gelled short hair, while Ken's head is a black mop. As a group, we have better hair than our rivals. But they beat us with their wide legs. In our year away at college, wide legs have gone beyond our 24-inch leg openings. Twenty-six- to 30-inch jeans are becoming the norm. If wide legs get any bigger, they will start flying up like a skirt in an updraft.

8   We have better accessories, though. Chi sports a red North Face that gives him a rugged mountain-climber look because of the jungle of straps sprouting in the back. Someone once asked Chi, "Why is the school bag so important to one's cool?" He responded, "Cuz it's the last thing others see when you walk away from them or when they turn back to look at you after you walk past them." But the other crew has female members, which augments their points. The encounter between us ends in a stalemate. But at least the K.F.C. members are in college and are not true punks.

9   In the afternoon, we decide to eat at the Chinatown McDonald's for a change instead of the Chinese bakery Maria's, our dear old hangout spot. "Mickey D's is good sit," Nel says. I answer: "But the Whopper gots more fat and meat. It's even got more bun." Nel agrees. "True that," he says. I want the Big Mac, but I buy the two-cheeseburger meal because it has the same amount of meat but costs less.

10   We sit and talk about ghettoness again. We can never exactly articulate what being ghetto entails, but we know the spirit of it. In Chinatown toilet facilities we sometimes find footprints on the seats because F.O.B.'s (fresh off the boats) squat on them as they do over the holes in China. We see alternative brand names in stores like Dolo instead of Polo, and Mike instead of Nike.

11   We live by ghettoness. My friends and I walk from 80-something Street in Manhattan to the tip of the island to save a token. We

gorge ourselves at Gray's Papaya because the hot dogs are 50 cents each. But one cannot be stingy all the time. We leave good tips at Chinese restaurants because our parents are waiters and waitresses, too.

12   We sit for a long time in McDonald's, making sure that there is at least a half-inch of soda in our cups so that when the staff wants to kick us out, we can claim that we are not finished yet. Jack positions a mouse bite of cheeseburger in the center of a wrapper to support our claim.

13   After a few hours, the K.F.C. prepares to disband. I get in one of the no-license commuter vans on Canal Street that will take me to Sunset Park in Brooklyn, where my family lives now. All of my friends will leave Chinatown, for the Upper East Side and the Lower East Side, Forest Hills in Queens and Bensonhurst in Brooklyn. We live far apart, but we always come back together in Chinatown. For most of us, our homes used to be here and our world was here.

Organization and Ideas

1. The essay is set out in chronological order. What paragraphs cover what times?
2. What categories of kids does Lau describe? Where does the Crew fit?
3. Lau describes "grilling" in paragraphs 4–8. What is his point?
4. Lau may have moved away from Chinatown, but he is still very much a part of its community. How would you characterize that community and its values?
5. Is Lau's thesis explicit or implicit? How can you phrase it in your own words?

Technique and Style

1. Look up the term *comma splice* in a handbook of grammar and usage, and check what you find against Lau's first sentence. Why is it a legitimate comma splice?
2. Lau uses dialogue in paragraphs 8 and 9. What does it add to the essay?
3. The essay piles on details and information that lead up to a definition of *ghetto*. State that definition in your own words.
4. *Ghetto* usually has a negative connotation. How does Lau make it positive?
5. The essay is written in standard American English. Why might Lau have chosen to write it that way instead of in "ghetto"?

Suggestions for Writing

Journal

1. If you met the Kung Fu Crew on the street, you might find yourself ignoring them, "grilling" them, admiring them, but no matter what, you'd have some sort of reaction. Describe how you would react.

2. Look up the word *intimidation* in an unabridged dictionary, and think about times in your experience when you were intimidated or when you intimidated someone else. Use your journal to define how you felt.

Essay

1. People spend a lot of time analyzing what's in and what's out. For some, those in advertising or fashion, for instance, it's a business, but all of us are affected by it. Perhaps you would find a lot to say in an essay about what it means to be "in" or "cool" or the opposite. Think about a category (some suggestions are listed below), choose a subject, and then start jotting down details such as the particulars of language (spoken and body), appearance, attitudes, and likes and dislikes that define your central term.

music
films or television shows
dates
schools
cars

As you draft your essay, try to keep your focus on definition. It's natural to lean toward comparisons, but, like Lau, make sure you use them to support what you are defining.

2. Each generation usually ends up with at least one label or tag—the Baby Boomers, Gen X, or some such. What label works for your generation? Write an essay that explains your choice, providing examples to prove your point.

Getting Angry Can Be a Good Thing

Cecilia Muñoz

Cecilia Muñoz tells you a fair amount about herself in her essay, but you may not know much about the organization she works for, the National Council of La Raza—a nonprofit group that fights for the civil rights of Hispanic-Americans. At La Raza, Muñoz is the vice president of the Office of Research, Advocacy and Legislation. Her essay describes some of that work but makes no mention of her having been awarded a MacArthur Fellowship in 2000. Arguably the most prized of fellowships, it recognizes those who have "shown extraordinary originality and dedication in their creative pursuits and a marked capacity for self-direction." That dedication comes through clearly in Muñoz's essay. It was written for the "This I Believe" segment on National Public Radio, where Muñoz read it as part of the "Morning Edition" broadcast on September 26, 2005.

What to Look For   Repetition is often something writers are warned about, but it can be used in a positive way. Read Muñoz's essay and ask yourself if repetition leaps off the page. Then reread the essay, marking each use of *outrage* so you can evaluate just how often it occurs as well as the various effects it creates.

1 I believe that a little outrage can take you a long way.

2   I remember the exact moment when I discovered outrage as a kind of fuel. It was about 1980. I was 17, the daughter of Bolivian immigrants growing up in suburban Detroit. After a dinner table conversation with my family about the wars going on in Central America and the involvement of the United States (my country by birth and my parents' country by choice), a good friend said the thing that set me off. He told me that he thought the U.S. might someday go to war somewhere in Latin America. He looked me in the eye and told me that if it happens, he believes my parents belong in an internment camp just like the Japanese-Americans during World War II.

3   Now this was someone who knew us, who had sat at our table and knew how American we are. We are a little exotic maybe, but it never occurred to me that we were anything but an American family. For my friend, as for many others, there will always be doubt as to whether we really belong in this country, which is our home, enough doubt to justify taking away our freedom. My outrage that day became the propellant of my life, driving me straight to the civil rights movement, where I've worked ever since.

4   I guess outrage got me pretty far. I found jobs in the immigrant rights movement. I moved to Washington to work as an advocate. I found plenty more to be angry about along the way and built something of a reputation for being strident. Someone once sent my mom an article about my work. She was proud and everything but wanted to know why her baby was described as "ferocious."

5   Anger has a way, though, of hollowing out your insides. In my first job, if we helped 50 immigrant families in a day, the faces of the five who didn't qualify haunted my dreams at night. When I helped pass a bill in Congress to help Americans reunite with their immigrant families, I could only think of my cousin who didn't qualify and who had to wait another decade to get her immigration papers.

6   It's like that every day. You have victories but your defeats outnumber them by far, and you remember the names and faces of those who lost. I still have the article about the farm worker who took his life after we lost a political fight. I have not forgotten his name—and not just because his last name was the same as mine. His story reminds me of why I do this work and how little I can really do.

7   I am deeply familiar with that hollow place that outrage carves in your soul. I've fed off of it to sustain my work for many years. But it hasn't eaten me away completely, maybe because the hollow place gets filled with other, more powerful things like compassion, faith, family, music, the goodness of people around me. These things fill me up and temper my outrage with a deep sense of gratitude that I have the privilege of doing my small part to make things better.

Organization and Ideas

1. In paragraph 2, Muñoz uses a personal narrative. What is her point? How does she generalize about it in paragraph 3?
2. How would you characterize the essay's organization? To what extent is it chronological, dramatic, or particular to general?

3. What do you associate with the word *outrage?* Explain the word's denotations and connotations.
4. Muñoz's last paragraph examines the negative and positive aspects of *outrage,* describing its effects on her and how they are countered. How believable is she?
5. To what extent is the opening sentence the essay's thesis? Why is it, or why isn't it?

TECHNIQUE AND STYLE

1. Reread Muñoz's essay, marking every word that relates to *outrage.* Why might she have chosen the words she did?
2. How credible is Muñoz's claim that for her outrage was "a kind of fuel"?
3. Though most of the essay is written in the first person, Muñoz brings in *your* and *you* in paragraphs 5, 6, and 7. To whom is Munoz referring? Why might she have switched the point of view?
4. In your own words, describe Muñoz's persona—the image of herself that she projects through the essay's prose.
5. Immigration is a hot topic for many readers. To what extent does the essay show that Muñoz is aware that her readers may have set opinions on the subject, many of them negative?

SUGGESTIONS FOR WRITING

Journal

1. What other titles can you think of for Muñoz's essay? Which do you prefer and why?
2. Think of your own experience in terms of *outrage.* Select one example and explain it. What caused it and what was its effect?

Essay

1. Muñoz deals with a number of abstract words in her essay:
   pride
   compassion
   faith
   family
   gratitude
   Choose one and explore its various meanings. Think of synonyms and the ways in which the word can be used, both negatively and positively. Like Muñoz, you will want to explore its causes and effects.
2. Muñoz explains the role *outrage* has played in her life, showing how an emotion that has negative connotations can have positive results.

Consider how a seemingly negative emotion has had a positive effect in your own experience. Like Muñoz, you will want to keep careful control over your persona. You might think of words such as *fear, shock, despair, anger,* and the like.

The Handicap of Definition

William Raspberry

William Raspberry left the small and segregated town in Mississippi where he grew up to take a summer job with the Indianapolis Reporter, *moving on in 1962 to* The Washington Post. *Although he now teaches at Duke University, where he is the Knight Chair in Communications and Journalism, he is better known as a writer for* The Washington Post *and as the author of a syndicated column that runs in more than 200 newspapers. His commentary on issues such as rap music, crime, and AIDS earned him a Pulitzer Prize in 1994. In the essay that follows, he writes about the terms* black *and* white, *words that have connotations we don't often think about. Raspberry shows us that if we stop to think about* black, *we'll see that it has so narrow a definition that it is "one of the heaviest burdens black Americans—and black children in particular— have to bear." Not much has changed since 1982, when this essay first appeared in Raspberry's syndicated column.*

What to Look For   Somewhere along the line, we've all been warned never to begin a sentence with a conjunction such as *and, but,* and the like. But as long as you know how to avoid the trap of a sentence fragment, beginning a sentence with a conjunction can lend a conversational tone to your essay. As you read Raspberry's essay, notice how often he uses this technique.

1   I know all about bad schools, mean politicians, economic deprivation and racism. Still, it occurs to me that one of the heaviest burdens black Americans—and black children in particular—have to bear is the handicap of definition: the question of what it means to be black.

2   Let me explain quickly what I mean. If a basketball fan says that the Boston Celtics' Larry Bird plays "black," the fan intends it—and Bird probably accepts it—as a compliment. Tell pop singer Tom Jones he moves "black" and he might grin in appreciation. Say to Teena Marie or The Average White Band that they sound "black" and they'll thank you.

3   But name one pursuit, aside from athletics, entertainment or sexual performance in which a white practitioner will feel complimented to be told he does it "black." Tell a white broadcaster he talks "black," and he'll sign up for diction lessons. Tell a white reporter he writes "black" and he'll take a writing course. Tell a white lawyer he reasons "black" and he might sue you for slander.

4   What we have here is a tragically limited definition of blackness, and it isn't only white people who buy it.

5   Think of all the ways black children can put one another down with charges of "whiteness." For many of these children, hard study and hard work are "white." Trying to please a teacher might be criticized as acting "white." Speaking correct English is "white." Scrimping today in the interest of tomorrow's goals is "white." Educational toys and games are "white."

6   An incredible array of habits and attitudes that are conducive to success in business, in academia, in the nonentertainment professions are likely to be thought of as somehow "white." Even economic success, unless it involves such "black" undertakings as numbers banking, is defined as "white."

7   And the results are devastating. I wouldn't deny that blacks often are better entertainers and athletes. My point is the harm that comes from too narrow a definition of what is black.

8   One reason black youngsters tend to do better at basketball, for instance, is that they assume they can learn to do it well, and so they practice constantly to prove themselves right.

9   Wouldn't it be wonderful if we could infect black children with the notion that excellence in math is "black" rather than white, or possibly Chinese? Wouldn't it be of enormous value if we could create the myth that morality, strong families, determination, courage and love of learning are traits brought by slaves from Mother Africa and therefore quintessentially black?

10   There is no doubt in my mind that most black youngsters could develop their mathematical reasoning, their elocution and their attitudes the way they develop their jump shots and their dance

steps: by the combination of sustained, enthusiastic practice and the unquestioned belief that they can do it.

11   In one sense, what I am talking about is the importance of developing positive ethnic traditions. Maybe Jews have an innate talent for communication; maybe Chinese are born with a gift for mathematical reasoning; maybe blacks are naturally blessed with athletic grace. I doubt it. What is at work, I suspect, is assumption, inculcated early in their lives, that this is a thing our people do well.

12   Unfortunately, many of the things about which blacks make this assumption are things that do not contribute to their career success—except for that handful of the truly gifted who can make it as entertainers and athletes. And many of the things we concede to whites are the things that are essential to economic security.

13   So it is with a number of assumptions black youngsters make about what it is to be a "man": physical aggressiveness, sexual prowess, the refusal to submit to authority. The prisons are full of people who, by this perverted definition, are unmistakably men.

14   But the real problem is not so much that the things defined as "black" are negative. The problem is that the definition is much too narrow.

15   Somehow, we have to make our children understand that they are intelligent, competent people, capable of doing whatever they put their minds to and making it in the American mainstream, not just in a black subculture.

16   What we seem to be doing, instead, is raising up yet another generation of young blacks who will be failures—by definition.

ORGANIZATION AND IDEAS

1. Examine paragraphs 1–4, 5–7, and 8–11. Each functions as a unit. What sentence is the major assertion for each group of paragraphs?

2. Examine paragraphs 12–16 as a concluding paragraph block. What is the relationship between paragraph 12 and the preceding paragraphs?

3. Consider the controlling ideas that guide the paragraph blocks and the conclusions Raspberry draws from the examples that support those assertions. Stated fully, what is Raspberry's thesis?

4. A militant who reads this essay would argue that Raspberry is trying to make blacks "better" by making them white. Is there any evidence to support this view? Explain.

5. A feminist who reads the essay might argue that it is sexist. Is there any evidence to support this view? Explain.

TECHNIQUE AND STYLE

1. This essay was one of Raspberry's syndicated columns; as a result, it appeared in a large number of newspapers with equally large readerships, mostly white. What evidence can you find that Raspberry is trying to inform his white audience and persuade his black readers?
2. How and where does Raspberry establish his credibility as a writer on this subject? What grammatical point of view does he use?
3. Where in the essay does he qualify or modulate his statements? What is the effect of that technique?
4. Paragraphs 3, 7, 13, and 14 all begin with a conjunction. What effect does this technique achieve? Consult a handbook of grammar and usage for a discussion of this device. To what extent does Raspberry's usage conform to the handbook's advice?
5. Paragraph 16 is an example of a rhetorical paragraph, a one-sentence paragraph that gives dramatic emphasis to a point. If you eliminate the dash or substitute a comma for it, what happens to the dramatic effect? What does the pun add?

SUGGESTIONS FOR WRITING

Journal

1. Raspberry's essay was published in 1982. Write a journal entry explaining whether his point holds true today.
2. Write down any examples you can think of that can substitute for those Raspberry uses, but focus on women. In a paragraph or two, explain how the substitutions would add to or detract from his point.

Essay

1. Find a word that has accumulated broad connotations and then see what definitions have evolved and their effect. Like Raspberry, you may want to consider two terms but emphasize only one. Possibilities:

   man
   hero
   student
   woman
   worker
   lover
   politician

2. Raspberry says "we have to make our children understand that they are intelligent, competent people, capable of doing whatever they put their minds to..." (paragraph 15). But *intelligent* and *competent* mean different things to different people. Select one of the words and write an

essay in which you define what the word means to you. As you think about your topic, remember that it can be useful to define something by what it is not, by comparisons.

Crippled by Their Culture

Thomas Sowell

As one would expect of a senior fellow at Stanford University's Hoover Institution, Thomas Sowell's academic credentials are impressive: AB (magna cum laude) from Harvard, AM from Columbia University, and PhD from the University of Chicago, all in the field of economics. Author of more than 20 books, Sowell notes, "I write only when I have something to say." And as his books attest, he has lots to say and on various topics, among them justice, law, culture, ethnicity, race, and affirmative action. He also has a lot to say about writing, and you might enjoy reading what he has to say about it at his Web site, http://www.tsowell.com/About_Writing.html. Sowell's most recent books are Black Rednecks and White Liberals *(2005),* On Classical Economics *(2006),* A Conflict of Visions, *rev. ed. (2007),* Basic Economics: A Common Sense Guide to the Economy, *3rd ed. (2007),* A Man of Letters *(2007), and* Economic Facts and Fallacies *(2008). The essay that follows defines "black rednecks" and was published by* The Wall Street Journal *on April 26, 2005.*

What to Look For   As you read Sowell's essay, look for the ways he bolsters his ideas by using the results of his research. Like Sowell, you can strengthen your points and make yourself credible by researching your subject. Your readers will be apt to find your essay more interesting and your point more believable.

1   For most of the history of this country, differences between the black and the white population—whether in income, IQ, crime rates, or whatever—have been attributed to either race or racism. For much of the first half of the 20th century, these differences

were attributed to race—that is, to an assumption that blacks just did not have it in their genes to do as well as white people. The tide began to turn in the second half of the 20th century, when the assumption developed that black-white differences were due to racism on the part of whites.

2   Three decades of my own research lead me to believe that neither of those explanations will stand up under scrutiny of the facts. As one small example, a study published last year indicated that most of the black alumni of Harvard were from either the West Indies or Africa, or were the children of West Indian or African immigrants. These people are the same race as American blacks, who greatly outnumber either or both.

3   If this disparity is not due to race, it is equally hard to explain by racism. To a racist, one black is pretty much the same as another. But, even if a racist somehow let his racism stop at the water's edge, how could he tell which student was the son or daughter of someone born in the West Indies or in Africa, especially since their American-born offspring probably do not even have a foreign accent?

4   What then could explain such large disparities in demographic "representation" among these three groups of blacks? Perhaps they have different patterns of behavior and different cultures and values behind their behavior.

5   There have always been large disparities, even within the native black population of the U.S. Those blacks whose ancestors were "free persons of color" in 1850 have fared far better in income, occupation, and family stability than those blacks whose ancestors were freed in the next decade by Abraham Lincoln.

6   What is not nearly as widely known is that there were also very large disparties within the white population of the pre–Civil War South and the white population of the Northern states. Although Southern whites were only about one-third of the white population of the U.S., an absolute majority of all the illiterate whites in the country were in the South.

7   The North had four times as many schools as the South, attended by more than four times as many students. Children in Massachusetts spent more than twice as many years in school as children in Virginia. Such disparities obviously produce other disparities. Northern newspapers had more than four times the circulation of Southern newspapers. Only 8% of the patents issued in 1851 went to Southerners. Even though agriculture was

the principal economic activity of the antebellum South at the time, the vast majority of the patents for agricultural inventions went to Northerners. Even the cotton gin was invented by a Northerner.

8   Disparities between Southern whites and Northern whites extended across the board from rates of violence to rates of illegitimacy. American writers from both the antebellum South and the North commented on the great differences between the white people in the two regions. So did famed French visitor Alexis de Tocqueville.

9   None of these disparities can be attributed to either race or racism. Many contemporary observers attributed these differences to the existence of slavery in the South, as many in later times would likewise attribute both the difference between Northern and Southern whites, and between blacks and whites nationwide, to slavery. But slavery doesn't stand up under scrutiny of historical facts any better than race or racism as explanations of North-South differences or black-white differences. The people who settled in the South came from different regions of Britain than the people who settled in the North—and they differed as radically on the other side of the Atlantic as they did here—that is, before they had ever seen a black slave.

10   Slavery also cannot explain the difference between American blacks and West Indian blacks living in the United States because the ancestors of both were enslaved. When race, racism, and slavery all fail the empirical test, what is left?

11   Culture is left.

12   The culture of the people who were called "rednecks" and "crackers" before they ever got on the boats to cross the Atlantic was a culture that produced far lower levels of intellectual and economic achievement, as well as far higher levels of violence and sexual promiscuity. That culture had its own way of talking, not only in the pronunciation of particular words but also in a loud, dramatic style of oratory with vivid imagery, repetitive phrases and repetitive cadences.

13   Although that style originated on the other side of the Atlantic in centuries past, it became for generations the style of both religious oratory and political oratory among Southern whites and among Southern blacks—not only in the South but in the Northern ghettos in which Southern blacks settled. It was a style used by Southern

white politicians in the era of Jim Crow and later by black civil rights leaders fighting Jim Crow. Martin Luther King's famous speech at the Lincoln Memorial in 1963 was a classic example of that style.

14   While a third of the white population of the U.S. lived within the redneck culture, more than 90% of the black population did. Although that culture eroded away over the generations, it did so at different rates in different places and among different people. It eroded away much faster in Britain than in the U.S. and somewhat faster among Southern whites than among Southern blacks, who had fewer opportunities for education or for the rewards that came with escape from that counterproductive culture.

15   Nevertheless the process took a long time. As late as the First World War, white soldiers from Georgia, Arkansas, Kentucky and Mississippi scored lower on mental tests than black soldiers from Ohio, Illinois, New York and Pennsylvania. Again, neither race nor racism can explain that—and neither can slavery.

16   The redneck culture proved to be a major handicap for both whites and blacks who absorbed it. Today, the last remnants of that culture can still be found in the worst of the black ghettos, whether in the North or the South, for the ghettos of the North were settled by blacks from the South. The counterproductive and self-destructive culture of black rednecks in today's ghettos is regarded by many as the only "authentic" black culture—and, for that reason, something not to be tampered with. Their talk, their attitudes, and their behavior are regarded as sacrosanct.

17   The people who take this view may think of themselves as friends of blacks. But they are the kinds of friends who can do more harm than enemies.

ORGANIZATION AND IDEAS

1. What paragraph or paragraphs provide the essay's introduction? Its conclusion? What reasons do you have for your choices?
2. The essay poses a question in paragraph 4. What is Sowell's answer?
3. Where in the essay does Sowell use comparisons? What do they add?
4. How does Sowell define "redneck culture"? What examples does he use and how effective are they?
5. In paragraph 16, Sowell states: "The counterproductive and self-destructive culture of black rednecks in today's ghettos is regarded

by many as the only 'authentic' black culture—and, for that reason, something not to be tampered with. Their talk, their attitudes, and their behavior are regarded as sacrosanct." How true do you find these statements?

TECHNIQUE AND STYLE

1. Paragraph 11 consists of three words. Rewrite paragraph 10 to include them. What is lost? Gained?
2. How does Sowell take some of the sting out of the word *redneck*? What, if anything, is positive about that "redneck culture"?
3. Paragraphs 12–16 trace the evolution of "redneck culture." What does that explanation add to Sowell's main point?
4. Sowell spends the first ten paragraphs arguing that neither race nor racism explains the disparities between blacks and whites but only six paragraphs on "redneck culture." What reasons can you think of for that decision?
5. Race and racism are explosive subjects, and anyone writing about them must tread carefully. How careful is Sowell? To what extent does his caution or lack of it hurt or strengthen the essay?

SUGGESTIONS FOR WRITING

Journal

1. Use your journal to record your responses to Sowell's ideas. What do you agree or disagree with and why? Cite examples to support your opinion.
2. At no point in the essay does Sowell mention that he is black. Use your journal to explore whether that fact is relevant to his argument. How would including it change the essay?

Essay

1. In paragraph 16, Sowell states that a culture is expressed in a person's "talk...attitudes...and behavior." Use your library or a Web resource to dig deeper into what is meant by *culture*. For the Web, you might start by looking up the word in Wikipedia (www.en.wikipedia.org) or the Encyclopaedia Brittanica (www.eb.com). Given a broader definition of *culture,* choose a subject whose culture you can analyze. Suggestions:
   sports fans
   poker players

cheerleaders
video game players
celebrities

2. Though Sowell focuses on "redneck culture" as it applies to urban blacks, he sees it at work in the white world as well. Write an essay in which you define "redneck culture" as it exists in the white population. You will probably want to narrow down that population by age group, location, occupation, or some other characteristic. Make sure you give examples to illustrate your points and keep in mind that your readership may include someone in the group you select. As in the first suggestion above, you would do well to start by looking up the key word.

Speed Bump

Dave Coverly

Dave Coverly's career started when he was a child, developed when his cartoons were published in his high school newspaper, and became serious when he was a student at Eastern Michigan University, majoring in philosophy and imaginative writing. That career then was polished at Indiana University, where he earned a graduate degree in creative writing, and it can now be followed in some 200 newspapers. You can see his work in papers as varied as The Washington Post, Chicago Tribune, Irish Times *(Dublin), and* The Observer *(London), as well as in* The New Yorker *and* Esquire. *If the heading says "Speed Bump," that's Coverly. Many of his cartoons are available in book form:* Speed Bump: A Collection of Cartoon Skidmarks *(2000). In 1995 and again in 2003, he received the National Cartoonists Society's Reuben Award for Best Newspaper Panel. Father of two daughters and friend of animals, Coverly is a contributing cartoonist for PETA's magazines,* Animal Times, *and* Grrr!

Speed Bump

FOR DISCUSSION

1. Why might Coverly have chosen the two figures he uses in the cartoon? Who are they?
2. What does the cartoon imply by the setting for the older character's advice? What do the details in the drawing imply? The name Coverly chose for his cartoons?
3. What reasons can you think of for Coverly's choice of "the purple people and the orange people"? Change the terms and judge their impact.

4. In what ways does the cartoon comment on the essays by Raspberry and Sowell?

5. In what ways does the cartoon comment on the essays by Muñoz and Lau?

SUGGESTIONS FOR WRITING

Journal

The general subject of Coverly's cartoon is that of differences. What other subjects does the cartoon suggest? Which has the greatest impact and why?

Essay

Advice from a member of one generation to another sometimes begins, "If we lived in a perfect world, then..." Think about similar statements you have heard or advice that you have read and choose one to evaluate. What was the context? What is the advice intended to imply about the speaker? The person to whom it is addressed? What effect did it have? How wise was it? How much good did it do? If you put yourself in the position of the one giving the advice, what would it be?

On Using
Comparison
and Contrast

5

1   It's fair to say that Japanese people are unbelievably busy. Working 10 hours a day, and often coming in on days off, they rarely take a vacation of more than three or four days. A straight week is a hedonistic luxury. Students have less than a month for summer vacation, and even then they have all kinds of assignments to do.

2   Watching people live like this, with almost no time for themselves, makes an American like me wonder why more of them don't throw themselves under subway trains. But I seem to have far more anxiety about free time than my Japanese friends do—even though, compared to them, I have much more of it. Why doesn't this cradle-to-grave, manic scheduling bother them?

Right away, you know Lynnika Butler is an American who has spent a fair amount of time in Japan, where she was struck by the differences between the two cultures, time being one of the major ones. The introduction to her essay first uses details to describe ways in which the Japanese are "unbelievably busy," then shifts to what strikes her as odd, that "I seem to have far more anxiety about free time than my Japanese friends do—even though, compared to them, I have much more of it." She then poses a question that she answers in the rest of her essay by comparing how the two cultures treat the concept of time.

"What's the difference?" gets at the heart of **comparison and contrast,** and it is a question that can fit into any context. In college, it often turns up in the form of essay questions; in day-to-day life, it implies the process behind most decisions: "What shall I wear?" "Which movie will I see?" "Should I change jobs?" All these questions involve choices that draw on comparison and contrast. Like description, narration, example, and classification, comparison and contrast forces you to observe, but here you are looking for similarities and differences.

Whether you stress differences or similarities, you need to be sure that the comparison is fair. Deciding where to go out to dinner often depends on how much you are willing to spend, so comparing a fast-food place to an elegant French restaurant doesn't have much of a point unless you want to treat the comparison humorously. If neither is worth the money, however, you've established a similarity that gives you a serious assertion to work with.

Essays that depend primarily on other modes, such as description, narration, and definition, often use comparison and contrast to heighten a difference or clarify a point, but the selections in this chapter rely on comparison and contrast as their main principle of organization, even though their purposes differ, to say nothing of what they compare. Butler deals with two cultures' attitudes toward time, while the other writers in this section analyze living together versus marriage, an elephant's vocal range versus a human's, reality TV versus sports, and American news coverage versus that of Al Jazeera.

How can you shape comparison and contrast for your readers?   Often you may want only to inform your reader; that gives you at least three possible theses:

x is better or worse than *y.*
x has a lot in common with *y,* though not obviously so.
x is quite different from *y,* though superficially similar.

Butler doesn't take a stand in her first two paragraphs, but when you read the rest of the essay, you can decide which of the three directions she takes. Her introductory two paragraphs, however, make clear that the two cultures' use of time differs radically. Butler ends this introduction with an ironic idea: The Japanese have little free time but that doesn't bother them; Americans (at least Butler) have much more free time but it creates anxiety. The twist captures the reader's attention, which is vital if the reader is to keep on reading.

If you were writing on the same or similar subject, you could easily take a stand and write an essay to persuade your audience that too many Americans fill their free time with chores and that idleness has much to be said for it. But comparison can also be used to entertain your readers. A seemingly simple job such as washing the dog can be as much of a challenge as performing major surgery. At least at hospitals, you don't have to catch the patient first.

How can you use analogy?   An analogy is an extended **metaphor** or **simile** in which a primary term is equated with another quite dissimilar term. An **analogy** can emphasize a point or illuminate an idea. If you are writing about an abstraction, for example, you can make it more familiar by using an analogy to make it concrete and, therefore, more understandable. For Butler, free time may be like being in a very foreign country where she's glad to be, but it makes her nervous; for the Japanese, free time may be like money one has to spend for the good of the community. Extend those similes and you'd have an analogy.

How can you structure your essay?   Comparison and contrast essays group information so that the comparison is made by **blocks** or **point by point** or by a combination of the two. If you were to write an essay explaining the differences between an American feast, such as Thanksgiving, and a Chinese one, here is what the two major types of organization would look like in outline form:

Type	**Structure**	**Content**
Block	Paragraph 1	Introduction
	Block A, paragraphs 2–4	American culture
	Point 1	Preparation
	Point 2	Courses and types of food
	Point 3	Manners
	Block B, paragraphs 5–7	Chinese culture
	Point 1	Preparation
	Point 2	Courses and types of food
	Point 3	Manners
	Paragraph 8	Conclusion
Point by point	Paragraph 1	Introduction
	Point 1, paragraph 2	Preparation
		Chinese
		American
	Point 2, paragraph 3	Courses and types of food
		Chinese
		American

And so on. As you can see, sticking rigorously to one type of organization can become boring or predictable, so writers often mix the two.

In this chapter you'll find essays organized by block, point by point, and by a combination of these. Outlining an essay readily reveals which type of organization the writer uses. In your own writing, you might first try what comes easiest; then, in a later draft, you might mix the organization a bit to see which is the more effective.

How can you apply what you've learned from earlier chapters?
A close look at any of the essays that follow will show how you can use other modes, such as description, narration, and cause and effect, to help flesh out the comparison and contrast. A brief narrative or anecdote is often a good way to begin an essay, as it usually sets a conversational tone and establishes a link between writer and reader. Examples can clarify your points and description can make them memorable, while exploring why the differences or similarities exist or what effect they may have will lead you into pondering cause-and-effect relationships.

Where should you place your thesis? The one-sentence thesis placed at the end of an introductory paragraph certainly informs your readers of your subject and stance, but you might find your paper more effective if you treat your thesis more subtly, trying it out in different forms and positions. While some of the essays in this chapter save their major assertion until last, others combine ideas from various points in the essay to form a thesis. And, of course, not all theses are explicit; but if you want to imply yours, you have to be sure your implication is clear or the reader may miss the point.

Although some writers begin the writing process with a thesis clearly set out, many find that it is easier to write their way into one. As a result, you may find that the last paragraph in your draft will make a very good introductory one, for by the time you write it, you have refined your thesis. At that point, you'll find coming up with a new introduction isn't the task it was to begin with; you already know where you ended up and how you got there.

Useful Terms

Analogy An analogy examines a subject by comparing it point by point to something seemingly unlike but more commonplace and less complex. An analogy is also an extended metaphor.

Block comparison A comparison of x to y by grouping all that is to be compared under x and then following with the same information under y.

Comparison and contrast An examination of two or more subjects by exploring their similarities and differences. Similarities and differences are usually developed through literal and logical comparisons within like categories.

Metaphor An implied but direct comparison in which the primary term is made more vivid by associating it with a quite dissimilar term. "Life is no bed of roses" is a familiar metaphor. Link the two elements being compared with *like* or *as* and the result is a **simile.**

Point-by-point comparison A comparison that examines one or more points by stating the point, then comparing subject *x* to subject *y,* and then continuing to the next point.

Pointers for Using Comparison and Contrast

Exploring the Topic

1. **What are the similarities?** What characteristics do your two subjects share? Are the two so similar that you have little to distinguish them? If so, try another subject; if not, pare down your list of similarities to the most important ones.

2. **What are the differences?** In what ways are your two subjects different? Are they so different that they have little in common? If so, make sure you can handle a humorous tone or try another subject; if not, pare down your list of differences to the most important ones.

3. **Should you emphasize similarities or differences?** Which pattern of organization best fits your material? Block? Point by point? A combination of the two?

4. **What examples will work best?** If your reader isn't familiar with your topic, what examples might be familiar? What examples will make clear what may be unfamiliar?

5. **What metaphor does your subject suggest?** Given the metaphor and your subject, what characteristics match? How can the metaphor be extended into an analogy? How can you outline the analogy as an equation? What equals what?

6. **What other modes are appropriate?** What modes can you draw on to help support your comparison and the organization of the essay? Do you need to define? Where can you use description? Narration? Example? Do any of your comparisons involve cause and effect?

7. **What is your point? Your purpose?** Do you want to entertain, inform, persuade? Given your point as a tentative thesis, should you spell it out in the essay or imply it? If you are writing to inform,

what information do you want to present? If you are writing to persuade, what do you want your reader to believe or do?

8. **What persona do you want to create?** Is it best for you to be a part of the comparison and contrast or to be an observer? Do you have a strongly held conviction about your subject? Do you want it to show? Does your persona fit your audience, purpose, and material?

Drafting the Paper

1. **Know your reader.** Use your first paragraph to set out your major terms and your general focus and to prepare the reader for the pattern of organization and tone that will follow. Reexamine your list of similarities and differences to see which ones may be unfamiliar to your reader. Jot down an illustration or brief description by each characteristic that the reader may not be familiar with. If your reader is part of the group you are examining, tread carefully, and if your teacher may have a bias about your topic, try to figure out what the bias is so you can counter it. Reread your paper from the perspective of the reader who is biased so that you can check your diction as well as your choice of examples and assertions.

2. **Know your purpose.** If you are writing to persuade, keep in mind the reader's possible bias or neutral view and see how you can use your persona as well as logical and emotional appeals to get the reader on your side. Informative papers run the risk of telling readers something they already know, so use description, detail, example, and diction to present your information in a new light. If your paper's main purpose is to entertain, these techniques become even more crucial. Try adding alliteration, allusions, paradox, and puns to the other techniques you draw on.

3. **If you use an analogy, double-check it.** Make sure your analogy is an extended metaphor, not a statement of fact. See what you want to emphasize. Also make sure the placement is effective by trying out the analogy in different positions. Perhaps it works best as a framing device or standing alone in a sentence or paragraph.

(Continued)

POINTERS FOR USING COMPARISON
AND CONTRAST *(Continued)*

4. **Use other modes to support your comparison.** Description and example are probably the most obvious modes to use, but consider narration, cause and effect, definition, and analogy as well. Perhaps a short narrative would add interest to your paper, or perhaps cause and effect enters into your comparisons. Definition may be vital to your thesis, and analogy may help clarify or expand a point.

5. **Check your pattern of organization.** If you are using block comparison, make sure you have introduced your two subjects and that your conclusion brings them back together. In the body of the paper, make sure that what you cover for one, you also cover for the other. In point-by-point comparison, check to see that your points are clearly set out. You may want to use both types of organization, though one will probably predominate.

6. **Make a point.** Perhaps you want to use your comparison to make a comment on the way we live, perhaps to clarify two items that people easily confuse, perhaps to argue that one thing is better than the other. Whatever your point, check it to make sure it is an assertion, not a mere fact. Whether your purpose is to inform or to persuade, take a stand and make sure that your thesis clearly implies or states it.

Living on Tokyo Time

Lynnika Butler

During the five years Lynnika Butler spent in Japan, she taught English, worked as a coordinator for international relations, and volunteered as an interpreter—experience that made her an astute observer of how the Japanese treat time. That experience, together with her BA in English and Spanish, may have also contributed to her decision to pursue a graduate degree in linguistics, earning a PhD from the University of Arizona. Her goal is "to use what I am learning about the science of language to help communities who are trying to preserve or revitalize their native languages." She is now engaged in research on dormant American Indian languages. Butler's essay was first published in the Salt *Journal,* Fall 2001, *and then reprinted in the* Utne Reader's January–February 2003 *issue.*

What to Look For The concept of time is a slippery one, but Butler explains it clearly. As you read her essay, be aware of how she leads into it and then explains how the two cultures view it.

1 It's fair to say that Japanese people are unbelievably busy. Working 10 hours a day, and often coming in on days off, they rarely take a vacation of more than three or four days. A straight week is a hedonistic luxury. Students have less than a month for summer vacation, and even then they have all kinds of assignments to do.

2 Watching people live like this, with almost no time for themselves, makes an American like me wonder why more of them don't throw themselves under subway trains. But I seem to have far more anxiety about free time than my Japanese friends do—even though, compared to them, I have much more of it. Why doesn't this cradle-to-grave, manic scheduling bother them?

3 A lot of Westerners make the glib assumption that Japanese people are simply submissive, unoriginal, or masochistic enough to put up with such a punishing system. I don't think that's it. In Japan, time is measured in the same hours and minutes and days as anywhere else, but it is experienced as a fundamentally different phenomenon. In the West, we save time, spend time, invest time, even kill time—all of which implies that it belongs to us in the first place. We might find

ourselves obliged to trade huge chunks of our time for a steady salary, but most of us resent this as something stolen from us, and we take it for granted that our spare hours are none of our teachers' or bosses' business.

4   The Japanese grow up with a sense of time as a communal resource, like the company motor pool. If you get permission, you can borrow a little for your own use, but the main priority is to serve the institution—in this case, society as a whole. Club activities, overtime, drinks with the boss, and invitations to the boring weddings of people you hardly know are not seen as intruding on your free time—they are the *shikata ga nai* (nothing you can do about it) duties that turn the wheels of society. "Free" time (*hima*) is something that only comes into existence when these obligations have all been fulfilled. This is nicely borne out by an expression my boss uses whenever he leaves work a little early: *chotto hima morau* ("I'm going to receive a little free time").

5   Though I can't pretend I like living on a Japanese schedule, I try hard not to make judgments. *Oku ga fukai*—things are more complicated than they appear. The Japanese sacrifice their private time to society, but in return they get national health insurance, a wonderful train system, sushi, the two thousand temples of Kyoto, and traditional culture so rich that every back-water village seems to have its own unique festivals, seasonal dishes, legends, and even dialect. All of which are invaluable social goods that I would not trade for a lifetime of free hours.

ORGANIZATION AND IDEAS

1. Butler opens by stating that the Japanese are "busy." How effective are the examples that support her statement?
2. In paragraph 2, Butler poses a question. What is the answer?
3. Sum up the Japanese attitude toward time. What is the American one?
4. Of the two views of time, which does Butler prefer and why?
5. Butler says that Americans treat time as though "it belongs to us" (paragraph 3). How accurate do you find that statement?

TECHNIQUE AND STYLE

1. Butler states a paradox in paragraph 2. How effective is it?
2. The essay opens with a description of Japanese "busyness" and follows it with a paragraph that gives Butler's reaction to it. To what extent is her response similar to the reader's?

3. Think about the simile Butler uses in paragraph 4. How effective is it?

4. Butler occasionally uses a Japanese term that she then translates. What does her use of the Japanese add to the essay?

5. Reread the last paragraph. Given your sense of what a conclusion should do, how effective is it?

SUGGESTIONS FOR WRITING

Journal

1. To what extent do you share the American sense of time being a personal possession?

2. How difficult would it be for you to adapt to the Japanese sense of time? Explain.

Essay

1. You can use Butler's essay as a model for your own, one in which you compare and contrast two groups' attitudes toward something. Think, for instance, of the difference between how you and your parents view vacations. For your own topic, consider first two different groups and then think your way into their attitudes toward *x*, with *x* standing for what they differ about. Suggestions for different categories:

generations

regions, for example, North and South

city and country residents

males and females

teachers and students

2. Butler contrasts the various intrusions on what Americans would think of as their free time to what Japanese see as "duties that turn the wheels of society" (paragraph 4). Think about your own sense of obligation and those things you do and do not feel a sense of duty toward. Write an essay in which you define your sense of duty by contrasting examples of where it does and does not apply.

Who's Watching? Reality TV and Sports

Frank Deford

It's hard to find something Frank Deford doesn't do and do well: If you read Sports Illustrated, *you've probably seen his byline; if you listen to National Public Radio's "Morning Edition," you've heard his commentary; if you watch Bryant Gumbel's "RealSports" on HBO, you've even seen him. Deford taught at Princeton University before he took up journalism as his career, and he has won almost every prize for sports writing there is to win: the National Magazine Award, the U.S. Sportswriter of the Year, the Christopher Award, and the Peabody Award. The author of several screenplays and 14 books, he has had two books made into films and one into a Broadway musical. His latest work is a novel* The Entitled *(2007), a look at baseball, sex, and celebrity. Hailed by* GQ *as "the world's greatest sportswriter," Deford read the piece that follows on NPR on June 2, 2004.*

What to Look For   Though Deford depends on comparison and contrast to examine his subject, be on the lookout for how he also uses examples and explains causal relationships—why *x* happened and the results. Note how these other modes support the main one.

1   It would seem to me that reality TV is nothing more than a form of sport. It's a competition, a game, but on a coast-to-coast basis it's more emotionally appealing than many of our sports. So I have to believe that as many people get more interested in the reality shows, they lose some interest in the old-fashioned sports.

2   The constant problem that sports in this country suffers from is that there are just too many teams playing too many games. People, especially local fans, can follow their teams, but only the hard-core zealots monitor a whole sport. As a consequence, especially in the team sports with myriad games—baseball, basketball and hockey—home attendance may remain high, while at the same time ratings for national games decrease. That may sound contradictory, but it makes sense.

3   Let's just take one city as example. The good people in Dallas may have cared passionately about their basketball and hockey teams, but as soon as the Stars and the Mavericks were eliminated in the playoffs, I would suspect that a goodly number of the Dallas fans dropped their interest altogether in the NBA and NHL playoffs and started devoting their attention to the local baseball team, the Texas Rangers.

4   Reality TV focuses. There are only a small number of competitors and we get to meet them and know them well, a whole lot better than our friends in Dallas ever got to know the Calgary Flames or the Milwaukee Bucks during the regular season. In many respects, in fact, reality TV shows essentially start with the elimination play-offs, which concentrate the mind without having to bother us with the long, boring regular season. Reality television shows also are scheduled for just once a week. Every competition becomes important, in TV language, "appointment viewing."

5   Football has become the one traditional team sport that continues to have a growing national audience, and a large reason for that is that there are only a limited number of games, with the vast majority taking place on the weekends. It's no coincidence, I think, that the one sport which has shown great ratings gains in the last few years is NASCAR, which follows the once-a-week NFL model. NASCAR is like an all-star reality show every week. Everybody who follows the sport knows all the major drivers. Contrast NASCAR, say, to the PGA, where each week there are different contenders. The casual fan can't keep them all straight, so he only stays tuned when Tiger Woods has a chance.

6   Familiarity is so important when we are watching any kind of game. If we know the contestants, we can decide whether we want to root for them or against them. That's why the NFL and the NBA drafts are more interesting to more people than most actual games. We become familiar with the prospects before the draft and get involved.

7   Anyway, with all the competition from the new once-a-week television competitions, maybe major-league baseball, the NBA and the NHL are just going to have to settle for having intense local fol-lowings with declining national impact, and the hero that a nation turns its lonely eyes to is not going to be a great star who hits home runs or scores baskets, but some guy who sings songs or picks a bride or gets a job with Donald Trump. Yes, indeed, your new American idol, but that's reality.

ORGANIZATION AND IDEAS

1. What paragraph or paragraphs function as the introduction? How much information does it give you?
2. Deford cites examples in paragraphs 3 and 4. How apt are they?
3. In what ways are reality shows and sports similar? Different? What kind of organizational pattern does Deford use?
4. Reread the essay to see how many examples of sports Deford provides and how many of reality shows. How fair is his comparison?
5. Think about what Deford says about NASCAR (paragraph 5). Is that also true of the World Series? The Super Bowl? Why or why not?

TECHNIQUE AND STYLE

1. How important is Deford's use of cause and effect in supporting his points? Explain what it adds to or detracts from the essay.
2. What is Deford's purpose? Is he writing to argue, explain, speculate, lament, complain, what?
3. Consider the examples Deford draws from sports. What definition can you deduce for his concept of what is covered by the word *sports*?
4. Deford's essay was written to be heard on radio. What can you spot that shows he was aware of how his essay would sound?
5. How would you describe Deford's persona? What examples can you cite to support your view?

SUGGESTIONS FOR WRITING

Journal

1. What are your least and most favorite sports and why?
2. What are your least and most favorite television shows and why?

Essay

1. "Reality show" is a broad label, but Deford does bring out some of the shows' characteristics. Think about them and think also of the various kinds of shows that appear on television:
   quiz shows
   major sports events (Indy 500, Kentucky Derby)
   survival shows
   talent shows
   talk shows (such as Oprah, Conan O'Brien, Jay Leno,
   David Letterman)
   Select two programs within a category and compare them, analyzing the kind of "reality" that is being presented. What conclusion can you draw? State it as an assertion and you have your thesis.

2. If you think about the word *sports,* you'll find it covers a large group of activities. Aside from the obvious ones, the term can also be applied to many that are less obvious, such as fencing, synchronized swimming, logrolling, and fox hunting. Take your own favorite sport and compare it to one that you don't think deserves the name. The essay that results will use comparison and contrast to explain what you mean by *sport.*

Playing House

Denise Leight

As a student at Middlesex County College in Edison, New Jersey, Denise Leight wrote "Playing House" in response to Daniel Zimmerman's research assignment for his English class. The essay was then published in the Spring 2001 issue of Becoming Writers, *one of the English Department's three journals. The collection, according to its editors, "celebrates the achievements of our students, who worked hard over the past semester to translate the insights and responses of full and busy lives into the well-crafted and thoughtfully imagined essays reprinted here. As writers we know it is never easy to find the words and form that most accurately communicate what we know, and the finished piece almost never emerges in the shape we originally imagined it. But it is in the struggle to express ourselves that our thoughts become fully ours, and the battle is always a richly rewarding process."* Becoming Writers *is an appropriate title for such a collection.*

What to Look For   As you read Denise Leight's essay, figure out if she is explaining her subject or arguing for a specific position or something in between.

1   More and more couples today live together or "play house" before taking the matrimonial plunge. Living together before marriage has become so popular that approximately half the couples in America participate in this activity (Gorrell 16). Some couples choose to live together to test their compatibility and possibly avoid an unsuccessful marriage. With the number of marriages ending in divorce these days,

it sounds reasonable that many couples want to give marriage a trial run before making any formal commitment. But do the chances of a successful marriage actually improve by cohabiting?

2   "Cohabitation isn't marriage," says sociology professor Linda Waite of the University of Chicago (qtd. in Jabusch 14). Married and cohabiting couples do not have the same characteristics. According to Professor Waite, cohabiting couples lack both specialization and commitment in their relationships (Jabusch 14). Unwed cohabitants generally live more financially and emotionally independent of one another to allow themselves the freedom to leave. This often results in less monogamous, short-term relationships.

3   Married couples specialize—while one partner might take over the cooking, the other might specialize in cleaning. They pool their money, time, and other resources, creating a higher quality lifestyle. Unmarried couples find it much harder to trust each other financially without the legal bond and, therefore, do not move quickly to pool those resources. While marriage does not ensure monogamy, married couples have more invested in their relationship and think longer before acting on their impulses and stepping outside of the relationship. Unmarried couples do not operate as a partnership, says Waite: "they are being two separate people—it is trading off freedom and low levels of commitment for fewer benefits than you get from commitment" (qtd. in Jabusch 15).

4   Many singles believe that by practicing marriage they will receive the commitment they desire. With this in mind, they move in together intending to tie the knot eventually. Time passes and the couple rarely talks seriously about finalizing the commitment. And so, they often end up cohabiting for a few years until eventually someone gets tired of waiting and leaves. Cohabitation can suppress the development of a higher level of commitment.

5   Sometimes, one or both of the people involved become complacent in the relationship, and without any pressure to move forward, they won't. As social psychologist Dr. Julia Hare puts it, "Why would you go to the store to buy some milk with the cow standing in the living room?" (qtd. in "Why...Marriage?" 53). Certainly, to call a marriage successful, it must actually take place.

6   A study conducted by an assistant professor of human development and family studies at Pennsylvania State University, Catherine Cohan, Ph.D., found that those who had lived together before marriage "displayed more negative and fewer positive problem solving and support behaviors than couples that had not cohabitated prior

to marriage" (Gorrell 16). For example, if one partner of a cohabiting couple diagnosed a particular topic as a problem, the other would express more negative behaviors such as forcefulness and attempts to control. Women who had lived with their partners before marriage generally exhibited more verbal aggressiveness than those in the couples without premarital cohabitation.

7   One cannot ignore the possibility that cohabitants as a group may have certain distinguishable characteristics that make them more likely to divorce. The type of people who would choose to cohabit before marriage may simply be less willing to put the full amount of effort required into a relationship. However, a recent study determined that "the cohabitor selectivity reflected in four sociodemographic variables—parental divorce, marital status homogamy, age homogamy, and stepchildren—is unable to materially account for the cohabitation effect" (Hall and Zhao 424). In other words, the study did not show that these predisposing factors contributed greatly to the marriage dissolution of cohabiting couples.

8   Cohabiting does not necessarily equal the tragic end of a relationship, but couples who do marry after living together have higher rates of separation and divorce (Gorrell 16). The lack of commitment in such a relationship plays a large role in this scenario. If a couple wishes to have a successful marriage, they should show their commitment to each other from the beginning. If they trust each other enough not to cohabit before marriage, their marriage already has a higher probability of success.

Works Cited

Gorrell, Carin. "Live-in and Learn." *Psychology Today*. Nov. 2000: 16.

Hall, David R., and John Z. Zhao. "Cohabitation and Divorce in Canada: Testing the Selectivity Hypothesis." *Journal of Marriage & the Family* 57.2 (1995): 421–27.

Jabusch, Willard F. "The Myth of Cohabitation." *America* 7 Oct. 2000: 14–16.

"Why Are So Many Couples Living Together Before Marriage?" *Jet* 3 Aug. 1998: 52–55.

ORGANIZATION AND IDEAS

1. Leight poses a question in paragraph 1. What is it and what is her answer?

2. What are the characteristics of a cohabiting couple? A married couple?

3. What is Leight's view of cohabitation versus marriage? What evidence supports your opinion?
4. As expected in a research paper, you find Leight cites evidence throughout. Is it sufficient? Why or why not?
5. What arguments or loopholes can you think of that Leight does not mention?

TECHNIQUE AND STYLE

1. In what ways is the title a pun?
2. What is the function of paragraph 7 and how necessary is it?
3. How would you describe Leight's level of diction? How appropriate is it for the assignment?
4. Think about what Leight lists as works cited. What conclusions can you draw from her list?
5. What is the essay's aim—to explain, argue, both? What evidence can you find to back up your view?

SUGGESTIONS FOR WRITING

Journal

1. Set a timer for 15 minutes and use your journal to explore the extent to which you are convinced by Leight's essay.
2. How would you describe Leight's persona, the person behind the writing? Quote from the essay to illustrate your impressions.

Essay

1. Leight's essay focuses on an important decision that many people face. Think about the decisions you have made between two choices, choose one, and write an essay in which you explain the choice and analyze whether it was the correct one. Suggestions:
   to go to college
   to take a particular job
   to pick a major
   to stand up for a friend
   to take a risk
2. Write your own version of "Playing House," using your library or the Web to research the subject, then selecting your own sources, using Leight's essay as an additional source. Argue for your own point of view.

Singing Like Yma Sumac

Cheryl Merrill

Cheryl Merrill has always been fascinated with pictures and words, a fascination you can appreciate in both her photography and poems. Her poems have been published in journals such as Northwest Review, Ghoti, Paintbrush, *and* Willow Springs *and collected in a chapbook* Cheat Grass *(1975). Her nonfiction work has been published in* Isotope, Pilgrimage, Fourth Genre, *and* Brevity. *The essay that follows was chosen for the collection* The Best of Brevity *(2005). The essay evolved from the time she spent in the Okavango Delta in Botswana with three elephants. Morula, whom you will meet in her essay, was one of them. Merrill has combined her interests in photography, prose, and elephants in a series published in the* Iron Horse Literary Review *and* The Drexel Online Journal, *and she is now at work on a book about elephants, appropriately called* Shades of Gray.

What to Look For You may be as unfamiliar with the mechanics of sound as you are with elephants, so notice the ways Merrill describes them so they are understandable. One way to do that is to mark every comparison you find in the essay.

1   Standing on a termite mound, face-to-trunk with an elephant, I place the flat of my hand against Morula's fluttering forehead, a forehead as cool and rough as tree bark. She's burbling, a contented rumble that has the sound of water gurgling in a drainpipe, but she is also making sounds that I cannot hear yet can feel. Right at the point where her nasal passage enters her skull, her skin pulses beneath my hand, vibrations that reverberate in my chest cavity, drum against my heart. Muscular ground-swells of sound roll full and luxuriously out into the bush, bumping into hippos, giraffes, zebras, lions, hyenas, birds, snakes and tsetse flies.

2   But only the elephants raise their heads and listen.

3   Most of Morula's vocalizations are rumbles, which fall partially or entirely in the infrasonic range of 5 to 30 hertz—throbbing, quaking

air for which we humans have no auditory perception. Such low-frequency rumbles usually have harmonics and overtones, both of which can be selectively emphasized. As in whale song, each individual elephant has a signature sound, one like no other elephant—their voices as different from each other as ours are different from each other.

4   *Are you there?*

5   *Yes, I am here, right behind you.*

6   When we speak, our vocal cords vibrate with forced, small explosions of air from our lungs. We shape words with our mouths and tongues. Expelled from a chestful of wind, words float around us like little clouds, each one a separate exhalation, creating an atmosphere of meaning, thickening language one word after another.

7   Sounds unfold in time, in agreeable waves pulsing against our ears. When *we* are listening to and lost within a *piece* of pleasurable music, time even suspends itself. Songs hang on our bones.

8   Standing on a termite mound, I close my eyes. A palm weevil drones by, a miniature bomber on short, stubby wings. Buried deep within a thicket, glossy starlings cheerfully *teer-teeer-teer-teer* at us. The afternoon has an eloquent cadence. Morula is immobile, as if listening, as if deeply immersed in translation. There is music here, if only I had the ears for it.

9   I open my eyes. *"MO-RU-LA,"* I sing.

10   My voice, like hers, originates in my vocal cords. But my vocal range is barely an octave, limping through the air at 220 hertz. Morula's range is tremendous, more than 10 octaves, from 5 to 9,000 hertz. The most athletic human voice in history was that of a Peruvian, Yma Sumac, who had a self-proclaimed range of 5 octaves and a recorded range of 4.5, from *B* below low-C to *A* above high-C, from about 123 to 1,760 hertz, as high-pitched as an elephant's trumpet. This is a woman who could occasionally hit a triple-trill and whose voice equaled that of an upright bass. Morula would find her vocalizations a lot more fascinating than mine are.

11   Like all elephants, Morula is able to produce low-frequency sounds just because she is big: The larger the resonating chamber (think cello compared to violin), the lower the frequency of its sound. Morula also has long and loose vocal chords and a flexible arrangement of bones attached to her tongue and larynx. In addition to a loose voice box, she also has another special structure at

the back of her throat called a pharyngeal pouch, which not only affects her low-frequency tones but also holds an emergency supply of water.

12   Imagine a vocal instrument that is equal parts cello, double bass, violin, tuba and trumpet, one whose entire body is an expanding and contracting resonating chamber, one that can sing with a throat full of water and triple-trill a rumble, a roar and infrasound, all in one 3-second call. Yma Sumac would be horribly jealous.

13   As I stand on the termite mound, a soothing mantle of high-pitched insect noise drapes over my shoulders. I lean against the afternoon, a lizard thawing, a gluttonous lion sleeping off a meal. Morula slaps her canvas ears against her shoulders. Beyond that dull sound, I can almost hear the leaves on the trees breathe. The single piccolo note of a boubou shrike rings out. A bleating warbler cries, *Help-me, help-me, help-me, help-me!* The burbling beneath my hand goes on and on and on. My whole body tingles; I listen as if I am a young species, as if my life depends on it.

ORGANIZATION AND IDEAS

   1. Merrill focuses on the particular—Morula and herself—but also uses the particular to generalize about elephants and people. Which paragraphs focus on Morula and elephants? Which focus on Merrill and people?

   2. Given your answers to the questions above, how would you describe Merrill's pattern of organization—point by point, block, or a mixture of the two?

   3. What do you learn about Merrill? How would you describe her? What examples can you find to support your opinion?

   4. Using your own words, what does the essay imply about elephants? People? Nature? Vocalization?

   5. Considering your response to the previous questions and the idea that Merrill's thesis is implied, what is it?

TECHNIQUE AND STYLE

   1. Reread the essay's first paragraph so that you can evaluate its effectiveness as an introduction. What comparisons strike you? What word choice? How well does she bring the scene to life?

   2. Paragraph 2 consists of one sentence. In what way does it round out paragraph 1? Why might she have chosen a one-sentence paragraph?

3. You know that Merrill is both a photographer and a poet. In what ways might the essay reflect those talents? What examples can you find?

4. Aside from the structure of the essay, comparison in the form of metaphor, simile, analogy, and simple description play a major role. What examples can you find and what do they add?

5. Think about how you would describe the atmosphere Merrill creates in the essay and then reread Merrill's last paragraph, paying particular attention to the last sentence. In what ways does the paragraph conclude the essay? How effective is the conclusion?

SUGGESTIONS FOR WRITING

Journal

1. To what extent does Merrill recreate the scene? In your own words, how would you describe it?

2. Paragraphs 1, 10, and 11 include specific details that you might expect to see in a scientific journal, not an informal essay. Explain what they add to the essay.

Essay

1. Merrill's essay focuses on a subject you may not know much about and uses comparison to bring the unfamiliar into the realm of the familiar. Think of something you know well that may be foreign to most of your readers, and explain it using comparisons. Like Merrill you may want to analyze a sound you are very familiar with. For suggestions, you might think of a particular

    song
    musical instrument
    animal
    classroom or lab
    job environment

2. More likely than not, you have traveled to some place that to some may seem foreign or at the least very different from the ordinary. Perhaps it was a foreign country or a city or place in this country that was unusual. Think first of what was strange or exotic and then for each example, come up with a familiar term that can be used for comparison. Based upon what you come up with, write an essay in which you explain your subject.

World and America Watching Different Wars

Danna Harman

Any newspaper would be hard-pressed to find someone as quali-fied to cover the war in Iraq as Danna Harman. After earning a BA in history from Harvard, she studied economics and Arabic at the University of California, Berkeley, and received an MPhil from Cambridge University in Islamic Studies. Now a freelance writer, Harman has been the Latin America bureau chief for USA Today *and* The Christian Science Monitor. *Harman has served as the* Monitor's *Africa correspondent with special assignments in Egypt, Israel, Yemen, Jordan, and Iraq. Her work has also been published in* The New Republic, The London Times, The Sunday Times, The Chicago Sun Times, *and* Elle. *Sent to cover the war for the* Monitor, *she was stationed in Egypt. There, she says, "I spent the whole month with the TV tuned to the local channels and went out to talk to people in the street as much as possible about what they believed was going on—and found the gap between the perceptions here and in the U.S. of what was happening pretty amazing." You'll see what she means. Her piece was published in the* Monitor *on March 25, 2003, where she also acknowledges the assistance of special correspondent Dan Murphy in Jakarta, Indonesia, and Alexandra Marks in New York.*

What to Look For As you read Harman's piece, keep in mind that it was written for a newspaper. The paragraphs are set to fit a news column, and the subheadings guide the reader through the story. Look to see how they help.

1 CAIRO, EGYPT—The Hamouda family is gathered around the TV, sipping sugary tea and glued to the pictures of captured U.S. soldiers being interrogated by Iraqis on the popular Qatar-based satellite station Al Jazeera.

2 "What's your name?" A terrified young female POW is asked. "How old are you?" The camera moves to her feet, which are bloody and bare.

3   "Yieee!" cheers eldest son Ahmed, knocking over a fake geranium plant as he shoots up from the couch in excitement. "Show it how it is!"

4   It is not that they are happy to see suffering, says Hellmy, the father, somewhat apologetically, as the camera weaves between several bodies. "But the other side of the story needs to be told."

5   The gruesome video shown Sunday on Al Jazeera—reaching 35 million Arab-speakers worldwide, including about 20 percent of the Egyptian population—will probably never be seen by the average American TV viewer.

6   In fact, American audiences are seeing and reading about a different war than the rest of the world. The news coverage in Europe, the Middle East, and Asia, reflects and defines the widening perception gap about the motives for this war. Surveys show that an increasing number of Americans believe this is a just war, while most of the world's Arabs and Muslims see it as a war of aggression. Media coverage does not necessarily create these leanings, say analysts, but it works to cement them.

7   "The difference in coverage between the United States and the rest of the world helped contribute to the situation that we're in now," says Kim Spencer, president of WorldLink TV, a U.S. satellite channel devoted to airing foreign news. "Americans have been unable to see how they're perceived."

8   For example, most Americans, watching CNN, Fox, or the U.S. television networks, are not seeing as much coverage of injured Iraqi citizens, or being given more than a glimpse of the antiwar protests now raging in the Muslim world and beyond.

9   In the Middle East, Europe, and parts of Asia, by comparison, the rapid progress made by U.S.-led troops has been played down. And many aspects of the conflict being highlighted in the U.S.—such as the large number of Iraqi troops surrendering, the cooperation between U.S.-led forces and various Gulf states, commentary on America's superior weapons technology, and the human interest angles on soldier life in the desert—are almost totally absent from coverage outside the U.S.

10   "Sure, the news we get in the Arab world is slanted," admits Hussein Amin, chair of the department of journalism and mass communication at Cairo's American University. "In the same way the news received in the U.S. is biased."

The View from Europe

11 Some analysts note that European press ownership is less concentrated than its counterparts in the U.S. and is seen as providing more perspectives than either the Arab or American outlets. In Frankfurt, for example, readers have access to 16 different German-language newspapers—many of which present different vantage points, which makes for a more lively and varied debate.

12 European journalists also seem to ask different, more skeptical, questions of this war, often being the ones at White House and Pentagon press conferences to ask whether the invasion of Iraq has turned up any of the weapons of mass destruction that used to justify the invasion—even as their American counterparts repeatedly focus on such questions as whether Saddam Hussein is alive or dead.

13 Media watchers say the European press has tended to be more balanced than the U.S. media in dealing with the war, in part because Europe is so much closer to the Muslim world. John Schmidt, a former reporter for the *International Herald Tribune*, who has just returned from Europe, notes that in Marseille, France, 30 percent of the population is Muslim. In Berlin, the biggest minority population is the Turks.

14 "These are countries in Europe that live cheek by jowl with Islamic people, they know how deep the dislike for the West can be, they know how sensitively some of these issues have to be transmitted," says Mr. Schmidt, who is now an economics writer for the *Milwaukee Journal Sentinel.*

15 "There are really two stories unfolding here, one is the war and its progress and the second one is the progress of world opinion," says Tom Patterson, a media expert at Harvard University's Kennedy School of Government. "That second dimension is there in the American press, but it's clearly way underreported."

16 For instance, American media outlets may report on the demonstrations in other countries, particularly if there are violent clashes. But they don't devote as many resources to covering in depth the growing anti-American sentiment—even among American allies—or its implications for the future, says Professor Patterson.

Reporter or Soldier?

17 Back in his Cairo living room, the elder Mr. Hamouda flips to CNN for a moment, over cries of protest from the rest of the family. It is vaguely possible to make out U.S. troop maneuvers on a grainy

green screen. In the corner there is a small photo of a middle-aged man in an Army jacket.

18   Nadia, the great-grandmother in the family, wonders aloud who CNN correspondent Walter Rogers is and what he is doing with the troops. "He is in bed with them," says an English speaking nephew, laughing at the well-worn joke, a pun on "embedding," in which the Pentagon allows journalists to report from within military units. Nadia has no idea what the boy is talking about. "Turn it back to Al Jazeera," she demands, adjusting her false teeth, "let's see those bodies again."

19   Across the globe, in Indonesia, student leader and antiwar activist Muhammad Hermawan has seen these same pictures on his local channel, which pirates Al Jazeera's signal and adds simultaneous Indonesian translation. "The more these pictures are shown, the more people will understand America's brutal aggression," he says. "People will learn, and we'll see bigger and bigger protests."

20   Interest in the war has been so high that Indonesia's TV7 began pirating Al Jazeera's signal shortly before the start of the war. The new station carries the Arab-language broadcast with simultaneous Indonesian translation. Though Al Jazeera is only shown from 10 in the evening until 11 in the morning an official at TV7 says the news department is receiving about 100 calls a day from viewers, up from "almost zero" before the U.S. invasion began.

21   The news broadcasts in Indonesia, the world's most populous Muslim nation, have been tamer than the news in the Middle East, focusing on protests against the war at home, with official statements against the war from abroad.

22   But they have also carried some stories sympathetic to U.S. soldiers, including an interview with Anecita Hudson of Alamogordo, Texas. Mrs. Hudson says her son, 23 year-old Army Specialist Joseph Hudson, was one of the prisoners of war shown on Al Jazeera. She said seeing her son captured was "like a bad dream."

23   Mrs. Hudson didn't see her son on American news outlets. She spotted him on a Filipino cable channel she subscribes to. She is originally from the Philippines.

24   The pictures of U.S. troops drew condemnation from U.S. Defense Secretary Donald Rumsfeld and other officials. "It seems to me that showing a few pictures on the screen, not knowing who they are and being communicated by Al Jazeera, which is not a perfect instrument of communication, obviously is part of Iraqi propaganda," Mr. Rumsfeld told CBS.

25   "War is ugly by nature and we did not create these pictures—we are only there to reflect reality on the ground," says Jihad Ali Ballout, Al Jazeera's media relations head. "Truth is sometimes unpleasant and gruesome, and I feel distressed when people ask me to dress it up."

Washington Watches Al Jazeera

26   The Bush administration sees Al Jazeera—the cable news channel made famous for its airing of Osama Bin Laden tapes—as having an anti-American bias. But, since the seven-year-old Al Jazeera has grown from six to 24 hours of daily programming and reaches more than 35 million Arab speakers around the world, including 150,000 in the United States, Washington seems to be attempting to work more closely with the network.

27   The Pentagon offered Al Jazeera four choice spots for its reporters to be embedded with U.S. military units and assigned it a special media liaison officer, and both National Security Adviser Condoleezza Rice and Defense Secretary Donald Rumsfeld have given extensive interviews to Al Jazeera in recent days. Al-Arabiya and Abu Dhabi, two other 24-hour Arab-language stations, have received similar attention from the administration.

28   Al Jazeera says that it has two of its correspondents "embedded" with U.S. units—but the units in question are in Kuwait. It has no reporters with U.S. troops directly participating in the invasion.

Variety Breeds Objectivity?

29   Professor Amin in Cairo argues that while watching this war unfold in the various media outlets is a good example of how bias clearly exists on all sides, there are nonetheless positive signs that international media are collectively moving toward becoming more objective, by force of necessity.

30   "The fact that the common man has access to different sources today means that it's harder for one source to get away with showing only one side of the story. You can piece together a broader, more accurate story yourself," he says.

31   There is some awareness in the Hamouda living room that Arab broadcasters may also spread propaganda.

32   In 1967, four days after Israel had won the war against Egypt, Egyptian radio was still declaring victory, recalls Hellmy Hamouda. "I was in the Suez Canal at the time and I had seen some of the war

with my own eyes," he says, "I had a hunch that radio was not telling the truth."

33   "Today, we can find the better truth by simply changing channels or going on the Internet," says Hamouda. He then flips back to Al Jazeera at the demand of grandma Nadia, "If we want to."

ORGANIZATION AND IDEAS

1. Harman covers a lot of topics in her essay—the media, bias, anti-American sentiment, the war in Iraq, pro-Muslim sentiment. What is her primary subject and what evidence supports your view?
2. In what ways does the American media differ from that in the Middle East, Europe, and much of Asia?
3. When published, the piece was subtitled "CNN vs. Al Jazeera: Seeing is Often Believing." What evidence can you find to support that idea?
4. To what extent is Harman explaining the situation? Arguing for a particular point of view?
5. In one sentence, state Harman's thesis. How valid is it now?

TECHNIQUE AND STYLE

1. Throughout the piece, Harman makes extensive use of sources with both quotations and summaries. What do they contribute to the essay?
2. The Hamouda family appears in paragraphs 1–4, 17 and 18, and again in 31–33. What do they add to the piece?
3. Look again at the subheadings. To what extent do they work to guide you through the essay?
4. In what ways is Harman's essay appropriate for the *Christian Science Monitor*?
5. The story opens and closes with a narrative. What does it add?

SUGGESTIONS FOR WRITING

Journal

1. Would you call Harman optimistic, pessimistic, something in between? Explain.
2. How do you obtain world news? To what extent do you find the source credible and why?

Essay

1. The media is often accused of bias or sensationalism, but other considerations are also at work—time constraints, availability of sources, concerns of the readership, and so on. Use a recent major event to analyze

the accuracy and depth of its reporting. You might compare the same story as covered in two

national daily newspapers
national evening television news shows
weekly news magazines
national Sunday newspapers
daily Web news reports

2. Choose a political news story of some importance and read about it—start to finish—in a major American newspaper and one from Great Britain, using print versions from the library or available on the Web. What differences do you note? What, if any, biases can you find? Where does the truth lie?

On Using Division and Classification

6

Russell Baker aptly titles his essay "The Plot Against People":

1   Inanimate objects are classified into three major categories—those that
     don't work, those that break down and those that get lost.

2   The goal of all inanimate objects is to resist man and ultimately to
     defeat him, and the three major classifications are based on the
     method each object uses to achieve its purpose. As a general rule, any
     object capable of breaking down at the moment when it is most
     needed will do so. The automobile is typical of the category.

Not only does Baker clearly set out his system of classification, but he
also establishes his purpose—to explain the "plot against people"—sets
up a humorous tone, and implies the structure that will follow. He also
suggests his thesis: By breaking down, getting lost, and not working,
inanimate objects resist and ultimately defeat people.

To divide a subject and then classify examples into categories or
classes that result from division you need to examine a subject from
several angles:

How can it be divided?
How can you classify your examples by differences?
How can you classify them by similarities?

In two short paragraphs, Baker implies a division between animate and
inanimate objects, hones in on the latter, names his categories, points out
their differences, and highlights their central similarity, their shared
"goal." All of the essays in this chapter use **division and classification**
to explore a variety of topics: Baker's inanimate objects as well as retail
stores, religions, and kinds of friends.

What is your purpose? Knowing the effect you want to have on your readers will help you devise your system of classification and sharpen your thesis. If you want to inform your audience, you may need to define some of your terms. Writing about the ways in which a one-year-old can both annoy and delight you, for instance, you may want to define what you mean by *annoy* and *delight.* You then can link the definitions to your audience's experiences, so that even if some of your readers have never spent much time around a baby, they can still appreciate your points. For *annoy,* you might define your reaction as similar to hearing a car alarm going off in the middle of the night, and for *delight,* you might remind your readers of how they felt when opening an unexpected but perfect present. Both definitions help explain and draw on common experiences.

Should you tackle that same topic with a humorous tone, you will not only be informing your audience but entertaining them as well. But humor comes in many forms, evoking everything from belly laughs to giggles to knowing smiles. To produce these responses, you may find yourself using exaggeration (also known as **hyperbole**), **irony, sarcasm,** or a combination of all three and more. Your title can tip off your readers to your tone: "Baby Destructo" (exaggeration); "Little Baby, Big Problem" (irony); "The Unsung Joys of Parenthood" (sarcasm).

You can also use division and classification to explore a topic and then argue a point. Thinking of ways in which a driver can be distracted, you might first divide the subject into people and gadgets. Under gadgets, you come up with cell phones, MP3 players, and navigation systems, as well as the car's standard dials and gauges. Perhaps you want to argue technology has made driving a hazard.

What is your system of classification? To work effectively, a system of classification must be thorough and logical. The system that governs how goods are arranged in a supermarket needs to be broad enough to cover everything a supermarket might sell, and it needs to make sense. Can openers should be with kitchen implements, not with vegetables; cans of peas should be with other canned goods, not with milk.

But the system need not be airtight. Baker, for instance, qualifies his categorization later in his essay: "things that get lost hardly ever break down." The "hardly ever" allows an exception to his general statement.

How do you organize your draft? Some writers begin by first dividing the subject into their system of classification, then moving on to focus on one of the classes. Say you chose as a topic the electronic objects we often take for granted. You might have found yourself making notes that include a huge list. Thinking through that list you might have noticed that you can divide it into machines that can be controlled with a remote device and those that cannot, or at least not yet. In one category are items such as microwaves and computers, and in the other you've lumped together CD players, television sets, and DVDs.

You sketch out notes that may look like this:

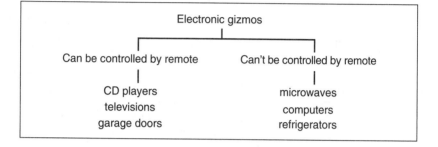

Electronic gizmos

Can be controlled by remote	Can't be controlled by remote
CD players	microwaves
televisions	computers
garage doors	refrigerators

The more you think about it, the longer the list for remote-controlled objects becomes; so instead of writing about both categories, you stick to one, speculating on a world with the ultimate universal remote.

On the other hand, you may find your central question so intriguing that you want to get right to it, in which case you wouldn't need to discuss the division at all; instead, you can leap straight into presenting the category of remote-controlled objects, illustrating it with multiple examples. If that's your choice, then think of division and classification as an extended version of comparison and contrast, one in which you compare more than two categories.

Perhaps the greatest trap in writing an essay that uses division and classification is having a string of examples that don't lead anywhere. All your examples are well developed, yes, but they don't support an assertion. It's the cardinal sin—an essay without a thesis.

If you find yourself headed in that direction, try answering your own questions. In the course of thinking about your subject, you may well have come up with a solid, focused, central question, such as "What kind of life will the American consumer have in a remote-controlled world?" Your one-sentence answer to that question can be your thesis.

If you are using division or classification to develop only one part of your paper, then where you place it depends on where you think it would be most effective. But if your essay, like most of those in this chapter, is structured primarily by division and classification, then you would do best to use a straightforward pattern of organization, devoting the body of the paper to developing the category or categories involved. Your reader can then follow your reasoning and understand how it supports your thesis. Because readers can get lost in a tangle of examples, you may opt for an explicit thesis in an obvious place, such as at the end of your introduction.

Useful Terms

Division and classification Methods of examining a subject. Division involves the process of separating, first dividing the subject into groups so that they can be sorted out—classified— into categories; classification focuses on shared characteristics, sorting items into categories that share a similar feature.

Hyperbole Obvious overstatement, exaggeration.

Irony A statement or action in which the intended meaning or occurrence is the opposite of the surface one.

Sarcasm A caustic or sneering remark or tone that is usually ironic as well.

POINTERS FOR USING DIVISION AND CLASSIFICATION

Exploring the Topic

1. **How can your topic be divided?** What divisions apply? Of those you list, which one is the best suited?
2. **What examples can you think of?** What characteristics do your examples have in common? Which do you have the most to say about?
3. **Are your categories for classification appropriate?** Are the categories parallel? Do they overlap? Do you need to make any adjustments?
4. **Do your examples fit your categories?** Are you sure the examples have enough in common? Are they obvious? Which are not?
5. **What is your principle for classification?** Have you applied it consistently to each category?
6. **Are your categories complete?** Do they cover the topic? Do they contain enough examples?

(Continued)

POINTERS FOR USING DIVISION
AND CLASSIFICATION *(Continued)*

7. How can your categories be sequenced? From simple to complex? Least to most important? Least to most effective?

8. What is your point? What assertion are you making? Does your system of classification support it? Are your examples appropriate?

9. What is your purpose? Are you primarily making your point to express your feelings, to inform, to persuade, or to entertain?

Drafting the Paper

1. Know your reader. Where does your reader stand in relation to your system of classification? Is the reader part of it? If so, how? If the reader is not part of your system, is he or she on your side, say a fellow student looking at teachers? What does your audience know about your topic? About your system of classification? What does the reader not know? Your audience might be biased toward or against your subject and classification system. How can you best foster or combat the bias?

2. Know your purpose. If your primary purpose is to express your feelings, make sure that you are not just writing to yourself and that you are not treading on the toes of your audience. Similarly, if you are writing to persuade, make sure you are not convincing only yourself. Check to see that you are using material that may convince someone who disagrees with you or who, at the least, is either sitting on the fence or hasn't given the matter much thought. Writing to inform is probably the easiest here, for though your subject may be familiar, your system of classification is probably new. On the other hand, writing to entertain is difficult and requires a deft use of persona.

3. Set up your system of classification early in the paper. You may find that a definition is in order or that some background information is necessary, but make your system clear and bring it out early.

4. Explain the principle behind the system. To give your system credibility, you need to provide an explanation for your means of selection. The explanation can be brief—a phrase or two—but it should be there.

5. Select appropriate examples. Perhaps you can best illustrate a class by one extended example, or maybe it would be better to pile on examples. If your examples are apt to be unfamiliar to your audience, make sure you give enough detail so that they are explained by their contexts.

6. Make a point. Remember that what you have to say about your subject is infinitely more interesting than the subject itself. So, too, your major assertion is more important than your system of classification: It is what your system of classification adds up to. It's easy, in writing this kind of paper, to mistake the means for the end; so make sure that you use classification to support an overall assertion.

What Are Friends For?

Marion Winik

*A graduate of Brown University with an MFA from Brooklyn University, Marion Winik now is on the faculty of the University of Baltimore, where she teaches in the MFA program in Creative Writing and Publishing Arts. In the interval between her taking courses and teaching them, she wrote poetry—*Nonstop *(1981) and* BoyCrazy *(1986)— before moving to essays, first for the* Austin Chronicle *and then for National Public Radio. In addition to the memoir* First Comes Love *(1996), Winik has written about her experience as a single mother in* The Lunch-Box Chronicles: Notes from the Parenting Underground *(1998) and provided advice in* Rules for the Unruly: Living an Unconventional Life *(2001). Her essays have been collected in* Telling *(1984) and her latest book* Above Us Only Sky *(2005). Together with Ericka Lutz, the fiction editor of* Literary Mama, *Winik has set down the "Top Ten Myths and Truths of the Writer's Life." You can find them at http://www.literarymama.com/profiles/archives/000890.html. The following essay comes from her collection* Telling.

What to Look For   Tone—a writer's attitude toward the subject and audience—can run through the same wide range as a person's voice. As you read Winik's essay, you'll find that her tone differs from many of the writers in this book. Think about her tone first in terms of a scale that runs from informal to formal and ask yourself where you would put it. Then try to describe her tone as fully as you can. Thinking along these lines will help you identify the kind of tone you want in your own writing.

1   I was thinking about how everybody can't be everything to each other, but some people can be something to each other, thank God, from the ones whose shoulder you cry on to the ones whose half-slips you borrow to the nameless ones you chat with in the grocery line.

2   Buddies, for example, are the workhorses of the friendship world, the people out there on the front lines, defending you from loneliness and boredom. They call you up, they listen to your

complaints, they celebrate your successes and curse your misfortunes, and you do the same for them in return. They hold out through innumerable crises before concluding that the person you're dating is no good, and even then understand if you ignore their good counsel. They accompany you to a movie with subtitles or to see the diving pig at Aquarena Springs. They feed your cat when you are out of town and pick you up from the airport when you get back. They come over to help you decide what to wear on a date. Even if it is with that creep.

3   What about family members? Most of them are people you just got stuck with, and though you love them, you may not have very much in common. But there is that rare exception, the Relative Friend. It is your cousin, your brother, maybe even your aunt. The two of you share the same views of the other family members. Meg never should have divorced Martin. He was the best thing that ever happened to her. You can confirm each other's memories of things that happened a long time ago. Don't you remember when Uncle Hank and Daddy had that awful fight in the middle of Thanksgiving dinner? Grandma always hated Grandpa's stamp collection; she probably left the windows open during the hurricane on purpose.

4   While so many family relationships are tinged with guilt and obligation, a relationship with a Relative Friend is relatively worry-free. You don't even have to hide your vices from this delightful person. When you slip out Aunt Joan's back door for a cigarette, she is already there.

5   Then there is that special guy at work. Like all the other people at the job site, at first he's just part of the scenery. But gradually he starts to stand out from the crowd. Your friendship is cemented by jokes about co-workers and thoughtful favors around the office. Did you see Ryan's hair? Want half my bagel? Soon you know the names of his turtles, what he did last Friday night, exactly which model CD player he wants for his birthday. His handwriting is as familiar to you as your own.

6   Though you invite each other to parties, you somehow don't quite fit into each other's outside lives. For this reason, the friendship may not survive a job change. Company gossip, once an infallible source of entertainment, soon awkwardly accentuates the distance between you. But wait. Like School Friends, Work Friends share certain memories which acquire a nostalgic glow after about a decade.

7   A Faraway Friend is someone you grew up with or went to school with or lived in the same town as until one of you moved away.

Without a Faraway Friend, you would never get any mail addressed in handwriting. A Faraway Friend calls late at night, invites you to her wedding, always says she is coming to visit but rarely shows up. An actual visit from a Faraway Friend is a cause for celebration and binges of all kinds. Cigarettes, Chips Ahoy, bottles of tequila.

8   Faraway Friends go through phases of intense communication, then may be out of touch for many months. Either way, the connection is always there. A conversation with your Faraway Friend always helps to put your life in perspective: when you feel you've hit a dead end, come to a confusing fork in the road, or gotten lost in some crackerbox subdivision of your life, the advice of the Faraway Friend—who has the big picture, who is so well acquainted with the route that brought you to this place—is indispensable.

9   Another useful function of the Faraway Friend is to help you remember things from a long time ago, like the name of your seventh-grade history teacher, what was in that really good stir-fry, or exactly what happened that night on the boat with the guys from Florida.

10   Ah, the Former Friend. A sad thing. At best a wistful memory, at worst a dangerous enemy who is in possession of many of your deepest secrets. But what was it that drove you apart? A misunderstanding, a betrayed confidence, an unrepaid loan, an ill-conceived flirtation. A poor choice of spouse can do in a friendship just like that. Going into business together can be a serious mistake. Time, money, distance, cult religions: all noted friendship killers. You quit doing drugs, you're not such good friends with your dealer anymore.

11   And lest we forget, there are the Friends You Love to Hate. They call at inopportune times. They say stupid things. They butt in, they boss you around, they embarrass you in public. They invite themselves over. They take advantage. You've done the best you can, but they need professional help. On top of all this, they love you to death and are convinced they're your best friend on the planet.

12   So why do you continue to be involved with these people? Why do you tolerate them? On the contrary, the real question is, What would you do without them? Without Friends You Love to Hate, there would be nothing to talk about with your other friends. Their problems and their irritating stunts provide a reliable source of conversation for everyone they know. What's more, Friends You Love to Hate make you feel good about yourself, since you are obviously in so much better shape than they are. No matter what

these people do, you will never get rid of them. As much as they need you, you need them too.

13   At the other end of the spectrum are Hero Friends. These people are better than the rest of us, that's all there is to it. Their career is something you wanted to be when you grew up—painter, forest ranger, tireless doer of good. They have beautiful homes filled with special handmade things presented to them by villagers in the remote areas they have visited in their extensive travels. Yet they are modest. They never gossip. They are always helping others, especially those who have suffered a death in the family or an illness. You would think people like this would just make you sick, but somehow they don't.

14   A New Friend is a tonic unlike any other. Say you meet her at a party. In your bowling league. At a Japanese conversation class, perhaps. Wherever, whenever, there's that spark of recognition. The first time you talk, you can't believe how much you have in common. Suddenly, your life story is interesting again, your insights fresh, your opinion valued. Your various shortcomings are as yet completely invisible.

15   It's almost like falling in love.

ORGANIZATION AND IDEAS

1. Reread the essay jotting down the focus of each of the 15 paragraphs. Which provides the essay's introduction? Its conclusion?

2. Which kinds of friends get the most attention? Which get the least? What reasons can you think of for that emphasis? For the order in which they appear?

3. To what extent does Winik use examples? How necessary are they? How effective?

4. Do any of the kinds of friends Winik describes ring false in your experience? How so?

5. Look again at the title and at the types of friends Winik describes. What is her thesis?

TECHNIQUE AND STYLE

1. Throughout the essay, Winik uses the pronoun *you.* To whom is she referring? In your own words, describe who the *you* stands for. Why might she have chosen that pronoun and how effective is her choice?

2. What examples can you find to suggest that Winik's style is a feminine one? To what extent is gender important to the essay?

3. Take another look at the essay with particular attention to Winik's use of initial capitals. What do you notice? What do they contribute? How effective is the device?
4. Paragraphs 3 and 5 contain questions representing hypothetical dialogue. What would be the effect of using actual dialogue? Which is preferable and why?
5. How effective is Winik's last paragraph? Would it be more or less effective if it were more fully developed?

Suggestions for Writing

Journal

1. Think about your own friends and choose one who fits one of Winik's categories. Describe that person in detail.
2. Look at the list you made of Winik's types of friends. What others can you come up with? Choose one and describe the type in much the same way as Winik does.

Essay

1. Given that people's personalities range over a continuum with extremes at either end, the extremes can be good subjects for an essay that uses division and classification. Think about virtually any activity people are involved in and identify the behavior that represents the two extremes, thus dividing the subject. Then choose one of those groups and consider the categories your choice can be classified into. Here are some suggestions:

    drivers
    readers
    writers
    parents

2. Think about the various kinds of teachers you have had and have heard about. What categories can they be sorted into? Write an essay in which you explain those categories, giving examples for each. The categories you choose and the examples you give for them will determine your thesis.

The Plot Against People

Russell Baker

Russell Baker grew up in poverty, enlisted in the U.S. Navy for pilot training in World War II, then returned to finish his degree at Johns Hopkins University and take up a career as a journalist. He is best known for his light tone, one that many readers enjoyed during the 36 years he was a regular columnist for The New York Times. *Winner of two Pulitzer Prizes, one for biography and another for commentary, Baker is the author of several collections of essays and autobiographical books, among them* So This Is Depravity *(1980),* Growing Up *(1982),* The Good Times *(1989),* There's a Country in My Cellar: The Best of Russell Baker *(1991). Baker is also the editor of* The Norton Book of Light Verse *(1986) and* Russell Baker's Book of American Humor *(1993). The essay that follows typifies the humorous side of Baker's style, for he has discovered the principles behind the continuing battle between humans and inanimate objects. He discusses these principles as he neatly divides things into three categories and then places objects into his classifications.*

What to Look For Transitions between paragraphs can be wooden, so obvious that they leap off the page to say "Look at me! I'm a transition." The more effective variety is subtle, and one way to bring that about is to pick up a key word from the previous sentence and repeat it in the first sentence of the paragraph that follows. After you've read Baker's essay, go back over it searching for his transitions between paragraphs.

1   Inanimate objects are classified into three major categories—those that don't work, those that break down and those that get lost.

2   The goal of all inanimate objects is to resist man and ultimately to defeat him, and the three major classifications are based on the method each object uses to achieve its purpose. As a general rule, any object capable of breaking down at the moment when it is most needed will do so. The automobile is typical of the category.

3   With the cunning typical of its breed, the automobile never breaks down while entering a filling station with a large staff of idle mechanics. It waits until it reaches a downtown intersection in the middle of the rush hour, or until it is fully loaded with family and luggage on the Ohio Turnpike.

4   Thus it creates maximum misery, inconvenience, frustration and irritability among its human cargo, thereby reducing its owner's life span.

5   Washing machines, garbage disposals, lawn mowers, light bulbs, automatic laundry dryers, water pipes, furnaces, electrical fuses, television tubes, hose nozzles, tape recorders, slide projectors—all are in league with the automobile to take their turn at breaking down whenever life threatens to flow smoothly for their human enemies.

6   Many inanimate objects, of course, find it extremely difficult to break down. Pliers, for example, and gloves and keys are almost totally incapable of breaking down. Therefore, they have had to evolve a different technique for resisting man.

7   They get lost. Science has still not solved the mystery of how they do it, and no man has ever caught one of them in the act of getting lost. The most plausible theory is that they have developed a secret method of locomotion which they are able to conceal the instant a human eye falls upon them.

8   It is not uncommon for a pair of pliers to climb all the way from the cellar to the attic in its single-minded determination to raise its owner's blood pressure. Keys have been known to burrow three feet under mattresses. Women's purses, despite their great weight, frequently travel through six or seven rooms to find a hiding space under a couch.

9   Scientists have been struck by the fact that things that break down virtually never get lost, while things that get lost hardly ever break down.

10   A furnace, for example, will invariably break down at the depth of the first winter cold wave, but it will never get lost. A woman's purse, which after all does have some inherent capacity for breaking down, hardly ever does; it almost invariably chooses to get lost.

11   Some persons believe this constitutes evidence that inanimate objects are not entirely hostile to man, and that a negotiated peace is possible. After all, they point out, a furnace could infuriate a man even more thoroughly by getting lost than by breaking down, just as a glove could upset him far more by breaking down than by getting lost.

12   Not everyone agrees, however, that this indicates a conciliatory attitude among inanimate objects. Many say it merely proves that furnaces, gloves and pliers are incredibly stupid.

13   The third class of objects—those that don't work—is the most curious of all. These include such objects as barometers, car clocks, cigarette lighters, flashlights, and toy train locomotives. It is inaccurate, of course, to say that they never work. They work once, usually for the first few hours after being brought home, and then quit. Thereafter, they never work again.

14   In fact, it is widely assumed that they are built for the purpose of not working. Some people have reached advanced ages without ever seeing some of these objects—barometers, for example—in working order.

15   Science is utterly baffled by the entire category. There are many theories about it. The most interesting holds that the things that don't work have attained the highest state possible for an inanimate object, the state to which things that break down and things that get lost can still only aspire.

16   They have truly defeated man by conditioning him never to expect anything of them, and in return they have given man the only peace he receives from inanimate society. He does not expect his barometer to work, his electric locomotive to run, his cigarette lighter to light or his flashlight to illuminate, and when they don't, it does not raise his blood pressure.

17   He cannot attain that peace with furnaces and keys and cars and women's purses as long as he demands that they work for their keep.

Organization and Ideas

1. Paragraphs 3–6 explain the first category. What effects does the automobile achieve by breaking down? How do those effects support Baker's contention about "the goal of all inanimate objects"? What other examples does Baker put into his first category? What example does not fit?

2. Paragraphs 7–12 present the second classification. What causes, reasons, or motives are attributed to the examples in this group?

3. Paragraphs 13–16 describe the third group. What are its qualities? Why might Baker have chosen to list it last? What principle of organization can you discern beneath Baker's ordering of the three groups?

4. Consider how each group frustrates and defeats people together with the first sentence of paragraph 2. Combine this information into a sentence that states the author's thesis.

5. To what extent does Baker use the absurd in his essay? How is it appropriate?

Technique and Style

1. In part, the essay's humor arises from Baker's use of anthropomorphism, attributing human qualities to inanimate objects. How effectively does he use the technique?

2. Baker has a keen eye for the absurd, as illustrated by paragraph 10. What other examples can you find? What does this technique contribute to the essay?

3. Baker's stance, tone, and line of reasoning, while patently tongue-in-cheek, are also mock-scientific. Where can you find examples of Baker's explicit or implied "scientific" trappings?

4. The essay's transitions are carefully wrought. What links paragraph 3 to paragraph 2? Paragraph 7 to paragraph 6? Paragraph 10 to paragraph 9? Paragraph 12 to paragraph 11?

5. How an essay achieves unity is a more subtle thing. What links paragraph 8 to paragraph 6? Paragraph 9 to paragraphs 3–6? Paragraph 16 to paragraph 2? Paragraph 17 to paragraphs 10–12 and paragraphs 3–5?

Suggestions for Writing

Journal

1. Describe a fight you have had with an inanimate object.

2. Of all the inanimate objects that can frustrate you, which one tops the list and why?

Essay

1. Write your own "plot" essay, imagining something else plotting against people. Like Baker, you can take a "scientific" stance or you may prefer your own humorous tone. Suggestions:

    clothes
    food
    pets
    the weather
    plants
    traffic

2. It's no news that we live in a highly technological society; it's also no news that at times that technology is frustrating. You may, for instance, have a number of objects that display the time—DVD, clock, stove, answering machine—but when the electricity goes off, getting them back in sync is a challenge. Choose a category and write an essay in which you explore whether that particular group of technological advances is good, bad, or somewhere in between.

The Search for Human Life in the Maze of Retail Stores

Michelle Higgins

Michelle Higgins joined The Wall Street Journal *as an intern for the popular Friday* Weekend Journal *in 1999 and quickly moved up to staff reporter. At* Weekend Journal, *she authored a weekly travel column, "Takeoffs & Landings" and wrote cover stories on everything from the online travel business to theme park vacations. In April 2002, Ms. Higgins began writing for the newspaper's new "Personal Journal" section. Featured as the "Cranky Consumer," her stories have included consumer issues covering everything from online banking to 401(k) accounts to summer camp. Higgins has since moved to* The New York Times, *where she writes the "Practical Traveler" column on topics such as the price of airline food and how to get bumped. The review that follows was published in the May 6, 2003, issue of* The Wall Street Journal.

What to Look For   A report on retail stores that critiques their ability to help shoppers find what they are looking for could be very dull indeed, but Michelle Higgins keeps it from being so. As you read, look for the ways she keeps her reader's interest.

1   When Jonathan Gordon went shopping at a Macy's in New Jersey for a vacuum cleaner recently, he couldn't find anyone to answer his questions. After a 10-minute search, he solved his problem by standing in the aisle and shouting, "Is there anybody here who can help me?"

2   Finally, a staffer appeared—who couldn't tell him anything he couldn't already read on the box.

3   Attention, shoppers: It is getting even tougher to get help in the aisles. The nation's third-largest discount retailer, **Kmart,** is expected to come out of bankruptcy Tuesday, and retailers overall are anticipating a postwar sales boost. But many are still in retrenching mode. In January, **Toys "R" Us** cut 700 positions in 400 stores. The next

month, **Circuit City** eliminated 4.8% of its work force, including an average of three salespeople per store. Overall last year, the number of employees in retail fell for the first time in a decade, according to the Bureau of Labor Statistics.

4   All this comes on top of a major effort in recent years by retailers to build ever-more-colossal shops—while simultaneously redesigning them to encourage people to serve themselves instead of getting help from the staff.

5   To see just how tough it is out there, we recently went shopping at six retailers. They included two big discounters Kmart and **Wal-Mart Stores,** the home-improvement giants **Lowe's** and **Home Depot**—and what is often the lion's den of retail: sprawling, kid-packed toy stores.

6   We picked stores in six different cities and visited them all on a Saturday between the busy hours of one and five. At each place we tried to find an employee who would help us locate two items we knew the store stocked. To see how much staff knew about their merchandise, we also asked for help with a specific task; for example, we asked at the toy stores for gift suggestions for a smart 10-year-old boy—but nothing too nerdy.

7   Our experience varied widely. At **KB Toys,** we were out the door in eight minutes with our three purchases: A Furreal Friend robotic cat, Shrinky Dinks and a basketball-player action figure. But at Wal-Mart, it took us 30 minutes and conversations with 10 people—and still, we left without finding one of the three things we wanted (a fondue pot) because the staff didn't know where they were.

8   KB Toys stores, of course, are small in comparison to warehouse-style Wal-Marts. But the staff was among the most helpful: One person even offered to carry our purchases for us while we kept shopping.

9   The retail business, struggling through its worst slump in years, can ill afford to be alienating shoppers. The pace of annual sales growth has tumbled from a high of 6.7% four years ago to just 2.9% last year. The outlook continues to look grim. The month of March was the weakest for U.S. retailers since 1995, according to a survey by Bank of Tokyo-Mitsubishi Ltd.

10   "In the past year, customer service has absolutely become dreadful," says Judson Rees of Brand Marketing, a company that dispatches "mystery shoppers" to test service at stores and restaurants. In a survey of shoppers, he said, more than three-quarters

reported that it's "common" to see salespeople ignoring customers this year, up from 39% last year.

11   It turns out there are a few ways to beat the system. Though we passed over it the first time, for example, Lowe's has buzzers in its stores to summon a staffer. Toys "R" Us has phones scattered around that you can pick up and ask for help.

12   We got off to a rocky start at a Toys "R" Us in Colma, California, when we asked where to find a Furreal Friend robotic cat. "It's right there," the staffer told us—pointing about 30 yards away and wagging his finger. "Right there! Right there!"

13   But later, the same guy warmed up and complimented us on our toys. While we had his attention, we asked where to find Shrinky Dinks. He consulted his walkie-talkie and announced: "The Imaginarium. Follow me." We were done shopping in 21 minutes.

14   A Toys "R" Us official said the first salesman should have been more polite.

15   The Lowe's we visited had a people-greeter at the front door, who deflected our question about a squirrel-proof birdfeeder to a customer-service desk that was already swarming with impatient shoppers. But after being directed to the right department, a staffer there told us Lowe's doesn't sell them—even though we later noticed that he was standing right in front of one. (Admittedly, it was on a very high shelf.)

16   After that, service picked up. Another employee got off a forklift and gave us detailed help after we asked for advice on closet organizers. He even drew us a sketch.

17   At a nearby Home Depot, we shopped for the same items and got efficient service. A cashier who was clocking out for the day even hung around to assist us.

18   Wal-Mart, Lowe's and Kmart said they are focusing on improving service.

19   Service was mixed at a Kmart in New York City. We asked the first employee we saw, a woman with an armful of clothes, for help finding a foot spa. She asked, "What is that?" before pointing us to the right department. There we asked another guy for help—who simply grunted and started walking away from us. We followed, on the chance that he intended us to, and he led us to the foot spas.

20   A third staffer helped us find cleaning products to take out a ketchup stain. "This one has a brush, so you can, shhh, shhh," he said, making a helpful brushing motion. We took it and said thanks. "You're welcome, sweetie," was the reply.

ORGANIZATION AND IDEAS

1. Outline the system of division and classification in an outline similar to the one on page 156.
2. In paragraph 6, Higgins outlines her methodology behind her system and examples. How trustworthy is it?
3. Higgins uses a framing device, beginning and ending the piece with narratives. In what ways are they similar? Different?
4. Higgins is careful to point out the stores' problems as well as those of the shopper. In what ways are the two sets of problems related?
5. If you constructed a chart to accompany the essay, what information would be in the columns? The rows? What would the chart add?

TECHNIQUE AND STYLE

1. What is Higgins' primary purpose: to entertain, inform, persuade? Some combination of the three?
2. Higgins wrote under the title of the Cranky Consumer. How apt is the title?
3. What devices and techniques does Higgins use to keep the piece from being dry?
4. In what ways is the selection an appropriate article for *The Wall Street Journal*?
5. How appropriate is the article's title?

SUGGESTIONS FOR WRITING

Journal

1. Higgins uses a lot of examples in her article. Which do you find the most interesting and why?
2. In a way, the article seems to stop instead of end. Write a concluding paragraph for it.

Essay

1. Write your own division and classification essay, using retail stores as a general subject. One of two ways to divide the topic is to think about the people you would see in them, dividing the general "people in retail stores" into
    shoppers
    sales personnel
    cashiers
Or if you'd prefer a more abstract system, you can use the general "large retail stores" and divide it into

efficiency
convenience
variety of merchandise

Choose one of these divisions or your own and consider the possible classifications. While you do not need to begin with a thesis, one will probably evolve as you write about your topic.

2. One of the arguments against the megastores such as the ones Higgins writes about is that they undercut and in many cases destroy the smaller mom-and-pop stores. Think about the kinds of stores that fall into the mom-and-pop category and write an essay that describes them. Research will help you here, so you might do a Web search for the key terms. Depending on what you find and your analysis of it, your thesis can be linked to the smaller stores' value to the community or lack of it.

Desert Religions

Richard Rodriguez

The son of Mexican immigrants, Richard Rodriguez did not learn English until he went to school, but he learned it well. He earned a BA from Stanford University and a PhD in English literature from the University of California at Berkeley. His public stands against bilingual education and affirmative action put him at odds with segments of the Chicano community, but he is best known for his writing, particularly his memoirs: Hunger of Memory *(1982),* Days of Obligation: An Argument with My Mexican Father *(1992), and* Brown: The Last Discovery of America *(2002). A contributing editor at* Harper's *and the* Los Angeles Times, *Rodriguez has been called the "best American essayist" by* The Village Voice. *You might have heard his own voice on* The News Hour with Jim Lehrer *where he is a regular contributor. For his "outstanding achievement" there he won a Peabody Award, the most coveted honor in television. The essay reprinted here was first aired on that show on July 8, 2002.*

What to Look For When you think about placing items in categories, you are analyzing their shared characteristics, their similarities. That's exactly what Rodriguez does, so as you read, look for the ways he tracks what the three "desert religions" have in common.

1   The Catholic priest is under arrest, accused of raping altar boys. The Muslim shouts out the name of Allah as the jetliner plows into the skyscraper. The Jewish settler's biblical claim to build on the West Bank is supported by fundamentalist Protestants who dream of the last days.

2   These have been months of shame and violence among the three great desert religions—Judaism, Christianity, and Islam—the religions to which most Americans adhere. These desert religions are sister religions in fact, but more commonly they have been brother religions, united and divided by a masculine sense of faith. Mullahs, priests, rabbis—the business of religion was traditionally the male's. It was the male's task to understand how God exists in our lives.

3   Judaism gave Christianity and Islam a notion both astonishing and radical, the notion that God acts in history. The desert religions became, in response to this idea, activist religions, ennobled at times by a sense of holy purpose, but also filled with a violence fed by the assumption that God is on my side and not yours. The history of the desert religions oft repeated by old men to boys, got told through stories of battles and crusades, sultans and emperors.

4   But within the three great desert faiths there was a feminine impulse, less strong but ever present, the tradition of absorption rather than assertion, service rather than authority, of play rather than dogmatic certitude. Think of the delicate poetry of the Song of Songs or the delicacy of the celebration of the maternal represented by the Renaissance Madonna or the architectural lines of the medieval mosques of Spain, light as music. And yet the louder, more persistent tradition has been male, concerned with power and blood and dogmatic points.

5   Now on the evening news, diplomats come and go speaking of [everything from] truces and terrorists to the price of oil. In truth, we are watching a religious war, Muslim versus Jew—a war disguised by the language of diplomacy. In decades and centuries past there have been Holocausts and crusades and violence as fierce among the members of a single religion, for example, Catholics contending with Protestant and Eastern Orthodox over heresies and questions of authority.

6   Yahweh, God, Allah—the desert Deity rarely expressed a feminine aspect as in Hinduism. The men who interpreted the Bible

or Koran rarely allowed themselves a sense of unknowing or paradox as in Buddhism. And not coincidentally I know many Americans who are turning away from the desert religions or are seeking to moderate the certitude of the desert religions by turning to the contemplative physics of yoga and the play of the Zen koan.

7   Meanwhile, in my own Catholic Church, there is the squalor of sexual scandal—men forcing themselves on boys. One hears conservative Catholics who speak of ridding the seminaries and the rectories of homosexuals. As one gay Catholic, a single man in this vast world, I tell you pedophilia is no more an expression of homosexuality than rape is an expression of heterosexuality. Pedophilia and rape are assertions of power. Polls indicate that a majority of American Catholics are more forgiving of the fallen priests than they are forgiving of the bishops and cardinals who have treated us like children, with their secret meetings and their clutch on power, apologizing but assuming no penance.

8   Polls indicate also that Catholics continue to go to church. We go to church because of the sacramental consolation our religion gives.

9   All of us now in our churches and synagogues and mosques, what knowledge unites us in this terrible season? Are we watching the male face of the desert religions merely reassert itself? Or are we watching the collapse of the tradition and the birth of—what?

10   I think of the women of America who have become priests and rabbis. I think of the women of Afghanistan who came to the school door the first morning after the Taliban had disappeared. I think of Mother Teresa whose name will be remembered long after we have forgotten the names of the cardinals in their silk robes. I think that we may be at the beginning of a feminine moment in the history of the desert religions, even while the tanks rumble and the priest is arrested and the girl, unblinking, straps explosives onto her body.

Organization and Ideas

1. Rodriguez divides desert religions into three groups and then traces the masculine and feminine impulses within them. How valid is his view of the masculine principle?
2. Paragraph 4 examines the feminine principle in the three religions. What other examples can you think of?
3. Reread the first and last paragraphs. In what ways do they frame the essay?

4. In paragraphs 8 and 9 Rodriguez speculates on why people still attend places of worship. What questions does he pose? What is his answer to those questions? How can you state it as a thesis?
5. The essay was aired in 2002, and many attitudes toward religion have changed since then. To what extent, if any, is it dated?

TECHNIQUE AND STYLE

1. In paragraph 4, Rodriguez defines what he means by the feminine impulse. How adequate is his definition?
2. The essay was written for television. What evidence can you find to show that Rodriguez shaped his prose to be heard instead of read?
3. Where in the essay does Rodriguez bring in his own experience? What does he achieve by doing so?
4. The details that Rodriguez uses, particularly those in paragraphs 1 and 9, are tied to the events of 2001 and 2002, times removed from that at which you are reading his essay. To what extent are those details still effective?
5. How would you describe the essay's overall tone: Pessimistic? Optimistic? Somewhere in between? What evidence supports your view?

SUGGESTIONS FOR WRITING

Journal

1. Think of your own religion or a religion you know well. Use your journal to write down examples of the masculine impulse.
2. Reread the essay, paying particular attention to Rodriguez's idea of the feminine impulse. To what extent does it apply to your religion or one that you know well?

Essay

1. Reread the essay, noting how Rodriguez defines the masculine and feminine impulses and the examples he uses to illustrate his definitions. Think about those impulses and consider how they operate in other areas or within other groups. If, for example, you were analyzing theme parks, you might think of all the kinds of rides, and then sort them into categories according to gender. Roller coasters would probably be masculine, ferris wheels feminine, and so on. Pick one of the suggestions below or one of your own and write an essay in which you analyze how masculine and feminine characteristics operate:
   musicians
   writers

comics
sports
food

2. The terms *masculine* and *feminine* are very broad, encompassing a wide variety of behavior. Arnold Schwarzenegger and Jay Leno would both be called masculine, though they are very different. Choose one of the terms and write an essay in which you analyze the variations within the general category. You may find the Web a good source for researching the names that occur to you. Just type the name into a search engine.

On Using
Process

7

Even the best of revolutions can go awry when we internalize the attitudes we are fighting. The class of 1992 is graduating into a violent backlash against the advances women have made over the last 20 years. This backlash ranges from a senator using "The Exorcist" against Anita Hill, to beer commercials with the "Swedish bikini team." Today I want to give you a backlash survival kit, a four-step manual to keep the dragons from taking up residence inside your own heads.

That is the opening paragraph of Naomi Wolf's address to the graduating class of women at Scripps College. She then relates an anecdote from the speech at her own commencement, one that made it a "Graduation from Hell," and presents her "backlash survival kit, a four-step manual." Wolf's "manual" takes the form of a **process analysis** whereby a subject—for Wolf, women's "survival"—is analyzed and then broken down into steps or stages.

We deal with this practical, how-to kind of process analysis every day in recipes, user's manuals, instruction booklets, and essays. Process analysis calls for:

- dividing the topic into the necessary steps
- describing each step in sufficient detail
- sequencing the steps so they are easy to follow
- anticipating trouble spots

Although process analysis is usually associated with specialized subjects—how to do *x*, how *y* works, or how *z* came about—it also finds its way into less formal prose. If you were to write about how you got interested in a hobby, you would be using process analysis, as you would if you were writing an explanatory research paper on the history of Coca-Cola. Process analysis can also be a means of discovery. If you were to analyze the process you go through to revise a draft, you might find out that you overemphasize a particular stage or leave out a step. Because process analysis is often equated with the simpler forms of how-to writing, it's easy to underrate it as a way of

178

thinking and expressing ideas. It can even be used to have fun with a subject, as several of the essays in this chapter show. Process analysis need not be dull.

How can you shape your subject for your reader? The concept of audience is crucial to process essays, for you must know just how familiar the reader is with the topic so you know what you need to explain and how to explain it. Familiar topics present you with a challenge; how can you interest your readers in a subject they already know about? The answer lies in what you have to say about that subject and how you say it. Naomi Wolf, for instance, begins by summarizing the "backlash" facing the graduating class, gives examples, and then explains her purpose: "I want to give you a backlash survival kit, a four-step manual to keep the dragons from taking up residence inside your own heads." From that point on, she has the attention of her listeners and readers—at least women.

Like Wolf, your purpose is apt to be informative and persuasive, but if you want your essay to be read by people who don't have to read it, then you need to make your approach to your subject interesting as well. Wolf's audience at the time she gave the talk was the graduating class of women, but the audience also included parents, relatives, and friends. For some of them, Wolf's advice might have come as a surprise.

Sometimes a writer explores a process to inform the reader and other times to persuade, but always the writer has an assertion in mind and is trying to affect the reader. If, for example, you enjoy scuba diving and you're trying to describe the physiological effects the body is subject to when diving, you might first describe the necessary equipment and then take the reader on a dive, emphasizing the different levels of atmospheric pressure—the instant and constant need to equalize the air pressure in your ears, the initial tightness of your mask as you sink to 10 feet, the gradual "shrinking" of your wet suit as the pressure increases with the depth of the dive. Then after a quick tour of the kinds of fish, sea creatures, and coral formations you see during the dive, you would return your reader to the surface, stopping at 15 feet to release the buildup of nitrogen in the blood. The whole process may strike your reader as not worth the risk, so you would want to make sure not only that your thesis counters that opinion, but also that you describe what you see so the attractions outweigh the hazards and momentary discomfort.

How can process organize your essay? The sequencing of steps—
chronology—is as crucial to process as it is to narration. In fact, it is
inflexible. A quick safety check of the necessary equipment has to come
before the dive. And then you must account for all the important steps. If
time is crucial, you have to account for it; although in a historical process
essay, time is apt to be compressed or deemphasized to underscore a
turning point. An essay on the civil rights movement, for instance, might
well begin with a brief account of the slave trade, even though the body
of the paper focuses on the 1950s and 1960s, culminating with the assas-
sination of Martin Luther King in 1968.

Undergirding the concept of sequence, of course, is the pattern of
cause and effect. Taking the previous example, you might want to explore
the effect of King's death on the civil rights movement. Wolf, in her last
paragraph, is careful to emphasize the positive effects of her plan. What's
most important to process analysis, however, is neither cause nor effect,
but the stages—the chronology of events. Without a set sequence or
chronology, neither cause nor effect would be clear.

To make the stages of the process clear, you will need to rely on logically placed transitions that lead the reader from one step to the next. Most
writers try to avoid depending only on obvious links, such as *first, next,
next,* and instead use chronology, shifts in tense, and other indicators to
spell out the sequence. The process itself may have markers that you can
use as transitions. An essay explaining a historical event, for instance, will
have specific dates or actions that you can use to indicate the next stage in
the sequence.

The body of a process essay almost organizes itself because it is made up
of the steps you have identified, and they must occur in a given sequence.
Introductions and conclusions are trickier, as is the thesis, for you must not
only set out a process but also make an assertion about it. Your thesis
should confront the reader with a point, implicit or explicit, about the
process involved, and in so doing, head off the lethal response, "So what?"

How can you apply what you've learned from earlier chapters?
In writing a process analysis, you will draw on the same skills you use for
description, narration, definition, and example papers, for without supporting details and examples, a process essay can be tedious indeed. An essay
on the civil rights movement would probably need to draw on statistics—
such as the percentage of the population held in slavery in 1860—as well as
examples of protests and boycotts in addition to quotations from those
involved, both for and against equal rights for African Americans. An essay
on scuba diving may need to define some terms and bring in examples

from mathematics and physiology, as well as from scientific articles on the relative health of coral reefs in the Caribbean.

As you read Naomi Wolf's piece, you'll not only find narratives, but also comparisons (of gender roles and earnings), examples (in the form of quotations and allusions), and cause-and-effect relationships. And, throughout you'll find details and descriptions. Wolf ends by predicting what may happen if you face "the worst" and choose to speak "your truth." You might try a look into the future to end one of your own essays.

Useful Terms

Chronology The time sequence involved in events; what occurred when.

Process analysis A type of analysis that examines a topic to discover the series of steps or acts that brought or will bring about a particular result. Whereas cause and effect analysis emphasizes *why*, process emphasizes *how*.

POINTERS FOR USING PROCESS

Exploring the Topic

1. **What kind of process are you presenting?** Is it a practical, "how-to" process? A historical one? A scientific one? Some mixture of types?
2. **What steps are involved?** Which are crucial? Can some be grouped together? Under what headings can they be grouped?
3. **What is the sequence of the steps?** Are you sure that each step logically follows the one before it?
4. **How familiar is your reader with your subject?** Within each step (or group of steps), what information does the reader need to know? What details can you use to make that information come alive? What examples? What connections can you make to what the reader already knows? Do you use any terms that need to be defined?

(Continued)

POINTERS FOR USING PROCESS *(Continued)*

5. Is setting or context important? If so, what details of the setting or context do you want to emphasize?

6. What is the point you want to make about the process? Is your point an assertion? Will it interest the reader?

Drafting the Paper

1. **Know your reader.** Using two columns, list what your reader may know about your topic in one and what your reader may not know in the other. If you are writing about a practical process, figure out what pitfalls your reader may be subject to. If you are writing about a historical or scientific process, make sure your diction suits your audience. Be on the lookout for events or actions that need further explanation to be understood by a general audience. If your reader is apt to have a bias against your topic, know what that bias is. If your topic is familiar, shape your first paragraph to enlist the reader's interest; if the topic is unfamiliar, use familiar images to explain it.

2. **Know your purpose.** If you are writing to inform, make sure you are presenting new information and that you are making an assertion about your topic. Don't dwell on information that the reader already knows if you can possibly avoid it. If you are writing to persuade, remember that you do not know whether your audience agrees with you. Use your persona to lend credibility to what you say, and use detail to arouse your reader's sympathies.

3. **Define your terms.** Think through the process you have chosen for your topic to make sure that your reader is familiar with all the terms associated with it. If any of those terms are technical or unusual ones, be sure you define them clearly.

4. **Present the steps in their correct sequence.** Make sure that you have accounted for all the important steps or stages in the process and that they are set out in order. If two or more steps occur at the same time, make sure you have made that clear. If time is crucial to your process, see that you have emphasized that point. If, on the other hand, the exact time at which an event occurred is less important than the event itself, make sure you have stressed the event and have subordinated the idea of time.

5. **Use details and examples.** Whether you are writing an informative or a persuasive essay, use details and examples that support your purpose. If you are explaining how to make your own ice cream, for example, draw on what the reader knows about various commercial brands and flavors to bolster the case for making your own. After all, your reader may not want to take the time and trouble to complete that process and may have to be enticed into trying it. Choose details and examples that combat your reader's negative associations.

6. **Double-check your transitions.** First mark your stages with obvious transitions or with numbers. After you have turned your notes into a working draft, review and revise the transitions you have used, checking to see that they exist, that they are clear, and that they are not overly repetitious or obvious. Make sure each important stage (or group of stages) is set off by a transition. See if you can indicate shifts by using verb tense or words and phrases that don't call attention to themselves as transitions.

7. **Make a point.** What you say about a subject is far more interesting than the subject itself, so even if you are writing a practical process essay, make sure you have a point. A paper on a topic such as "how to change a tire" becomes unbearable without a thesis. Given an assertion about changing a tire—"Changing my first flat was as horrible as I had expected it to be"—the paper at least has a chance.

Runner

Laura Carlson

Running has been a sport Laura Carlson has enjoyed for more than ten years, both on her own and for her school. As a junior at Valley City State University in Valley City, North Dakota, she wrote the essay that follows in a class taught by Noreen Braun, who reprinted the essay on a Web page devoted to what she titled "Some Fine Student Writing from Composition I, Fall Semester, 1997." Thinking about the essay and reading it over, Carlson comments: "I am really taken aback. I remember writing it and thinking that this is my favorite type of writing, descriptive, and that I could really do a good job on it—if I wanted to. It was really hard for me to sit down and write something with a due date. One thing I did was to basically forget that I had to do it for class, but that I had to write the essay for myself."

Stumped for a subject, Carlson thought about what she enjoyed and came up with the topic that is the title of the essay. She notes that the idea for the essay "came naturally to me. I actually went out that day to run." Thinking about that experience, she "tried to remember what it had been like; the feelings that I felt, the cold and the pictures in my mind, and I tried to incorporate them back into my writing. I think it really worked. I really just wrote about what I knew and how I really felt. Visualization was the key to my success with this essay." What worked for Laura may well work for you.

What to Look For   Not everyone knows what it feels like to run for a fairly long distance, and even those who do may not know what it's like to do that on a cold North Dakota morning. To make her experience come alive and to make it immediate, Carlson, therefore, chooses the present tense and descriptive details. The result is an essay that explains the process she goes through when she runs and makes the reader feel what Carlson feels.

1   When I wake up this morning, I can feel the chill of the air in my joints. I am almost reluctant to give up the warmth of my bed, but I know I need to. Slowly, I step out of my bed and quickly

throw on a sweatshirt and pants. Leaving my room, still tired, but slowly awakening, I yawn.

2   I stretch my tired limbs, first my arms, then my legs. Noticing a tightness in my right hip, I take a little extra time to stretch it. I am still moving slowly as if in a drugged stupor. Maybe I should just go back to bed. Before I change my mind, I hurry outside into the brisk early morning air. I take three or four breaths to acclimate myself to the cold, cold air. I can see my breath on the air in little white puffs. I want to reach out as if I could float away with the rising mist. It is still dark outside. The sun hasn't quite poked his head out to greet the day. The blue black sky is waiting to engulf me as his arms extend as far as I can see.

3   Running on an October morning is so exhilarating! I think it is only about 20 degrees this morning. I am so cold!

4   My steps are slow to start. I feel my legs tighten and restrain me, not wanting to exert the effort to propel me forward, yet I know that it is mind over matter and I am going to win this battle! I tell myself that I need to get ready for the big meet that is coming up at the end of the month. My adrenaline is pumping and my mind is whirling at a mile a minute taking in the frosty scenery that is surrounding me. The trees are covered in a fine layer of crystals forming together to make a wintry scene unlike any other I have seen yet this season. My breathing is accelerating and my pulse is beating in my ears. The biting cold is gnawing at my skin. I refuse to give into the cold of the air and the gripping of my lungs.

5   As I slowly retreat into a solid pace, my body is more aware of my feet steadily pounding on the pavement and of the crunching of the leaves and twigs as they collapse under the weight of my body. The burning in my lungs is lessening as my pace is increasing. The steady flow of traffic helps keep my mind from wandering and keeps me focused. I only have a couple of miles to go. My nose is running just as fast as my feet. I feel the slight burning as if the air were actually freezing the breath entering and exiting my nostrils.

6   I can tell by the landmarks of the city that I am closing in on my destination: home. I pass the fenced-in yard with the barking dog who chooses to torment me each time I pass. I keep running, my pace not faltering. As I come within three blocks of my house, I pick up my pace as if in a race. I am feeling winded as my stride lengthens and my breathing becomes much more shallow. I am almost home. The scenery is changing as the sun has finally approached

the horizon. The hues of the sky are changing rapidly with the approaching daylight.

7   My house is in sight. I slow my pace to a fast walk and slowly make my way to my driveway. I take deep breaths to get used to the different pace. I am done for another day. I feel refreshed and awakened. I am now ready to continue with another day.

ORGANIZATION AND IDEAS

1. Which paragraph or paragraphs make up the essay's introduction? What does it tell you?

2. Trace the process of the run itself. What paragraphs describe it?

3. One technique Carlson uses to avoid the stilted *first-next-then* marking of the essay's chronology is to use the progress of the sunlight. Where in the essay does she note that progress?

4. Is Carlson's thesis stated or implied? What evidence can you find to support your idea?

5. If you're a runner, how well does Carlson describe the experience? If you're not, to what extent does she convince you that running is a pleasure?

TECHNIQUE AND STYLE

1. Carlson gives the essay unity by frequently referring to the weather. What descriptive details does she use?

2. Throughout the essay, Carlson uses the first person *I*. Does she avoid overusing it or not? How can you back up your opinion?

3. In paragraph 2, Carlson personifies the sun and the sky by referring to them with the adjective *his*. What would be lost without that personification? What is gained?

4. The first sentence of paragraph 6 uses a colon. What other punctuation could be used? Which is the most effective and why?

5. Reread the last paragraph. How else might the essay have ended that would fit in with what has come before? Which is the more effective ending and why?

SUGGESTIONS FOR WRITING

Journal

1. Write your own last paragraph for the essay and then, briefly, explain why you think it is better or not as good as Carlson's.

2. Briefly describe the feelings you have when you are involved in a sport, either as a spectator or a participant.

Essay

1. Like Carlson, you might start by thinking about what you enjoy. Perhaps it's a sport or a hobby, but no matter what the subject, you can use Carlson's essay as a model to write your own description of the process involved. You may find it easiest to start with the process, jotting down the steps or stages. Then once you have a rough draft, you can decide on the kind of introduction and conclusion that would be most effective for the essay, and, of course, where best to put the thesis, if you want to state rather than imply it. Suggestions for a topic:

   playing a sport
   being involved with your hobby
   playing a card game
   cooking a favorite dish
   enjoying a "do nothing" day

2. Even though many people participate in sports, even more watch games on television. During play-offs and championships, watching television has almost turned into a ritual. Choose a sport you like or a television show you are addicted to and describe the process you go through to watch it.

Independence Day

Dave Barry

It's a rare columnist who can claim both a Pulitzer Prize and a television sitcom, but few things aren't unusual about Dave Barry. Barry was the focus of the show Dave's World, *which ran from 1993 to 1997 and was based on two of his many books, and in 1988, he won a Pulitzer for Commentary "for his consistently effective use of humor as a device for presenting fresh insights into serious concerns." A humor writer for* The Miami Herald, *his columns were carried by over 500 newspapers; now that his column has been retired, he continues to write humorous "Year in Review" surveys. A number of those surveys have been collected in his most recent book* Dave Barry's History of the Millennium (So Far) *(2007), but Barry has also written two novels:* Big Trouble *(1999) and* Tricky Business *(2002). His Web site (davebarry.com) notes that he "lives in Miami, Florida, with his wife, Michelle, a sportswriter. He has a son, Rob, and a daughter, Sophie, neither of whom thinks he's funny.*" "*Independence Day" first appeared in* Tropic *magazine and was reprinted in* Mirth of a Nation, *Michael J. Rosen, editor.*

What to Look For   As you read Barry's essay, look for the ways he avoids using obvious markers as he takes his readers through a typical Fourth of July celebration.

1   This year, why not hold an old-fashioned Fourth of July picnic?

2   Food poisoning is one good reason. After a few hours in the sun, ordinary potato salad can develop bacteria the size of raccoons. But don't let the threat of agonizingly painful death prevent you from celebrating the birth of our nation, just as Americans have been doing ever since that historic first July Fourth when our Founding Fathers— George Washington, Benjamin Franklin, Thomas Jefferson, Bob Dole and Tony Bennett—landed on Plymouth Rock.

3   Step one in planning your picnic is to decide on a menu. Martha Stewart has loads of innovative suggestions for unique, imaginative and tasty summer meals. So you can forget about her. "If Martha Stewart comes anywhere near my picnic, she's risking a barbecue fork to the eyeball" should be your patriotic motto. Because you're having a *traditional* Fourth of July picnic, and that means a menu of hot dogs charred into cylinders of industrial-grade carbon, and hamburgers so undercooked that when people try to eat them, they leap off the plate and frolic on the lawn like otters.

4   Dad should be in charge of the cooking, because only Dad, being a male of the masculine gender, has the mechanical "know-how" to operate a piece of technology as complex as a barbecue grill. To be truly traditional, the grill should be constructed of the following materials:

- 4 percent "rust-resistant" steel;
- 58 percent rust;
- 23 percent hardened black grill scunge from food cooked as far back as 1987 (the scunge should never be scraped off, because it is what is actually holding the grill together);
- 15 percent spiders.

5   If the grill uses charcoal as a fuel, Dad should remember to start lighting the fire early (no later than April 10) because charcoal, in

accordance with federal safety regulations, is a mineral that does not burn. The spiders get a huge kick out of watching Dad attempt to ignite it; they emit hearty spider chuckles and slap themselves on all eight knees. This is why many dads prefer the modern gas grill, which ignites at the press of a button and burns with a steady, even flame until you put food on it, at which time it runs out of gas.

6   While Dad is saying traditional bad words to the barbecue grill, Mom can organize the kids for a fun activity: making old-fashioned ice cream by hand, the way our grandparents' generation did. You'll need a hand-cranked ice-cream maker, which you can pick up at any antique store for $1,875. All you do is put in the ingredients, and start cranking! It makes no difference what specific ingredients you put in, because—I speak from bitter experience here—no matter how long you crank them, they will never, ever turn into ice cream. Scientists laugh at the very concept. "Ice cream is not formed by cranking," they point out. "Ice cream is formed by freezers." Our grandparents' generation wasted millions of man-hours trying to produce ice cream by hand; this is what caused the Great Depression.

7   When the kids get tired of trying to make ice cream (allow about twenty-five seconds for this) it's time to play some traditional July Fourth games. One of the most popular is the "sack race." All you need is a bunch of old-fashioned burlap sacks, which you can obtain from the J. Peterman catalog for $227.50 apiece. Call the kids outside, have them line up on the lawn and give each one a sack to climb into; then shout "GO!" and watch the hilarious antics begin as, one by one, the kids sneak back indoors and resume trying to locate pornography on the Internet.

8   Come nightfall, though, everybody will be drawn back outside by the sound of loud, traditional Fourth of July explosions coming from all around the neighborhood. These are caused by the fact that various dads, after consuming a number of traditionally fermented beverages, have given up on conventional charcoal-lighting products and escalated to gasoline. As the spectacular pyrotechnic show lights up the night sky, you begin to truly appreciate the patriotic meaning of the words to *The Star-Spangled Banner,* written by Francis Scott Key to commemorate the fledgling nation's first barbecue:

> And the grill parts' red glare;
> Flaming spiders in air;
> Someone call 911;
> There's burning scunge in Dad's hair.

9   After the traditional visit to the hospital emergency room, it's time to gather 'round and watch Uncle Bill set off the fireworks that he purchased from a roadside stand operated by people who spend way more on tattoos than dental hygiene. As Uncle Bill lights the firework fuse and scurries away, everybody is on pins and needles until, suddenly and dramatically, the fuse goes out. So Uncle Bill relights the fuse and scurries away again, and the fuse goes out again, and so on, with Uncle Bill scurrying back and forth with his Bic lighter like a deranged Olympic torchbearer until, finally, the fuse burns all the way down, and the firework, emitting a smoke puff the size of a grapefruit, makes a noise—"phut"—like a squirrel passing gas. Wow! What a fitting climax for your traditional old-fashioned July Fourth picnic!

10   Next year you'll go out for Chinese food.

ORGANIZATION AND IDEAS

1. You could describe Barry's essay as a "how-to" guide for a traditional celebration on the Fourth of July, but his breaking down the event into steps is subtle. How does he do it?
2. It's possible to argue that the essay is organized by process (steps), chronology (time), drama (least to most effective), or some combination. Make a case for the way you read the organization.
3. How effective is Barry's last paragraph?
4. Barry's essay is obviously a satire, but of what: the Fourth of July, family gatherings, American values, the consumer culture, American sense of history, tradition, or some combination? What in the essay supports your view?
5. Take a look at the biographical information and note the reason Barry was awarded a Pulitzer Prize. In what ways does that statement apply to this essay?

TECHNIQUE AND STYLE

1. Look up *hyperbole* (pp. 155, 157). To what extent does Barry use the device? How effective is it?
2. Barry includes contemporary figures (paragraphs 2 and 3). Why might he have done that and what effect does he achieve?
3. What is the point of the fractured "facts" in paragraph 2?
4. Granted that the essay is humorous, but what kind of humor? How would you describe Barry's tone?
5. Reread the essay marking every use of *traditional.* To what extent is the repetition effective? What is Barry's point in using it?

SUGGESTIONS FOR WRITING

Journal

1. In what ways is the title a pun?
2. What description do you find the most amusing and why? Quote from the essay to back up your view.

Essay

1. Write your own "how-to" essay on the preparations for a typical, traditional, or important time. Like Barry, you may want to remove yourself from the scene and generalize, or you may want to be part of it. Suggestions:
   Thanksgiving
   first date
   first day of classes
   looking cool
   dealing with a computer problem
2. Barry does an amusing job depicting the "typical" American family at play on a celebratory occasion. Think about the family gatherings you have attended, those of either your own family or someone else's, and write your own survivor's guide.

How to Write a Letter

Garrison Keillor

Even if you've never lived in or even been to the Midwest, you probably know the area through Garrison Keillor's Prairie Home Companion. *Storyteller, comedian, musician, and creator of Lake Woebegon and all its inhabitants, Keillor has become a radio institution and now reaches over three million listeners with his weekly show that airs on public radio stations across the country. Keillor got his start in radio when he was an English major at the University of Minnesota and with only a few interruptions has been on the air waves ever since. He has been awarded numerous prizes given by the media, including the coveted Peabody Award, and as a writer he has published over 19 books, his latest being* Liberty: A Lake Wobegon Novel *(2008). You may have seen the film* A Prairie Home Companion *(2006) that was based on his radio show, a film in which he played himself. The essay that follows is from his collection* We Are Still Married *(1989).*

What to Look For   When writers use imperatives—such as "Do this" or "Stop that"—they usually imply a harsh and unpleasant tone, so much so that these phrases almost demand exclamation points. But in Keillor's essay you'll find that he moderates his imperatives so that his tone is downright friendly. As you read the essay, be aware of how he does it, for it's a technique you may want to use in your own process essay.

1   We shy persons need to write a letter now and then, or else we'll dry up and blow away. It's true. And I speak as one who loves to reach for the phone, dial the number, and talk. I say, "Big Bopper here—what's shakin', babes?" The telephone is to shyness what Hawaii is to February, it's a way out of the woods, *and yet:* a letter is better.

2   Such a sweet gift—a piece of handmade writing, in an envelope that is not a bill, sitting in our friend's path when she trudges home from a long day spent among wahoos and savages, a day our words will help repair. They don't need to be immortal, just sincere. She can read them twice and again tomorrow: *You're someone I care about, Corinne, and think of often and every time I do you make me smile.*

3   We need to write, otherwise nobody will know who we are. They will have only a vague impression of us as A Nice Person, because, frankly, we don't shine at conversation, we lack the confidence to thrust our faces forward and say, "Hi, I'm Heather Hooten; let me tell you about my week." Mostly we say "Uh-huh" and "Oh, really." People smile and look over our shoulder, looking for someone else to meet.

4   So a shy person sits down and writes a letter. To be known by another person—to meet and talk freely on the page—to be close despite distance. To escape from anonymity and be our own sweet selves and express the music of our souls.

5   Same thing that moves a giant rock star to sing his heart out in front of 123,000 people moves us to take ballpoint in hand and write a few lines to our dear Aunt Eleanor. *We want to be known.* We want her to know that we have fallen in love, that we quit our

job, that we're moving to New York, and we want to say a few things that might not get said in casual conversation: *Thank you for what you've meant to me, I am very happy right now.*

6 The first step in writing letters is to get over the guilt of *not* writing. You don't "owe" anybody a letter. Letters are a gift. The burning shame you feel when you see unanswered mail makes it harder to pick up a pen and makes for a cheerless letter when you finally do. *I feel bad about not writing, but I've been so busy,* etc. Skip this. Few letters are obligatory, and they are *Thanks for the wonderful gift* and *I am terribly sorry to hear about George's death* and *Yes, you're welcome to stay with us next month,* and not many more than that. Write those promptly if you want to keep your friends. Don't worry about the others, except love letters, of course. When your true love writes, *Dear Light of My Life, Joy of My Heart, O Lovely Pulsating Core of My Sensate Life,* some response is called for.

7 Some of the best letters are tossed off in a burst of inspiration, so keep your writing stuff in one place where you can sit down for a few minutes and (*Dear Roy, I am in the middle of a book entitled* We Are Still Married *but thought I'd drop you a line. Hi to your sweetie, too.*) dash off a note to a pal. Envelopes, stamps, address book, everything in a drawer so you can write fast when the pen is hot.

8 A blank white eight-by-eleven sheet can look as big as Montana if the pen's not so hot—try a smaller page and write boldly. Or use a note card with a piece of fine art on the front; if your letter ain't good, at least they get the Matisse. Get a pen that makes a sensuous line, get a comfortable typewriter, a friendly word processor— whichever feels easy to the hand.

9 Sit for a few minutes with the blank sheet in front of you, and meditate on the person you will write to, let your friend come to mind until you can almost see her or him in the room with you. Remember the last time you saw each other and how your friend looked and what you said and what perhaps was unsaid between you, and when your friend becomes real to you, start to write.

10 Write the salutation—*Dear* You—and take a deep breath and plunge in. A simple declarative sentence will do, followed by another and another and another. Tell us what you're doing and tell it like you were talking to us. Don't think about grammar, don't think about lit'ry style, don't try to write dramatically, just give us your news. Where did you go, who did you see, what did they say, what do you think?

11 If you don't know where to begin, start with the present moment: *I'm sitting at the kitchen table on a rainy Saturday morning. Everyone*

is gone and the house is quiet. Let your simple description of the present moment lead to something else, let the letter drift gently along.

12   The toughest letter to crank out is one that is meant to impress, as we all know from writing job applications; if it's hard work to slip off a letter to a friend, maybe you're trying too hard to be terrific. A letter is only a report to someone who already likes you for reasons other than your brilliance. Take it easy.

13   Don't worry about form. It's not a term paper. When you come to the end of one episode, just start a new paragraph. You can go from a few lines about the sad state of pro football to the fight with your mother to your fond memories of Mexico to your cat's urinary-tract infection to a few thoughts on personal indebtedness and on to the kitchen sink and what's in it. The more you write, the easier it gets, and when you have a True True Friend to write to, a *compadre,* a soul sibling, then it's like driving a car down a country road, you just get behind the keyboard and press on the gas.

14   Don't tear up the page and start over when you write a bad line—try to write your way out of it. Make mistakes and plunge on. Let the letter cook along and let yourself be bold. Outrage, confusion, love—whatever is in your mind, let it find a way to the page. Writing is a means of discovery, always, and when you come to the end and write *Yours ever* or *Hugs and kisses,* you'll know something you didn't when you wrote *Dear Pal.*

15   Probably your friend will put your letter away, and it'll be read again a few years from now—and it will improve with age. And forty years from now, your friend's grandkids will dig it out of the attic and read it, a sweet and precious relic of the ancient eighties that gives them a sudden clear glimpse of you and her and the world we old-timers knew. You will then have created an object of art. Your simple lines about where you went, who you saw, what they said, will speak to those children and they will feel in their hearts the humanity of our times.

16   You can't pick up a phone and call the future and tell them about our times. You have to pick up a piece of paper.

ORGANIZATION AND IDEAS

1. What paragraph or paragraphs provide the essay's introduction? What evidence can you find to support your opinion?

2. Where in the essay does Keillor start describing the process of writing a letter? What are the steps he outlines?

3. One way to avoid writing a dull process essay is to cover not just what to do but also what not to do. What does Keillor include that fits that category? How necessary is it?

4. To what extent does Keillor use the pattern of division and classification? What does it add to the essay? Detract from its primary pattern?

5. Keillor's essay covers a number of topics—how to write a letter, kinds of letters, friends, writing in general, why people write, the joy of getting a letter, and several other subjects. Think about all the topics he hits and in your own words state his thesis.

TECHNIQUE AND STYLE

1. Keillor writes the essay from the position of a "shy person." How effectively does he create that persona? To what extent do you believe it?

2. What role does humor play in the essay? What examples can you find? Describe the kind of humor Keillor displays.

3. At various times, Keillor uses a metaphor, simile, or simple comparison. What examples can you find? What do his choices add to the essay's tone? To its expository purpose?

4. The advice is directed to "you," the reader. To what extent is the "you" meant to be a "shy person"? How well does Keillor's advice apply to the general reader?

5. To what extent does Keillor argue for the power of the written word? Where in the essay do you find support for that idea? How valid is his argument?

SUGGESTIONS FOR WRITING

Journal

1. Reread the essay so that you can evaluate the degree to which Keillor's advice about writing a letter applies to writing in general. What do you find?

2. What sorts of letters do you write? How does writing them make you feel—similar to the way Keillor feels or what?

Essay

1. Keillor deals with the kinds of letters we might write to a friend, relative, or lover, someone to whom "we want to be known." But there are other kinds of letters that take up our time. Imagine a context for one of those kinds and write an essay describing how to write the appropriate letter. Start with a description of the context and then follow with your advice. Suggestions:

      faulty product—complaint letter
      newspaper editorial—letter to the editor

job opening—cover letter for resumé
jury duty—inability to serve
present from relative—thank you note

2. New forms of communication—such as email, texting, and chat rooms—have made the kind of letter writing Keillor describes almost obsolete. Some declare that these new forms have eroded our use of language, made it sloppy, ambiguous; others maintain the effect has been positive, bringing immediacy and life to writing. Use the Web to research the debate and write an essay in which you take a stand on it, citing sources to back up your point.

A Woman's Place

Naomi Wolf

A graduate of Yale university and a Rhodes Scholar at Oxford University, Naomi Wolf was working on her PhD at Princeton University when she adapted her dissertation into The Beauty Myth: How Images of Beauty Are Used Against Women, *a best seller published in 1991. As the title implies, Wolf is concerned with issues that affect women, an interest that runs through all of her work as she tries to redefine feminism. She has explored the relationship between women and politics in* Fire with Fire: The New Female Power *(1993); girls, women, and sexuality in* Promiscuities: The Secret Struggle for Womanhood *(1997); women, childbirth, and the medical industry in* Misconceptions: Truth, Lies and the Unexpected on the Journey to Motherhood *(2001); and father/daughter relationships in* The Treehouse: Eccentric Wisdom from My Father on How to Live, Love, and See *(2005). Her essays have been published in print media as diverse as* Ms., Glamour, The Wall Street Journal, *and* The New Republic. The End of America: Letter of Warning to a Young Patriot *(2007), her latest book, reflects her concerns with progressive causes. The following essay was published in* The New York Times *on May 31, 1992, and is adapted from a commencement address she gave at Scripps College, a women's college in California.*

What to Look For   Many writers steer away from beginning a sentence with the word *and* because they are afraid of creating a sentence fragment. But as long as the sentence has a subject and main verb, it can begin with *and* (or, like this one, *but* or any other conjunction) and still be an independent clause, a complete sentence, with the conjunction serving as an informal transition. To see how effective that kind of sentence can be, notice Wolf's last paragraph.

1   Even the best of revolutions can go awry when we internalize the attitudes we are fighting. The class of 1992 is graduating into a violent backlash against the advances women have made over the last 20 years. This backlash ranges from a senator using "The Exorcist" against Anita Hill, to beer commercials with the "Swedish bikini team." Today I want to give you a backlash survival kit, a four-step manual to keep the dragons from taking up residence inside your own heads.

2   My own commencement, at Yale eight years ago, was the Graduation from Hell. The speaker was Dick Cavett, rumored to have been our president's "brother" in an all-male secret society.

3   Mr. Cavett took the microphone and paled at the sight of hundreds of female about-to-be Yale graduates. "When I was an undergraduate," I recall he said, "there were no women. The women went to Vassar. At Vassar, they had nude photographs taken of the women in gym class to check their posture. One year the photos were stolen, and turned up for sale in New Haven's redlight district." His punchline? "The photos found no buyers."

4   I'll never forget that moment. There we were, silent in our black gowns, our tassels, our brand new shoes. We dared not break the silence with hisses or boos, out of respect for our families, who'd come so far; and they kept still out of concern for us. Consciously or not, Mr. Cavett was using the beauty myth aspect of the backlash: when women come too close to masculine power, someone will draw critical attention to their bodies. We might be Elis, but we still wouldn't make pornography worth buying.

5   That afternoon, several hundred men were confirmed in the power of a powerful institution. But many of the women felt the shame of the powerless: the choking on silence, the complicity, the helplessness. We were orphaned from our institution.

6   I want to give you the commencement talk that was denied to me.

7   Message No. 1 in your survival kit: redefine "becoming a woman." Today you have "become women." But that sounds odd in ordinary

usage. What is usually meant by "You're a real woman now"? You "become a woman" when you menstruate for the first time, or when you lose your virginity, or when you have a child.

8   These biological definitions are very different from how we say boys become men. One "becomes a man" when he undertakes responsibility, or completes a quest. But you, too, in some ways more than your male friends graduating today, have moved into maturity through a solitary quest for the adult self.

9   We lack archetypes for the questing young woman, her trials by fire; for how one "becomes a woman" through the chrysalis of education, the difficult passage from one book, one idea to the next. Let's refuse to have our scholarship and our gender pitted against each other. In our definition, the scholar learns womanhood and the woman learns scholarship; Plato and Djuna Barnes, mediated to their own enrichment through the eyes of the female body with its wisdoms and its gifts.

10   I say that you have already shown courage: Many of you graduate today in spite of the post-traumatic stress syndrome of acquaintance rape, which one-fourth of female students undergo. Many of you were so weakened by anorexia and bulimia that it took every ounce of your will to get your work in. You negotiated private lives through a mine field of new strains of VD and the ascending shadow of AIDS. Triumphant survivors, you have already "become women."

11   Message No. 2 breaks the ultimate taboo for women: *Ask for money in your lives.* Expect it. Own it. Learn to use it. Little girls learn a debilitating fear of money—that it's not feminine to insure we are fairly paid for honest work. Meanwhile, women make 68 cents for every male dollar and half of marriages end in divorce, after which women's income drops precipitously.

12   Never choose a profession for material reasons. But whatever field your heart decides on, for god's sake get the most specialized training in it you can and hold out hard for just compensation, parental leave and child care. Resist your assignment to the class of highly competent, grossly underpaid women who run the show while others get the cash—and the credit.

13   Claim money not out of greed, but so you can tithe to women's political organizations, shelters and educational institutions. Sexist institutions won't yield power if we are just patient long enough. The only language the status quo understands is money, votes and public embarrassment.

14   When you have equity, you have influence—as sponsors, share-holders and alumnae. Use it to open opportunities to women who deserve the chances you've had. Your B.A. does not belong to you alone, just as the earth does not belong to its present tenants alone. Your education was lent to you by women of the past, and you will give some back to living women, and to your daughters seven generations from now.

15   Message No. 3: Never cook for or sleep with anyone who routinely puts you down.

16   Message No. 4: Become goddesses of disobedience. Virginia Woolf wrote that we must slay the Angel in the House, the censor within. Young women tell me of injustices, from campus rape coverups to classroom sexism. But at the thought of confrontation, they freeze into niceness. We are told that the worst thing we can do is cause conflict, even in the service of doing right. Antigone is imprisoned. Joan of Arc burns at the stake. And someone might call us unfeminine!

17   When I wrote a book that caused controversy, I saw how big a dragon was this paralysis by niceness. *The Beauty Myth* argues that newly rigid ideals of beauty are instruments of a backlash against feminism, designed to lower women's self-esteem for a political purpose. Many positive changes followed the debate. But all that would dwindle away when someone yelled at me—as, for instance, cosmetic surgeons did on TV, when I raised questions about silicone implants. Oh, no, I'd quail, people are mad at me!

18   Then I read something by the poet Audre Lorde. She'd been diagnosed with breast cancer. "I was going to die," she wrote, "sooner or later, whether or not I had ever spoken myself. My silences had not protected me. Your silences will not protect you.... What are the words you do not yet have? What are the tyrannies you swallow day by day and attempt to make your own, until you will sicken and die of them, still in silence? We have been socialized to respect fear more than our own need for language."

19   I began to ask each time: "What's the worst that could happen to me if I tell this truth?" Unlike women in other countries, our breaking silence is unlikely to have us jailed, "disappeared" or run off the road at night. Our speaking out will irritate some people, get us called bitchy or hypersensitive and disrupt some dinner parties. And then our speaking out will permit other women to speak, until laws are changed and lives are saved and the world is altered forever.

20   Next time, ask: What's the worst that will happen? Then push your-self a little further than you dare. Once you start to speak, people *will* yell at you. They *will* interrupt, put you down and suggest it's personal. And the world won't end.

21   And the speaking will get easier and easier. And you will find you have fallen in love with your own vision, which you may never have realized you had. And you will lose some friends and lovers, and real-ize you don't miss them. And new ones will find you and cherish you. And you will still flirt and paint your nails, dress up and party, be-cause as I think Emma Goldman said, "If I can't dance, I don't want to be part of your revolution." And at last you'll know with surpassing certainty that only one thing is more frightening than speaking your truth. And that is not speaking.

ORGANIZATION AND IDEAS

1. Wolf's essay could easily be retitled "How to Survive the Backlash." What is the backlash?
2. Why does Wolf include the anecdote about Dick Cavett? How is it related to the backlash?
3. What are the four steps for survival?
4. Wolf's essay gives advice and explains how to survive, but it also comments on women's place in society today. Combine those comments with her advice and the result will be the thesis.
5. The original audience for the essay was women, but it was republished for an audience that also includes men. Explain whether men would find the essay offensive. To what extent is it antimale? Dated?

TECHNIQUE AND STYLE

1. What saying does Wolf's title refer to? How does her title set up her essay?
2. Throughout the essay, Wolf uses allusion—Anita Hill (paragraph 1), Plato and Djuna Barnes (paragraph 9), Virginia Woolf (paragraph 16), Audre Lorde (paragraph 18), and Emma Goldman (paragraph 21). Use an ency-clopedia to look up one of these allusions so that you can explain to the class how it is (or is not) appropriate.
3. To explore the effect of Wolf's repeated use of *and* in her last para-graph, try rewriting it. What is gained? Lost?
4. What can you find in the prose that suggests that "A Woman's Place" was written to be heard, not read?
5. Wolf is obviously a feminist, but think of feminism as a continuum ranging from conservative to radical. Based on this essay, what kind of feminist is Wolf? What evidence can you find for your opinion?

SUGGESTIONS FOR WRITING

Journal

1. Choose one of Wolf's "messages" and test it out against your own experience. Do you find the advice helpful? Necessary?
2. Relate an experience in which you ran into sexism, either antimale or antifemale. You could use this entry later as the basis for an essay in which you explain how to cope with sexism.

Essay

1. All of us at one time or another have played a role we didn't believe in or didn't like. Those roles vary greatly. Think about the roles you have had to play and how you broke out of them. Choose one and draft a paper explaining "How to Survive" or "How to Break Out." Some roles to think about:

   dutiful daughter
   responsible sibling
   perfect husband (or wife)
   brave man
   happy homemaker

2. Write your own version of the essay but title it "A Student's Place" and create the advice and explanation to fit the title.

On Using Cause and Effect

8

1   My first victim was a woman—white, well-dressed, probably in her early twenties. I came upon her late one evening on a deserted street in Hyde Park, a relatively affluent neighborhood in an otherwise mean, impoverished section of Chicago. As I swung onto the avenue behind her, there seemed to be a discreet, uninflammatory distance between us. Not so. She cast back a worried glance. To her, the youngish black man—a broad 6 feet 2 inches with a beard and billowing hair, both hands shoved into the pockets of a bulky military jacket—seemed menacingly close. After a few more quick glimpses, she picked up her pace and was soon running in earnest. Within seconds she disappeared into a cross street.

2   That was more than a decade ago. I was 22 years old, a graduate student newly arrived at the University of Chicago. It was in the echo of that terrified woman's footfalls that I first began to know the unwieldy inheritance I'd come into—the ability to alter public space in ugly ways. It was clear that she thought herself the quarry of a mugger, a rapist, or worse. Suffering a bout of insomnia, however, I was stalking sleep, not defenseless wayfarers. As a softy who is scarcely able to take a knife to a raw chicken—let alone hold one to a person's throat—I was surprised, embarrassed, and dismayed all at once. Her flight made me feel like an accomplice in tyranny. It also made it clear that I was indistinguishable from the muggers who occasionally seeped into the area from the surrounding ghetto. That first encounter, and those that followed, signified that a vast, unnerving gulf lay between nighttime pedestrians—particularly women—and me. And I soon gathered that being perceived as dangerous is a hazard in itself. I only needed to turn a corner into a dicey situation, or crowd some frightened, armed person in a foyer somewhere, or make an errant move after being pulled over by a policeman. Where fear and weapons meet—and they often do in urban America—there is always the possibility of death.

These two paragraphs open Brent Staples' essay "Black Men and Public Space" and show how complex **cause-and-effect** relationships can be. Reduced to bare bones, here's how Staples' mingling of the two can be mapped out:

Paragraph	Cause	Effect
1	Staples' nighttime walk	Woman's fear
2	Staples' insomnia	Staples' nighttime walk
	Woman's fear	Staples' surprise and dismay
	Woman's flight	Staples' "an accomplice in tyranny"
	Staples "perceived as dangerous"	Perception a "hazard in itself"
	Fear and weapons	"Possibility of death"

You can see how causal analysis can be confusing in that a cause leads to an effect, which can then become another cause. Staples' sleeplessness causes his walk that then becomes the cause of the woman's fear.

Chapter 7 explains how process analysis focuses on *how*; causal analysis emphasizes *why*. Though some writers examine both cause and effect, most will stress one or the other. Causal analysis looks below the surface of the steps in a process and examines why they occur: why *x* happens and what results from *x*. As a way of thinking, causal analysis is a natural one. In this chapter, you'll see how it works with various topics—a fourth-grade encounter, music, technology, and iPods.

How can you explore a subject? You can avoid a confused causal analysis if you apply some of the skills you use in division and classification and in process analysis:

1. Divide your subject into two categories—causes and effects.
2. Think about the steps or stages that are involved and identify them as possible causes or effects.
3. List an example or two for each possible cause or effect.
4. Sort out each list by dividing the items into primary or secondary causes and effects—that is, those that are relatively important and those that are relatively unimportant.

When you reach this final point, you may discover that an item you have listed is only related to your subject by time, in which case you should cross it out.

If you were writing a paper on cheating in college, for instance, your notes might resemble these:

	Possibilities	**Examples**	**Importance**
Causes	Academic pressure	Student who needs an A	Primary
	Peer pressure	Everybody does it	Primary
	System	Teachers tolerate it No real penalty	Secondary
	Moral climate	Cheating on income taxes False insurance claims Infidelity Breakup of family unit	Secondary
Effects	Academic	Grades meaningless	Primary
	Peers	Degree meaningless	Primary
	System	Erodes system	Secondary
	Moral climate	Weakens moral climate	Secondary

The train of thought behind these notes chugs along nicely. Looking at them, you can see how thinking about the moral climate might lead to speculation about the cheating that goes undetected on tax and insurance forms, and for that matter, the cheating that occurs in a different context—that of marriage. The idea of infidelity then sets off a causal chain: Infidelity causes divorce, which causes the breakup of families. Pause there. If recent statistics show that a majority of students have cheated, and if recent statistics also reveal a large number of single-parent households, is it safe to conclude that one caused the other? No. The relationship is one of time, not cause. Mistaking a **temporal relationship** for a causal one is a **logical fallacy,** technically called **post hoc reasoning.**

It is also easy to mistake a **primary cause** or effect for a **secondary** one. If the notes above are for an essay that uses a narrative framework, and if the essay begins by relating an example of a student who was worried about having high enough grades to get into law school, the principle behind how the items are listed according to importance makes sense. To bring up his average, the student cheats on a math exam, justifying the action by thinking, "Everybody does it." The essay might then go on to speculate about the less apparent reasons behind the action—the system and the moral climate. For the student who cheated, the grade and peer pressure are the more immediate or primary causes; the system and climate are the more remote or secondary causes.

How can you shape cause and effect for your readers? Staples, for instance, may have made several assumptions about his readers: that most are white and might react the same way as the woman; that crime is an urban problem and creates fear. His first paragraph is a narrative that sets a scene those readers can identify with. His second paragraph, however, explores the event from the perspective of a black man, a perspective these readers have never experienced. To make them understand it, Staples uses precise diction: The only thing he was "stalking" was sleep; he's a "softy"; he was "surprised, embarrassed, and dismayed...an accomplice in tyranny," branded as "mugger." He then generalizes about his experience, concluding that "being perceived as dangerous is a hazard in itself."

An awareness of your readers and their possible preconceptions can also guide your approach to a topic. If, for example, your focus is the single-parent family, and you want to dispel some ideas about it that you think are misconceptions, you might assume that your audience regards single-parent families as at best incomplete and at worst irresponsible. It's obvious that you won't win your argument by suggesting that anyone with such ideas is a fool and possibly a bigot as well; it's also obvious that making your point while not offending some readers requires a subtle approach. One way to avoid offense is to put yourself in the shoes of the reader who has the negative associations. Then, just as you learned more about the topic and became enlightened, so, with any luck, may your reader.

How can you use examples? As noted earlier, it is easy to mistake a temporal relationship for a causal relationship and to assign significance to something relatively unimportant. That's another way of saying that evidence and logical reasoning are essential to cause-and-effect essays. If, for instance, you find yourself drawn to one example, you need to think about how to avoid resting your entire argument on that one case.

Writing about collegiate sports, for instance, you might have been struck by the story of a high school basketball star who wanted to play pro ball but wasn't good enough to go straight to the pros; yet he couldn't meet the admission requirements for an NCAA Division I basketball school. After playing at several junior colleges, he finally transferred to an NCAA

I institution. There, he was tutored and received a lot of individual attention, so he was able to maintain his academic eligibility. Then, one year short of graduation, all that support vanished because he had used up his time limit and was no longer eligible to play. The effect—no degree, little education, and few chances for review by pro scouts—was devastating. You want to write about it. You want to argue that college sports take advantage of high school athletes, but you have only one example. What to do?

You can use your one example as a narrative framework, one that is sure to interest your reader. But to make that example more than an attention-getting device that enlists the reader's emotions, you have a number of alternatives. If your research shows that a fair number of athletes have a similar story, then you have multiple examples to support your point. If only a few share the experience, you'll need to modify your thesis to argue that even a few is too many. And if you can't find any other examples, then you must narrow your focus to fit what you have, arguing that this particular individual was victimized. While you can ask how many more like him there may be, you cannot state that they exist.

Should your thesis emphasize cause or effect? Although a cause can lead to an effect that then becomes a cause leading to another effect and so on, most essays are organized around either one or the other: why high school students drop out, why a person returns to college, what happens if a college takes advantage of an athlete, what effect does a one-parent household have on children. That's not to say that if your essay focuses on cause, you have to avoid effect and vice versa; think of the complex interrelationships Staples sets out in his introduction. In your own writing, whichever one you don't emphasize can make a good conclusion. Your introduction, however, is a good place for your thesis; the reader can then follow the logical relationships between ideas as you develop your main point.

Useful Terms

Cause and effect An examination of a topic to discover, explain, or argue why a particular action, event, situation, or condition occurred.

Logical fallacy An error in reasoning. Assigning a causal relationship to a temporal one and reaching a general conclusion based on one example are both logical fallacies.

Post hoc reasoning A logical fallacy in which a temporal relationship is mistaken for a causal one. The fact that one event preceded another only establishes a temporal not a causal relationship.

Primary cause The most important cause or causes.

Secondary cause The less important cause or causes.

Temporal relationship Two or more events related by time rather than anything else.

POINTERS FOR USING CAUSE AND EFFECT

Exploring the Topic

1. **Have you stated the topic as a question that asks why *x* happened?** What are the possible causes? The probable causes? Rank the causes in order of priority.

2. **Have you stated the topic as a question that asks what results from *x?*** What are the possible effects? The probable effects? Rank the effects in order of priority.

3. **Is a temporal relationship involved?** Review your lists of causes and effects, and rule out any that have only a temporal relationship to your subject.

4. **Which do you want to emphasize—cause or effect?** Check to make sure your focus is clear.

5. **What is your point?** Are you trying to show that something is so or to explore your topic? Are you making an argument?

6. **What evidence can you use to support your point?** Do you need to cite authorities or quote statistics? If you depend on personal experience, are you sure your experience is valid, that is, representative of general experience?

7. **What does your reader think?** Does your audience have any preconceived ideas about your topic that you need to account for? What are they? How can you deal with them?

8. **Do you need to define any terms?** What words are crucial to your point? Are any of them abstract and, therefore, need to be defined? Have you used any technical terms that need definition?

9. **What role do you want to play in the essay?** Are you an observer or a participant? Do you intend to inform, persuade, or entertain? What point of view best serves your purpose?

(Continued)

POINTERS FOR USING CAUSE AND EFFECT *(Continued)*

Drafting the Paper

1. **Know your reader.** Figure out what attitudes your reader may have about your topic. If the causal relationship you are discussing is unusual, you might want to shape your initial attitude so that it is as skeptical as your reader's. On the other hand, you may want to start with a short narrative that immediately puts the reader on your side. How much does your reader know about your topic? If you are the expert, make sure you explain everything that needs to be explained without being condescending.

2. **Know your purpose.** Adjust your tone and persona to your purpose. If you are writing a persuasive paper, make sure your persona is credible and that you focus your ideas to change the mind of a reader or at least rethink a position. If you are writing an informative paper, choose a persona and tone that will interest the reader. Tone and persona are even more crucial to essays written to entertain, in which the tone can range from ironic to lighthearted.

3. **Emphasize a cause or effect.** Essays that focus on cause will probably cover a variety of reasons that explain the result. Though there may be only one effect or result, you may want to predict other possible effects in your conclusion. For instance, an essay that explores the causes of violence may examine a number of reasons or causes for it but may then conclude by speculating on the possible effects of a rising crime rate. On the other hand, essays that focus on effect will more than likely cover a number of possible effects that are produced by a single cause, though again you may want to speculate on other causes. If you are writing about the effects of smoking, at some point in the essay you may want to include other harmful substances in the air such as dust, hydrocarbons, and carbon monoxide.

4. **Check for validity.** Don't hesitate to include quotations, allusions, statistics, and studies. Choose your examples carefully to buttress the relationship you are trying to establish, and be sure you don't mistake a temporal relationship for a causal one.

5. Make a point. The cause-and-effect relationship you examine should support an assertion: video games not only entertain, they also stimulate the mind and improve coordination; video games are not only habit-forming, they are also addictive.

6. Proofread. Check to make sure you are using *affect* and *effect* correctly. While a handbook will provide a longer explanation, the short one is to think of *affect* as a verb and *effect* as a noun. That's not always true, but it is most of the time.

Tiffany Stephenson—An Apology

Bjorn Skogquist

Bjorn Skogquist came to Concordia College in Moorhead, Minnesota, with a firm interest in drama (having been in productions at Anoka High School that were recognized for excellence by the Kennedy Center for the Performing Arts) but a distinct aversion to writing. His freshman year, however, when his instructor, James Postema, encouraged him to "include anything I wanted, anything that I felt to be important," Skogquist "began to find it rather easy, and in a way, almost entertaining." He comments, "About halfway through, after I had written about various mishaps and comical incidents in my life, I decided to write about the things that a person would rather forget." The result is the essay that follows, although the name of the subject has been changed to Tiffany Stephenson. Skogquist relates "one of those things that I would rather forget, but instead of forgetting it, I apologized. It was something that I began and couldn't put down until I had finished."

What to Look For   If you find yourself thinking about an incident that occurred to you and mulling over its effect, you may well be on the way to an essay that takes a personal narrative and reexamines it through the lens of cause and effect. That is what Bjorn Skogquist does with what happened to him in the fourth grade. As you read the essay, look for the ways he handles different time periods—what had been happening before he entered his new school, his first day there, the incident that occurred, and the present.

1   When I was in the fourth grade, I moved from a small Lutheran school of 100 to a larger publicly funded elementary school. Lincoln Elementary. Wow. Lincoln was a big school, full of a thousand different attitudes about everything from eating lunch to how to treat a new kid. It was a tough time for me, my first year, and more than anything, I wanted to belong.

2   Many things were difficult; the move my family had just made, trying to make new friends, settling into a new home, accepting a new

stepfather. I remember crying a lot. I remember my parents fighting. They were having a difficult time with their marriage, and whether it was my stepfather's drinking, or my mother's stubbornness, it took an emotional toll on both me and my siblings. Despite all this, the thing that I remember most about the fourth grade is Tiffany Stephenson.

3   The first day of fourth grade at Lincoln Elementary School was an emptiness, and it felt enormous. I wasn't the only one who felt this way, but I was too absorbed in my own problems to notice anyone else's. I was upset that my father, my blood father, was in the hospital for abusing alcohol. Among other things, he was a schizophrenic. I was too young to understand these diseases, but I understood all too well that my daddy was very sick, and that I couldn't see him any more.

4   My first day at Lincoln was a very real moment in my life. The weather was both cloudy and intolerably sunny at the same time. Maybe it wasn't that the sun was so bright, maybe it was just that our eyes were still adjusted to morning shadows. It was one of those sequences that somehow stand out in my memory as unforgettable. I remember feeling gray inside. I think that all of us felt a little gray, and I would guess that most of us remember that first day as you might remember your grandmother's funeral, whether you liked it or not.

5   I walked in and sat near the back of the class, along with a few others. If you were different or weird or new, from another planet, you sat in the back because those were the only desks left. I sat at the far left of the room, in the back near the windows. For a while I just stared out into the playground, waiting for recess to come. Our teacher, Mrs. Bebow, came into the room and started talking to us. I don't remember exactly what she said that day, because I wasn't listening. I was numb to the world, concentrating solely on that playground. She seemed distant, far away, and I think that my whole day might have stayed numb if it weren't for a boy named Aaron Anderson.

6   Aaron, who sat to my right, leaned over and whispered, "My name's Aaron. And that's Tiffany Stephenson. Stay away from her. She's fat and ugly and she stinks." At that, a few others laughed, and I felt the numbness leaving me. Mrs. Bebow remarked that if we had something so terribly amusing to say, everyone had a right to know just what it was. Of course, we all quieted down. Then I asked which one was Tiffany, and Aaron pointed. There she was, coloring contentedly, sitting alone in the corner, in the very back, just like me.

She was not fat or ugly, and as far as I knew, she didn't stink either. I even remember thinking that she was cute, but I quickly dismissed the thought because I already had a new friendship, even though it was in the common disgust of Tiffany Stephenson.

7   While all this was happening, our teacher Mrs. Bebow managed to take roll, after which she proceeded to lecture the boys on good behavior and then the girls on being young ladies. Every time she turned her back, airplanes and garbage flew across the room at Tiffany, along with a giggle. I don't think Tiffany Stephenson thought too much of us, that day or ever.

8   A few days later, one of the girls passed Tiffany a note. It ended up making her cry, and it got the girl a half an hour of detention. I was too busy trying to fit in to notice though, or didn't notice, or was afraid to notice, or simply didn't care.

9   That fall, both the boys and girls would go up to Tiffany on the playground and taunt her. They made absurd accusations, accusations about eating boogers at lunch, or about neglecting to wear underwear that day. Interestingly, this was the only activity that we participated in where a teacher didn't command, "OK, boys and girls need to partner up!" What we did to Tiffany Stephenson was mean, but in using her we all became common allies. I wonder if the teachers knew what we were up to when we made our next move, or if they thought that we were actually getting along. I think they knew at first, but we got craftier as time passed. And Tiffany had quit telling the teacher what happened. She knew that when we were ratted on, her taunts got worse. And they did get worse. We were mean, but we kept on because there was no one to stand out and say, "Enough."

10   When I think about that year, and about Tiffany, I remember that she was almost always alone. Toward the second half of the year, a retarded girl named Sharon Olsen befriended her. Sharon and Tiffany were a lot alike. They spent most of their time together coloring and drawing pictures, and those pictures always found their way to the prize board at the end of the week. The teacher knew that they needed a little encouragement, but mostly that "encouragement" ended up making us hate them more. We picked on Sharon a lot too, but not as much as we targeted Tiffany.

11   Through the long winter, our taunts became hateful jeers, and our threats of pushing and shoving became real acts. We carried our threats out against Tiffany, but with no real reason to hate her. A couple of times when we walked down to lunch, we even pushed her

around the corner to an area under the stairs. We knew that if no other classes followed us, we could get away with our plan, which was to tease her until tears flowed. We always asked her if she was scared. She never gave us the right answer. In a quiet voice she would reply, "No. Now leave me alone." Sometimes we left her alone, and sometimes we just laughed. Tiffany must have felt so very scared and alone, but she had more than us, she had courage. We didn't care. The more we could scare her, the better, the closer, the stronger knit we somehow felt.

12   One afternoon, heading for lunch, a few of us stayed behind and blocked the doorway. Tiffany was there, alone again, and cornered by three boys. Looking back, I realized why we began pushing her around. We felt unbelievably close, so close to each other through our hatred. It was a feeling that I have experienced only a few times since. And not only was the experience ours to cherish, it was a delight for Mrs. Bebow's entire fourth grade class. We were a purpose that afternoon, and we knew it. Looking back to that moment, I feel more remorse for my coldness than I have felt for any other passing wrong. But then, there, I felt alive, unafraid, and strangely whole.

13   That afternoon changed me forever.

14   By the time we sent Tiffany Stephenson to the green linoleum, she was no longer a person. Her full name, given to her at birth as a loving gesture, was now a fat, smelly, ugly title. There, on the green linoleum of Mrs. Bebow's fourth grade classroom, amidst the decorations and smell of crayfish aquariums, Tiffany Stephenson received many kicks, punches and unkind words. We didn't kick or punch her very hard, and the things we said weren't especially foul, but they were inhuman. This event was the culmination of the inhumane hate and vengeance that had been growing inside of us all year long. And yet, if any one of us stopped for a second to look, to really take a good look at who it was lying there on the ground, curled up in a ball crying, we would have realized that she was one of us.

15   At the beginning of the year, all of us had felt like we were in the back of the room. We were all unknowns. But somehow during that year we had put ourselves above her by force, and I admit that for a long time I couldn't see my wrong. But I had wronged. I had caused someone pain for my own personal ambitions. I was now popular, and it was at Tiffany Stephenson's expense. I was a coward, stepping on her courage for one moment in the warm sunlight, above my own pale clouds.

16   Only recently do I realize my error. I wish I could have been the one to say, on that first fall afternoon, "Tiffany's not ugly, fat or stinky. She's just like you and me, and we're all here together." Really, I wish anyone would have said it. I know now that people need each other, and I wish I could tell the fourth grade that we could all be friends, that we could help each other with our problems. I wish that I could go back. But all I can do is apologize. So Tiffany, for all my shortcomings, and for sacrificing you for the sake of belonging, please forgive me.

ORGANIZATION AND IDEAS

1. What paragraph or paragraphs introduce the narrative?
2. Trace the causal relationships in paragraphs 1–5 and 6–14. What does the author feel and why?
3. Paragraphs 15 and 16 sum up the incident that occurred "that afternoon." What did the author realize then? Now?
4. Consider all the cause-and-effect relationships in the narrative and state the thesis of the essay.
5. What is the emotional effect of the essay? How does Skogquist achieve it?

TECHNIQUE AND STYLE

1. Tiffany Stephenson's name first appears in paragraph 2 but not again until paragraph 6. Explain what is gained by the delay.
2. How does the author try to connect his experience with that of the reader? Why might he have chosen to do that?
3. In paragraph 15 Skogquist says, "I was a coward, stepping on her courage for one moment in the warm sunlight, above my own pale clouds." What does he mean by "the warm sunlight, above my own pale clouds"?
4. Paragraph 13 consists of one sentence. Explain its function and effect.
5. Skogquist gives his audience a lot of information about his family. Explain why he may have chosen to do that and what it contributes to the essay.

SUGGESTIONS FOR WRITING

Journal

1. Do you identify with the author or with Tiffany Stephenson? Explain.
2. If you were Tiffany Stephenson, would you forgive Skogquist? Why or why not?

Essay

1. Write your own personal narrative about an experience in which you explore the effect it had on you. Like Skogquist, you will probably want to have a dual perspective: the effects then and now. For a subject, consider your first

   day at a new school
   attempt at a sport
   acquaintance with death
   friendship
   visit to the dentist or doctor or hospital

2. Place yourself in Tiffany Stephenson's position and write the essay from her point of view, looking back on the fourth grade from a time much later.

Black Men and Public Space

Brent Staples

Born in Chester, Pennsylvania, Staples was one of nine children in a blue-collar family that watched Chester slide into poverty and crime when the city's major industries closed. Though he hadn't thought of going to college, he was encouraged to do so by Eugene Sparrow, a black college professor, and was chosen for Project Prepare, a program aimed at providing bright undereducated students with the skills needed for college. Staples went on to graduate with honors from Widener University and then to earn an MA and PhD in psychology from the University of Chicago. A former reporter for the Chicago Sun-Times, *Staples became the assistant metropolitan editor of* The New York Times, *then editor of* The New York Times Book Review, *and now writer on education, race, and culture for* The New York Times *editorial board. Hailed as one of the best coming-of-age books in recent years,* Parallel Time: Growing Up in Black and White, *his memoir, was published in 1994.*

The essay reprinted here was first published in Harper's Magazine *in 1986. Any woman who walks along city streets at night knows the fear Brent Staples speaks of, but in this essay we learn how that fear can also affect the innocent. We see and feel what it is like to be a tall, strong, young black man who enjoys walking at night but innocently terrifies any lone woman. His solution to his night walking problems gives a nice twist to nonviolent resistance.*

What to Look For   Before you read the essay, look up the dash in a handbook of usage so you'll be on the lookout for Staples' use of it. He uses it in two different ways, but always appropriately.

1   **M**y first victim was a woman—white, well-dressed, probably in her early twenties. I came upon her late one evening on a deserted street in Hyde Park, a relatively affluent neighborhood in an otherwise mean, impoverished section of Chicago. As I swung onto the avenue behind her, there seemed to be a discreet, uninflammatory distance between us. Not so. She cast back a worried glance. To her, the youngish black man—a broad 6 feet 2 inches with a beard and billowing hair, both hands shoved into the pockets of a bulky military jacket—seemed menacingly close. After a few more quick glimpses, she picked up her pace and was soon running in earnest. Within seconds she disappeared into a cross street.

2   That was more than a decade ago. I was 22 years old, a graduate student newly arrived at the University of Chicago. It was in the echo of that terrified woman's footfalls that I first began to know the unwieldy inheritance I'd come into—the ability to alter public space in ugly ways. It was clear that she thought herself the quarry of a mugger, a rapist, or worse. Suffering a bout of insomnia, however, I was stalking sleep, not defenseless wayfarers. As a softy who is scarcely able to take a knife to a raw chicken—let alone hold one to a person's throat—I was surprised, embarrassed, and dismayed all at once. Her flight made me feel like an accomplice in tyranny. It also made it clear that I was indistinguishable from the muggers who occasionally seeped into the area from the surrounding ghetto. That first encounter, and those that followed, signified that a vast, unnerving gulf lay between nighttime pedestrians—particularly women—and me. And I soon gathered that being perceived as dangerous is a hazard in itself. I only needed to turn a corner into a dicey situation, or crowd some frightened, armed person in a foyer somewhere, or make an errant move after being pulled over by a policeman. Where fear and weapons meet—and they often do in urban America—there is always the possibility of death.

3   In that first year, my first away from my hometown, I was to become thoroughly familiar with the language of fear. At dark,

shadowy intersections, I could cross in front of a car stopped at a traffic light and elicit the *thunk, thunk, thunk, thunk* of the driver—black, white, male, or female—hammering down the door locks. On less traveled streets after dark, I grew accustomed to but never comfortable with people crossing to the other side of the street rather than pass me. Then there were the standard unpleasantries with policemen, doormen, bouncers, cabdrivers, and others whose business it is to screen out troublesome individuals *before* there is any nastiness.

4   I moved to New York nearly two years ago and I have remained an avid night walker. In central Manhattan, the near-constant crowd cover minimizes tense one-on-one street encounters. Elsewhere—in SoHo, for example, where sidewalks are narrow and tightly spaced buildings shut out the sky—things can get very taut indeed.

5   After dark, on the warrenlike streets of Brooklyn where I live, I often see women who fear the worst from me. They seem to have set their faces on neutral, and with their purse straps strung across their chests bandolier-style, they forge ahead as though bracing themselves against being tackled. I understand, of course, that the danger they perceive is not a hallucination. Women are particularly vulnerable to street violence, and young black males are drastically overrepresented among the perpetrators of that violence. Yet these truths are no solace against the kind of alienation that comes of being ever the suspect, a fearsome entity with whom pedestrians avoid making eye contact.

6   It is not altogether clear to me how I reached the ripe old age of 22 without being conscious of the lethality nighttime pedestrians attributed to me. Perhaps it was because in Chester, Pennsylvania, the small, angry industrial town where I came of age in the 1960s, I was scarcely noticeable against a backdrop of gang warfare, street knifings, and murders. I grew up one of the good boys, had perhaps a half-dozen fistfights. In retrospect, my shyness of combat has clear sources.

7   As a boy, I saw countless tough guys locked away; I have since buried several, too. They were babies, really—a teenage cousin, a brother of 22, a childhood friend in his mid-twenties—all gone down in episodes of bravado played out in the streets. I came to doubt the virtues of intimidation early on. I chose, perhaps unconsciously, to remain a shadow—timid, but a survivor.

8   The fearsomeness mistakenly attributed to me in public places often has a perilous flavor. The most frightening of these confusions

occurred in the late 1970s and early 1980s, when I worked as a journalist in Chicago. One day, rushing into the office of a magazine I was writing for with a deadline story in hand, I was mistaken for a burglar. The office manager called security and, with an ad hoc posse, pursued me through the labyrinthine halls, nearly to my editor's door. I had no way of proving who I was. I could only move briskly toward the company of someone who knew me.

9   Another time I was on assignment for a local paper and killing time before an interview. I entered a jewelry store on the city's affluent Near North Side. The proprietor excused herself and returned with an enormous red Doberman pinscher straining at the end of a leash. She stood, the dog extended toward me, silent to my questions, her eyes bulging nearly out of her head. I took a cursory look around, nodded, and bade her good night.

10   Relatively speaking, however, I never fared as badly as another black male journalist. He went to nearby Waukegan, Illinois, a couple of summers ago to work on a story about a murderer who was born there. Mistaking the reporter for the killer, police officers hauled him from his car at gunpoint and but for his press credentials would probably have tried to book him. Such episodes are not uncommon. Black men trade tales like this all the time.

11   Over the years, I learned to smother the rage I felt at so often being taken for a criminal. Not to do so would surely have led to madness. I now take precautions to make myself less threatening. I move about with care, particularly late in the evening. I give a wide berth to nervous people on subway platforms during the wee hours, particularly when I have exchanged business clothes for jeans. If I happen to be entering a building behind some people who appear skittish, I may walk by, letting them clear the lobby before I return, so as not to seem to be following them. I have been calm and extremely congenial on those rare occasions when I've been pulled over by the police.

12   And on late-evening constitutionals I employ what has proved to be an excellent tension-reducing measure: I whistle melodies from Beethoven and Vivaldi and the more popular classical composers. Even steely New Yorkers hunching toward nighttime destinations seem to relax, and occasionally they even join in the tune. Virtually everybody seems to sense that a mugger wouldn't be warbling bright, sunny selections from Vivaldi's *Four Seasons*. It is my equivalent of the cowbell that hikers wear when they know they are in bear country.

Organization and Ideas

1. Reread paragraph 1. What expectations does it evoke in the reader? For paragraph 2, state in your own words what Staples means by "unwieldy inheritance." What effects does that inheritance have?

2. The body of the essay breaks into three paragraph blocks. In paragraphs 3–5, what effects does the author's walking at night have on others? On himself?

3. In paragraphs 6 and 7, Staples refers to his childhood. Why had he been unaware of his effect on others? What effect did the streets he grew up on have on him?

4. Summarize the causes and effects Staples brings out in paragraphs 11 and 12, and in one sentence, make a general statement about them. What does that statement imply about being a black male? About urban life? About American culture? Consider your answers to those questions, and in one sentence state the thesis of the essay.

5. Who are the "victims" in Staples' essay? What are they victims of?

Technique and Style

1. A large part of the essay's impact lies in the ironic contrast between appearance and reality. What details does Staples bring out about himself that contrast with the stereotype of the mugger?

2. In paragraph 1, Staples illustrates the two uses of the dash. What function do they perform? Rewrite either of the two sentences so that you avoid the dash. Which sentence is better and why?

3. Trace Staples' use of time. Why does he start where he does? Try placing the time period mentioned in paragraphs 6 and 7 elsewhere in the essay. What advantages does their present placement have? What is the effect of ending the essay in the present?

4. Examine Staples' choice of verbs in the second sentence of paragraph 5. Rewrite the sentence using as many forms of the verb *to be* as possible. What differences do you note?

5. Staples concludes the essay with an analogy. In what ways is it ironic? How does the irony tie into the essay's thesis?

Suggestions for Writing

Journal

1. To what extent do you identify with the women in the essay? With Staples? With both? Explain.

2. Think about a time when, intentionally or unintentionally, you threatened or intimidated someone. Describe either the causes or effects.

Essay

1. You can develop either of the journal ideas above into a full-fledged essay. Or, if you prefer, think about a situation in which you have been stereotyped and that stereotype determined your effect on others. Among the physical characteristics that can spawn a stereotype are

   age
   race
   gender
   physique
   clothing

2. All of us have been in a situation in which we felt threatened. Select an incident that occurred to you and describe its effect on you.

When Music Heals Body and Soul

Oliver Sacks

For Oliver Sacks, medicine is a family tradition. Born in England to parents who were both physicians, he is one of three sons who became doctors. Armed with a medical degree from Oxford University, Sacks moved to the United States for his internship and residency and is now clinical professor of neurology at the Albert Einstein College of Medicine in New York. Sacks is probably best known for his book Awakenings *(1974), an account of his work with "frozen" patients that was made into a film in 1990, starring Robin Williams and Robert De Niro. Part of another of his clinical studies,* An Anthropologist on Mars *(1995), was made into* At First Sight, *starring Val Kilmer (1999). Other medical works include* The Man Who Mistook His Wife for a Hat *(1985) and* The Island of the Colorblind *(1998). Sacks' autobiographical books are* A Leg to Stand On *(1989) (where he recounts the accident he refers to in his essay that follows),* Uncle Tungsten: Memories of a Chemical Boyhood *(2001), and* Oaxaca Journal *(2002). Though Sacks calls himself a "lonely person, not at ease socially," it's obvious that he cares deeply about people in general and the link between "body and soul" in particular. He also emphasizes that link in* Musicophilia: Tales of Music and the Brain *(2008). The essay reprinted here was published in* Parade Magazine *on March 31, 2002.*

What to Look For It's often difficult for someone in a highly technical field to write in a way that is understood by ordinary readers. That's the problem Sacks faces when he describes a number of medical cases and neurological symptoms. As you read his essay, check to see if his prose is clear and comprehensible.

1   All of us have all sorts of personal experiences with music. We find ourselves calmed by it, excited by it, comforted by it, mystified by it and often haunted by it. It can lift us out of depression or move us to tears. I am no different. I need music to start the day and as company when I drive. I need it, propulsively, when I go for swims and runs. I need it, finally, to still my thoughts when I retire, to usher me into the world of dreams.

2   But it was only when I became a patient myself that I experienced a *physical* need for music. A bad fall while climbing a mountain in Norway had left me incapacitated by damage to the nerves and muscles of one leg. After surgery to repair the torn tendons in my leg, I settled down to await some return of function in the torn nerves.

3   With the leg effectively paralyzed, I lost all sense of its existence—indeed, I seemed to lose the very *idea* of moving it. The leg stayed nonfunctional for the longest 15 days of my life. These days were made longer and grimmer because there was no music in the hospital. Radio reception was bad. Finally, a friend brought me a tape recorder along with a tape of one of my favorite pieces: the Mendelssohn *Violin Concerto.*

4   Playing this over and over gave me great pleasure and a general sense of being alive and well. But the nerves in my damaged leg were still healing. Two weeks later, I began to get small twitches in the previously flaccid muscle and larger sudden, involuntary movements.

5   Strangely, however, I had no impulse to walk. I could barely remember how one would go about walking—until, unexpectedly, a day or two later, the *Violin Concerto* played itself in my mind. It seemed, suddenly, to lend me its own energy, and I recovered the lost rhythm of walking—like remembering a once-familiar but long-forgotten time. Only then did walking regain its natural, unconscious, kinetic melody and grace.

6   Music can have the same effect on the neurologically impaired. It may have a power beyond anything else to restore them to themselves—at least in the precious few minutes that it lasts.

7   For reasons we do not yet understand, musical abilities often are among the last to be lost, even in cases of widespread brain damage. Thus, someone who is disabled by a stroke or by Alzheimer's or another form of dementia may still be able to respond to music in ways that can seem almost miraculous.

8   After a stroke, patients may suffer from *aphasia,* the inability to use or comprehend words. But the ability to sing words is rarely affected, even if an aphasic cannot speak them. Some patients can even be "reminded" in this way of words and grammatical constructions they have "forgotten." This, in turn, may help them start to regain old neural pathways for accessing language or to build new pathways in their place. Music becomes a crucial first step in a sequence followed by spontaneous improvement and speech therapy.

9   Some of my patients with strokes or Alzheimer's are unable to carry out a complex chain of actions: to dress, for example. Here, music can work as a mnemonic—a series of promptings in the form of verse or song, as in the childhood rhyme "One, two, buckle my shoe."

10   My patient Dr. P. had lost the ability to recognize or identify even common objects, though he could see perfectly well. He was unable to recognize a glove or a flower when I handed it to him, and he once mistook his own wife for a hat. This condition was almost totally disabling—but he discovered that he could perform the needs and tasks of the day if they were organized in song. And so he had songs for dressing, songs for eating, songs for bathing, songs for everything.

11   As a result of a brain tumor, my patient Greg has not been able to retain any new memories since the 1970s. But if we talk about or play his favorite Grateful Dead songs, his amnesia is bypassed. He becomes vividly animated and can reminisce about their early concerts.

12   I first saw the immense therapeutic powers of music 30 years ago, in the postencephalitic patients I later wrote about in *Awakenings.* These 80 individuals all were victims of *encephalitis lethargica,* the viral sleeping sickness that swept the globe just after World War I. When I came to Beth Abraham Hospital in the Bronx in 1966, most of them had been "frozen," absolutely motionless, for decades.

13   Their voices, if they could speak, lacked tone and force; they were almost spectral. Yet these patients were able to *sing* loudly and clearly, with a normal range of expressiveness and tone. Among those who could walk and talk—though only in a jerky,

broken way—music gave their movement or speech the steadiness and control it usually lacked.

14   We could observe this effect on the patients' electroencephalograms. If we found music that worked, their EEGs—often exceedingly slow, reflecting their frozen states—would become faster and more regular. We noted this when patients listened to music or sang it or played it—even when they imagined it.

15   Take Rosalie B., a patient who had a severe form of parkinsonism. She tended to remain transfixed for hours a day, completely motionless, stuck, usually with one finger on her spectacles. But she knew all of Chopin's works by heart, and we had only to say "Opus 49" to see her whole body, posture and expression change. Her parkinsonism would vanish as soon as she even imagined Chopin's *Fantaisie in F minor*. Her EEG would become normal at the same instant the Chopin played itself in her mind.

16   Clearly, human brains are able to tenaciously hold and replay musical stimuli. This is why tunes may repeat themselves endlessly, sometimes maddeningly, in the mind. Musical hallucinations are far more common than visual hallucinations. There even seems to be a sort of normal "reminiscence" or "recycling" of early musical memories, especially in the aging brain.

17   To help, however, the music must be the right kind for each patient—music that has meaning and evokes feeling for that individual. Music therapists who work with a geriatric population often find that only old popular songs can bring such patients to life. While singing them, these patients are able to find a brief but intense sense of community and connectedness with their past lives—and perhaps a deep emotional catharsis.

18   This almost universal responsiveness to music is an essential part of our neural nature. Though analogies often are made to birdsong or animal cries, music in its full sense—including complexities of rhythm and harmony, of pace, timbre and tonality no less than of melody—seems to be confined to our own species, like language. Why this should be so is still a mystery. Our research is only now beginning to unlock those secrets.

ORGANIZATION AND IDEAS

1. What kind of music do you enjoy? How does it affect you?
2. To what extent are your responses similar to those Sacks describes in paragraph 1?

3. Trace the pattern of general and particular through the essay. How would you describe it?
4. How does music affect Sacks' recovery? Those who are neurologically damaged?
5. Consider all the effects Sacks shows that music can have on people and in one sentence state what you find to be his thesis.

TECHNIQUE AND STYLE

1. Paragraphs 10–15 set out a number of examples. What do they add to the essay?
2. You may be familiar with *Parade Magazine,* for it accompanies many a Sunday newspaper. Its readership is about as general as one can be, yet Sacks is very much a specialist. How well does he tailor his knowledge to his audience?
3. Sacks blends personal narrative with examples from his medical practice. How effective is his use of the subjective and the objective?
4. Sacks focuses on the effects of music. To what extent does he bring in causal analysis?
5. Paragraphs 16–18 provide the essay's conclusion. How satisfactory is it? Explain.

SUGGESTIONS FOR WRITING

Journal

1. In what ways is the title of the essay appropriate? What others can you think of?
2. What surprises you most in Sacks' essay? Explain why.

Essay

1. Almost everyone uses leisure time to relax by pursuing some form of pleasure. Think about what you do for day-to-day fun and make a list of what you come up with. Choose one subject and consider why you do it as well as its effects on you. Then draft an essay in which you explain what you do and why. You may want to emphasize cause rather than effect or vice versa. Suggestions:
   talking to friends
   playing a sport
   watching television
   pursuing a hobby
   exercising
2. Think about the ways in which music affects you and explore that subject in an essay. You might begin by defining the kind of music you like and then go on to analyze its effect.

Technology's Power to Narrow Our View

Samantha Power

Samantha Power refers to herself as a "thirtysomething anachronism" who prefers newspapers to the electronic media, but it's a preference backed up by her research and writing. A graduate of Yale University and Harvard Law School, Power's first book, A Problem from Hell: America and the Age of Genocide *(2002), began as a paper she wrote for law school and earned her a Pulitzer Prize for general nonfiction as well as a National Book Critics Circle Award. Prior to that time, she had been a correspondent for* U.S. News and World Report, The Boston Globe, *and* The New Republic, *reporting on the wars in what used to be Yugoslavia. Now the foreign affairs columnist for* Time, *she continues to write for other publications,* The Atlantic Monthly, The New Yorker, *and* The New York Review of Books *among them. Power teaches at the Carr Center for Human Rights Policy at Harvard's Kennedy School of Government, where she holds a title almost as long as her list of publications: Professor of Practice of Global Leadership and Public Policy. Her latest book is* Chasing the Flame: Sergio Vieira de Mello and the Fight to Save the World *(2008), a biography of the Chief of the United Nation's mission to Iraq who was killed in a bombing in Baghdad. Her essay that follows was published in the May 22, 2008, issue of* Time.

What to Look For Power's essay in a way is a personal one in that she uses her own experiences and *I*, the first person pronoun. As you read the essay, note how often she uses *I* and ask yourself whether the essay focuses primarily on Power. If it doesn't, who or what is the main focus?

1 Commencement season is upon us, when students across the nation make familiar pledges to go forth and change the world. The explosion of social networks on the Internet—Facebook users have affiliated with more than 80,000 causes—has emboldened them to believe their generation will make change. But does new technology make it more or less likely that young people today will commit themselves to do something for others?

2   Let me start by confessing that I am a thirtysomething anachronism. I still read the hard copies of the *New York Times* and the *Boston Globe*, and I refuse to consider changing my habits. My students marvel at me the way I once marveled at my mother for being slow to get an e-mail account. They don't understand why right-thinking people would willfully make their hands dirty every day when they don't have to. To them I am like a person who takes a shower in the morning and then decides to do gardening before work. True, smudge isn't great, but it seems a small price to pay for what the newspaper offers: serendipitous discovery and wide-angle perspective.

3   I would not be doing what I do today if not for two encounters I never would have sought out on my own. After my freshman year in college, I interned in the sports department of the CBS affiliate in Atlanta and spent my days taking notes on the then hapless Braves' baseball games. One day news from Tiananmen Square suddenly interrupted the CBS feed. Chinese soldiers mauled students and then lunged toward the CBS cameraman filming the scene. I sat looking at my clipboard, wondering what on earth I was doing with my life. Three years later, I got a second push when the nightly news (all three networks!) and the *New York Times* showed images of emaciated Bosnian men imprisoned in concentration camps in Europe. I went off to the Balkans to cover the war as a freelance journalist.

4   Much has been made of the convening and mobilizing power of today's technology. A person inspired by a cause can blog about their outrage and plot a response on Facebook with other similarly animated people. While any single congressional district might not produce a groundswell to demand a halt to global warming or killing in Darfur, a virtual community unmoored from geography can deliver a critical mass. And once converted, advocates are far better informed than a generation ago. They can hear the personal tales of aid workers over Skype. When the Western press steers clear, they can access and share local media reports. Thanks to what Chris Anderson called the "long tail," far more documentaries are available than when movie theaters and video stores catered only to the most popular side of the market. Netflix carries close to 7,500 documentaries, allowing people already immersed in a cause to deepen their knowledge and commitment—and enabling proselytizers to attract new adherents.

5   For many of us, though, technology has actually lowered the odds of bumping into inconvenient knowledge. If I had been setting up a

Google alert in 1989, mine would not have been for "China" or "human rights." In 1992, I certainly would not have asked for stories on "concentration camps." When I'm abroad these days and have to go without my newspaper, I often turn to the most e-mailed stories on news websites, which are generally opinion pieces (rather than news stories), from which I cherry-pick arguments or facts that comport with my pre-existing views. Reading this way, I rarely stray from the familiar and soothing.

6 Amid the hoopla over new media, it is worth considering the costs of the personalization of news. Sure, viral YouTube videos of global conflicts and tragedies will occasionally find an audience, and movements may grow up around iconic new-media images as they did around the old. But while the long tail ensures once obscure documentaries remain available, citizen advocacy may have a short tail, causing the number of viable causes to get winnowed to a handful of megacauses. Burma may achieve the requisite market share, while Burundi fails to penetrate at all.

7 Further, the screen on which people view the world will narrow. Spared the burden of considering multiple parts of the world at once, single-issue advocates may have a hard time seeing the relationship of one foreign policy challenge to another. Viewing issues à la carte, they might be unable or unwilling to prioritize. To be fair, if young advocates fail to see the way Guantánamo has undermined U.S. efforts in Darfur, they are being no more tunnel-visioned than the Bush Administration. But they are the ones we are counting on to help turn things around.

ORGANIZATION AND IDEAS

1. What paragraph or paragraphs work as the introduction to the essay? What reasons can you cite for your choice?
2. Paragraphs 3 and 4 concentrate on the positive effects of technology. Trace the cause-and-effect relationships.
3. Paragraphs 5–7 shift to the negative effects. Plot out what causes what. To what extent do you find the causal relationships valid ones? Do they sufficiently counter the ones set out in paragraphs 3 and 4?
4. Power poses a question at the end of her first paragraph: "But does new technology make it more or less likely that young people today will commit themselves to do something for others?" Given the rest of the essay, what is her answer?
5. How effective are the examples Power uses to back up her points?

TECHNIQUE AND STYLE

1. In paragraphs 4 and 6, Power alludes to Chris Anderson and the "long tail." Anderson is the editor of *Wired* who coined the term to represent electronic media's economic effect, one causing a shift from mass markets to niche ones. For a more detailed explanation, Anderson suggests you read about it on Wikipedia's Web site http://en.wikipedia.org/wiki/Long_Tail. How well do Power's allusions to the term work?

2. Reread the essay looking for places where Power qualifies her statements. What examples can you find? What does that sort of qualification add to the strength of her argument?

3. *Time Magazine* has a broad readership, but it can be pegged as a fairly well educated older one, one several years removed from the students Power mentions in paragraphs 1 and 7. To what extent is Power directing her argument to *Time*'s readership? To graduating students?

4. Given the brief biography preceding the essay and the essay itself, how would you describe Samantha Power? What evidence can you find to back up your opinion?

5. How would you describe the level of diction Powers uses? What do her word choices contribute to the essay? To her persona? What effect do they have?

SUGGESTIONS FOR WRITING

Journal

1. Given what Powers has to say in her essay, how effective is her title? What alternative titles can you think of? Which do you prefer and why?

2. In paragraph 6, Powers mentions "viral YouTube videos" and that can "occasionally find an audience." Evaluate the validity of her claim.

Essay

1. Think about the electronic media you use to get and convey information. What sources are readily available? Which one do you depend on and why? What effect does it have? Write an essay in which you explain what you use and its effect. Suggestions:

    YouTube
    Facebook
    Twitter
    MySpace
    Vimeo
    Skype

2. Blogs have become increasingly popular as a means of letting off steam, commenting on current events, setting out opinions, and various other

uses. Use the Web to research what the most popular blogs are and what kind of effect they may have. To make the subject more manageable, limit your search to a particular kind of blog—political (liberal/conservative/independent), media, entertainment, celebrities, sports, etc.

Retreat into the iWorld

Andrew Sullivan

Andrew Sullivan was born in England, where he graduated from Oxford University and then won a fellowship to the John F. Kennedy School of Government at Harvard. There he received an MA in public administration and, later, a PhD in political science. His career in journalism, however, started by interning for The Daily Telegraph *and at the conservative Centre for Policy Studies, both in London, and then in Washington, D.C., at* The New Republic, *where at the age of 27 he rose to editor. A frequent guest on radio and TV news and talk shows, Sullivan has written four books:* Virtually Normal *(1996),* Love Undetectable: Notes on Friendship, Sex, and Survival *(1999),* Same-Sex Marriage: Pro and Con *(2004), and* The Conservative Soul: How We Lost It, How to Get It Back *(2006). His blog—the* Daily Dish—*appears on* The Atlantic Online, *and his print journalism has appeared in* The Wall Street Journal, The Washington Post, *and* Esquire. *You may have seen him on one of many television shows, among them* Nightline, Meet the Press, Hardball, The O'Reilly Factor, *and* Hannity and Colmes. *Though he is still a senior editor at* The New Republic, *he also writes for* Time, The New York Times Book Review, *and the* Sunday Times *of* London, *where this essay appeared on February 20, 2005.*

What to Look For   If Sullivan is right, then most cities are full of iPod people, which means they are part of the audience for his essay. As you read it, keep track of how he tries not to alienate them.

1   I was visiting New York last week and noticed something I'd never thought I'd say about the city. Yes, nightlife is pretty much dead (and I'm in no way the first to notice that). But daylife—that

insane mishmash of yells, chatter, clatter, hustle and chutzpah that makes New York the urban equivalent of methamphetamine—was also a little different. It was quieter.

2 Manhattan's downtown is now a Disney-like string of malls, riverside parks and pretty upper-middle-class villages. But there was something else. And as I looked across the throngs on the pavements, I began to see why.

3 There were little white wires hanging down from their ears, or tucked into pockets, purses or jackets. The eyes were a little vacant. Each was in his or her own musical world, walking to their soundtrack, stars in their own music video, almost oblivious to the world around them. These are the iPod people.

4 Even without the white wires you can tell who they are. They walk down the street in their own MP3 cocoon, bumping into others, deaf to small social cues, shutting out anyone not in their bubble.

5 Every now and again some start unconsciously emitting strange tuneless squawks, like a badly tuned radio, and their fingers snap or their arms twitch to some strange soundless rhythm. When others say "Excuse me" there's no response. "Hi", ditto. It's strange to be among so many people and hear so little. Except that each one is hearing so much.

6 Yes, I might as well own up. I'm one of them. I witnessed the glazed New York looks through my own glazed pupils, my white wires peeping out of my ears. I joined the cult a few years ago: the sect of the little white box worshippers.

7 Every now and again I go to church—those huge, luminous Apple stores, pews in the rear, the clerics in their monastic uniforms all bustling around or sitting behind the "Genius Bars", like priests waiting to hear confessions.

8 Others began, as I did, with a Walkman—and then a kind of clunkier MP3 player. But the sleekness of the iPod won me over. Unlike other models it gave me my entire music collection to re-arrange as I saw fit—on the fly, in my pocket.

9 What was once an occasional musical diversion became a compulsive obsession. Now I have my iTunes in my iMac for my iPod in my iWorld. It's Narcissus heaven: we've finally put the "i" into Me.

10 And, like all addictive cults, it's spreading. There are now 22m iPod owners in the United States and Apple is becoming a mass-market company for the first time.

11 Walk through any airport in the United States these days and you will see person after person gliding through the social ether as if on

autopilot. Get on a subway and you're surrounded by a bunch of Stepford commuters staring into mid-space as if anaesthetised by technology. Don't ask, don't tell, don't overhear, don't observe. Just tune in and tune out.

12 It wouldn't be so worrying if it weren't part of something even bigger. Americans are beginning to narrow their lives.

13 You get your news from your favourite blogs, the ones that won't challenge your view of the world. You tune into a satellite radio service that also aims directly at a small market—for new age fanatics, liberal talk or Christian rock. Television is all cable. Culture is all subculture. Your cell phones can receive e-mail feeds of your favourite blogger's latest thoughts—seconds after he has posted them—get sports scores for your team or stock quotes of your portfolio.

14 Technology has given us a universe entirely for ourselves— where the serendipity of meeting a new stranger, hearing a piece of music we would never choose for ourselves or an opinion that might force us to change our mind about something are all effectively banished.

15 Atomisation by little white boxes and cell phones. Society without the social. Others who are chosen—not met at random. Human beings have never lived like this before. Yes, we have always had homes, retreats or places where we went to relax, unwind or shut out the world.

16 But we didn't walk around the world like hermit crabs with our isolation surgically attached.

17 Music was once the preserve of the living room or the concert hall. It was sometimes solitary but it was primarily a shared experience, something that brought people together, gave them the comfort of knowing that others too understood the pleasure of a Brahms symphony or that Beatles album.

18 But music is as atomised now as living is. And it's secret. That bloke next to you on the bus could be listening to heavy metal or a Gregorian chant. You'll never know. And so, bit by bit, you'll never really know him. And by his white wires, he is indicating he doesn't really want to know you.

19 What do we get from this? The awareness of more music, more often. The chance to slip away for a while from everydayness, to give our lives its own soundtrack, to still the monotony of the commute, to listen more closely and carefully to music that can lift you up and keep you going.

20   We become masters of our own interests, more connected to people like us over the internet, more instantly in touch with anything we want, need or think we want and think we need. Ever tried a Stairmaster in silence? But what are we missing? That hilarious shard of an overheard conversation that stays with you all day; the child whose chatter on the pavement takes you back to your early memories; birdsong; weather; accents; the laughter of others. And those thoughts that come not by filling your head with selected diversion, but by allowing your mind to wander aimlessly through the regular background noise of human and mechanical life.

21   External stimulation can crowd out the interior mind. Even the boredom that we flee has its uses. We are forced to find our own means to overcome it.

22   And so we enrich our life from within, rather than from white wires. It's hard to give up, though, isn't it.

23   Not so long ago I was on a trip and realised I had left my iPod behind. Panic. But then something else. I noticed the rhythms of others again, the sound of the airplane, the opinions of the taxi driver, the small social cues that had been obscured before. I noticed how others related to each other. And I felt just a little bit connected again and a little more aware.

24   Try it. There's a world out there. And it has a soundtrack all its own.

ORGANIZATION AND IDEAS

1. Sullivan begins with a personal narrative. Where else in the essay does he return to that mode? What effects does it achieve?

2. Reread Sullivan's essay, marking each instance of cause and of effect. Which predominates?

3. In paragraphs 17 and 18, Sullivan uses comparison and contrast. In what ways does that mode contribute to the primary one of cause and effect?

4. Sullivan states a bare-bones thesis in paragraph 12. Given the essay as a whole, how can you flesh it out?

5. Test Sullivan's thesis against your own experience. How valid is it?

TECHNIQUE AND STYLE

1. Sullivan refers to "Narcissus heaven" (paragraph 9) and "Stepford commuters" (paragraph 11). What does he mean by these allusions?

2. Reread the essay looking for unusual or striking words. How would you characterize Sullivan's diction? What does he achieve by using it?

3. In paragraph 7, Sullivan sets out an analogy. What is being compared? How effective is the comparison?
4. Sullivan begins paragraph 15 with three incomplete sentences that amount to a short list. Rewrite them to make one or more complete sentences. What is gained? Lost?
5. Where in the essay does Sullivan use metaphor? Choose the one you like best and explain what it adds to the essay.

SUGGESTIONS FOR WRITING

Journal

1. If you have an iPod, how accurate do you find Sullivan's essay? If you don't have one, explain why you would or would not want one.
2. In paragraph 20, Sullivan argues for "allowing your mind to wander aimlessly through the regular background noise of human and mechanical life." Explain to what extent you agree or disagree with the value of letting your mind wander.

Essay

1. It's a rare invention or technical advance that doesn't have some drawbacks, major or minor. Think about the electronic or mechanical innovations that are now available, choose one, and analyze its effects, both positive and negative. Once you've weighed those effects, you can form your thesis for an essay. Suggestions:

   camera phones
   chat rooms
   blogs
   digital cameras
   DVDs
   cell phone ring tones

2. Analyze Sullivan's essay to determine the extent to which he takes a stand. Is he arguing, explaining, speculating, musing, analyzing, what? Back up your interpretation with quotations and examples from the essay.

The Class of 2008

John Deering

Like many cartoonists, John Deering started young and kept going at a fast clip. After two years studying commercial and fine art at the University of Arkansas, he started work for the Arkansas Democrat-Gazette. *There, he progressed quickly from advertising layout to editorial cartoonist to chief editorial cartoonist and to two book collections—Deering's State of Mind (1990) and* We Knew Bill Clinton…Bill Clinton Was a Friend of Ours *(1993), the latter with Vic Harville (also with the* Democrat-Gazette*). Perhaps living in the same state as the Clintons and Governor Mike Huckabee provides ample fodder for cartoons. Deering's work become syndicated in two categories, as editorial cartoons and as a more free-ranging panel titled "Strange Brew." You can find his drawings reproduced in dailies such as* The New York Times *and* Los Angeles Times *and in magazines such as* Time *and* Newsweek. *Seven-time winner of the Arkansas Press Association's Best Editorial Cartoonist Award, Deering's work has been recognized nationally by the National Press Foundation's Berryman Award (1997). The editorial cartoon shown here was published on May 19, 2008.*

AS WE, THE CLASS OF 2008 GO FORTH, I'M REMINDED OF SOME WORDS FROM ONE OF THE TRULY GREAT TEXT MESSAGES...

For Discussion

1. Who is the speaker? Why is that choice crucial to the cartoon's intended humor?
2. Why might Deering have drawn the speaker the way he did? What does his depiction imply?
3. How typical is the opening of the speech? What words tip it off as typical?
4. What would be the cartoon's impact if the speaker were looking at her audience? At the sky? What does Deering gain by having her looking down?
5. In what ways does the cartoon comment on the essays by Power and Sullivan?

Suggestions for Writing

Journal

The general subject of Deering's cartoon is text messaging. What other subjects does the cartoon suggest? Which has the greatest impact and why?

Essay

Write your own graduation address on a subject that comes from popular culture. Perhaps you can find your "text" represented by a product, television show, musical group, or sports figure. No matter what you choose, you can use an ironic tone or a serious one or something in between. Your choice.

On Using
Argument

9

1   Quite a long time ago, having briefly joined the herd of 20-something backpackers that eternally roams Southeast Asia, I found myself in Bali. Like all of the other 20-somethings, I carefully read the Lonely Planet backpacker's guide to Indonesia and learned, among other things, that it was considered improper for women to wear shorts or trousers when entering Balinese temples. I dutifully purchased a Balinese sarong and, looking awkward and foreign, wore it while visiting temples. I didn't want to cause offense.

2   I thought of that long-ago incident during a visit last week to London, where a full-fledged shouting match has broken out over Muslim women who choose to wear the veil. This particular argument had begun because a teaching assistant in Yorkshire refused to remove her veil—a *niqab,* which covers the whole body except for the eyes—in the presence of male teachers, which was much of the time. She was fired; she went to court—and a clutch of senior British politicians entered the fray.

Anne Applebaum begins her essay "Veiled Insult" with a personal narrative and then compares her experience to what happened in England to a Muslim teaching assistant who insisted on wearing a full-face veil. That incident sets the stage for Applebaum's subject: the right to hide one's face. In the rest of the essay, Applebaum uses examples and comparisons drawn from her research to support her opinion on the topic. What she constructs is her argument.

In everyday speech, **argument** is so closely associated with *quarrel* or *fight* that it has a negative connotation, but that connotation does not apply to essays. When you read the rest of Applebaum's essay, you will be analyzing it by examining its argument: her major assertion and the weight of the evidence on which it rests. That's what you'll be looking for when you write your own argumentative essays. You want the reader to respond in one of several ways:

- to adopt your view
- to rethink his or her previous position
- to take a particular action
- to keep reading

Though the last goal may seem a small one, many of the subjects of argumentative essays are ones your readers already have an opinion about. That being the case, having someone who disagrees with you keep on reading means you have constructed a successful argument.

Because an argumentative essay bases its thesis primarily on reason, the word *logic* may pop into your mind and raise images of mathematical models and seemingly tricky statements stringing together sentences beginning with *ifs* and leading to one starting with *therefore.* Don't worry. The arguments you construct build on the kinds of essays you've written all along: Your thesis is the heart of your argument, and examples, definitions, descriptions, and the like provide supporting evidence.

In this chapter you will discover how to write a short argumentative essay and how to use the various modes to support that aim. The essays that follow are examples of argument, though the subjects differ widely: wearing full-face veils; banning dancing; lowering the legal drinking age; and controlling illegal immigration. Each of the last two topics is covered by two essays and two cartoons. Direct, current, often abrasive, and savagely funny, political cartoons and comic strips are readily accessible forms of argument. The artists who draw them consider all subjects fair game, so it's not surprising that the debates over underage drinking and immigration appeal to a great many political satirists.

How can you find a topic and support your argument? Often the best topic for an argumentative essay is the one you come up with on your own, but at times you may be assigned a topic. If so, your chances for success increase if you shape the topic so that you can connect to it. Because you already know something about the subject, you have done some thinking about it instead of starting from scratch or using secondhand opinions. Even abstract topics such as euthanasia can be made concrete and will be the better for it.

You may know little about mercy killing, but you may have had a member of your family who was terminally ill. Would euthanasia have been an appropriate alternative? Should it have been? In addition to using your own experience, research the topic. Newspaper accounts and editorials can help give form and focus to an abstract issue, as can book and periodical sources, all of which and more can be found on the Internet. The Web provides instant access to a huge and often unfiltered amount of information, so always check who or what is behind the information. Anyone can put anything on the Web. And does.

How can you shape your argument for your readers? Audience plays a greater role in argument than in any other type of writing, and therein lies a problem: You must adapt both form and content to fit your audience, while at the same time maintaining your integrity. If you shape your argumentative position according to its probable acceptance by your readers rather than your own belief, the result is propaganda or sensationalism, not argument. Knowingly playing false with an audience by omitting evidence or shaping facts to fit an assertion or by resorting to illogical notions are all dishonest tricks.

Within honest bounds, however, you have much to draw on, and a sense of what your audience may or may not know and of what the audience believes about a topic can guide you. Even if your topic is familiar, what you have to say about it will be new information. If your subject is one many readers know little about, you can begin by explaining the issue and its context, which is what Applebaum does in the two paragraphs included at the start of this chapter, paragraphs that also introduce her essay "Veiled Insult." When you read the rest of her essay, you'll see how she explores the various positions on the subject before she states her own stand.

What are logical fallacies and how can you avoid them? Argumentative writing ranges from the personal to the abstract and draws on the various patterns that can be used to structure an essay. For instance, waiting tables in a restaurant may have convinced you that tips should be automatically included in the bill. To make the case that the present system is unfair to those in a service trade, you might draw primarily on your own experience and that of others, though you need to make sure that your experience is representative. If you don't, your reader may discount your argument, thinking that one example isn't sufficient evidence. A quick check among others who are similarly employed and a look at government reports on employment statistics can support your example as typical and, therefore, to be trusted.

The technical term for an entire argument based on only one example is **hasty generalization,** one of many logical fallacies that can occur in argumentative writing. **Logical fallacies** are holes or lapses in reasoning and to be avoided. If you were to argue that the reader should consider only the present system of tipping or the one you propose, you will be guilty of **either–or reasoning,** which is false because it permits no middle ground such as requiring a minimum tip of 12 percent. Quote Kobe Bryant on the subject and you will be citing **false authority;** he knows basketball but not the restaurant industry. And obviously, if you call a 10-percent tipper a cheap idiot, you will be accused quite rightly of name calling, the **ad hominem** (to the person) fallacy.

Say you noticed one evening that as closing time loomed, your tips got smaller. Is that because people who dine late tip minimally or because your customers felt rushed or because someone miscalculated the tip or some unknown reason? If you conclude that people who dine late are poor tippers, you may well be mistaking a temporal relationship for a causal one. Two events may occur at times close to each other (small tip, late hour) without implying a valid cause-and-effect relationship. To confuse the two is called **post hoc reasoning.**

Advertising and political campaigns are good places to spot logical fallacies. A flyer asks you to vote for a candidate for the school board because she is a Vietnam veteran with a successful law practice, but the logic doesn't follow (a literal translation of the Latin term **non sequitur**). What does being a veteran and an attorney have to do with the duties of a member of the school board? And if the flyer goes on to maintain that because the candidate is a mother with three children she can understand the problems of students in public schools when you know that all three go to private schools, then you've spotted a **false analogy**—a double one: Public and private schools are quite different, and three children from the family of a lawyer are not typical of the public school student population.

Such a flyer is also guilty of **begging the question,** another fallacy. The main question for a school board election is "What can this person contribute?" Being a Vietnam veteran and the mother of three children doesn't answer that question. A **shifting definition** is another form of begging the question. If this hypothetical candidate also claims to be a "good citizen" and then goes on to define that term by example, citing service to her country and motherhood as proof, then as a voter you're left with a very narrow definition. Good citizenship involves much more.

Often when you read or hear about the holes in an argument, you may also hear the term **straw man.** With this technique (yet another form of begging the question), your attention is drawn away from the main point to focus on a minor one, with the hope that by demolishing it the main one will also suffer.

How can you appeal to reason, emotion, and persona?   The **appeal to reason,** what the ancient Greeks called *logos,* is crucial. To present a logical pattern of thought, you will probably find yourself drawing on one or more modes, particularly definition, comparison, and cause and effect. If, for instance, you have a part-time job at a fast-food franchise, you may have noticed that most of the other employees are also part-time. The situation may strike you as exploitive, and you want to write about it.

You might start sketching out a first draft with the example of your job, then define what part-time means, using cause and effect to argue that franchise companies that depend primarily on part-time labor exploit their workers to create greater profits for the company. As you work, you will find that you are laying out a line of reasoning, the assertions—probably the topic sentences for paragraphs or paragraph clusters—that support your thesis. You will also have to do some research so that you place your example in a larger context, showing that it is clearly typical. Then, armed with some facts and figures, you can test your thesis and supporting sentences:

1. Am I making an assertion? Test the sentence by checking to see if it states an opinion.
   If yes, go to question 2.
   If no, review pages 3–4 and 19 and revise the sentence.
2. Is the assertion supported by evidence? List the evidence and sources.
   If yes, go to question 3.
   If no, research the topic to gather more evidence.
3. Is the evidence sufficient? Check it to make sure it's directly related to the assertion.
   If yes, the assertion checks out.
   If no, gather more evidence.

If your thesis and supporting sentences check out, then you know your argument rests on reason.

Logical thinking must undergird all argumentative essays, even those that use an **appeal to emotion,** or *pathos*—an appeal that often rests on example, description, and narration. Paint a picture of a part-time worker who has two other jobs in order to pay the medical expenses of an autistic child and you may find yourself substituting emotion for reason.

The ethical appeal, or *ethos,* rests on a credible **persona** and is more subtle than the others; the writer is not appealing directly to the reader's emotions or intellect but instead is using his or her persona to lend credence to the essay's major assertion. To understand how persona functions, think of the last time you took an essay test. What you were writing was a mini argument maintaining that your answer to the question is a correct one. Your persona, which you probably didn't even think about, was intended to create a sense of authority, the idea that you knew what you were writing about. You are so used to writing within an academic context that the elements of your persona come naturally. The tone you use for essay tests is more formal than informal, which means that your choice of words, your diction, is more elevated than conversational. And if a technical vocabulary is appropriate—the vocabulary of physics, sociology, the arts, and the like—you use it.

Successful essay answers also use evidence and are tightly organized so that the line of thought is clear and compelling, all of which comes under the appeal of reason, but don't underestimate the appeal of persona. If two test answers contain the exact same information, the one that is written in the more analytical style that implies a more thoughtful response is apt to receive the higher grade.

How can you structure your argument? The thesis of an argumentative essay should be readily identifiable: It is the conviction that you want an audience to adopt. Sometimes the thesis may be stated in the title, but more often you will state your position early on, then back it up with evidence in the body of your essay. If you organize your ideas by moving from the general (the thesis) to the particular (the evidence), you are using **deductive reasoning.** Most of the argumentative essays you run across will be using this kind of logical organization. As for the order in which you choose to present the evidence on which your thesis rests, you'll probably arrange it from the least important to the most important so that the essay has some dramatic tension. Putting the most important first doesn't leave you anywhere to go, rather like knowing from the start that the butler did it.

Although sometimes you may want to put your thesis as your first sentence, usually you will want to lead up to it, *introduce* it in the literal sense. Often an argumentative essay will begin with a narrative or some explanation, ways of setting the scene so that when the thesis appears, it seems natural. As for the ending, you may want to return to the same narrative or information you started with, which is what Applebaum does, or call for action or point out what may happen unless your view is adopted.

Now and then, you'll find yourself reading an argument that is organized by moving from the particular to the general, from evidence to thesis. What you have then is called **inductive reasoning,** and it demands tight focus and control. Think of the essay's organization as a jigsaw puzzle. Your reader has to recognize each piece as a piece, and you have to build the evidence so that each one falls into a predetermined place. The completed picture is the thesis.

If you want to construct an essay using inductive reasoning, you may find it easier to do if in your first draft you state your thesis at the beginning, baldly, just so you stay on track. Then, when you've shaped the rest of the paper, you simply move the thesis from the beginning to the last paragraph, perhaps even the last sentence.

You'll find that the essays in this section represent both kinds of organization, so you'll have a chance to see how others have developed their ideas to argue a particular point.

Useful Terms

Ad hominem argument Name-calling, smearing the person instead of attacking the argument. A type of logical fallacy. Smearing the group the person belongs to instead of attacking the argument is called an *ad populum* logical fallacy.

Appeal to emotion Playing or appealing to the reader's emotions.

Appeal to persona The appeal of the writer's moral character that creates the impression that the writer can be trusted and, therefore, believed.

Appeal to reason Presenting evidence that is logical, well thought out, so as to be believed.

Argument The writer's major assertion and the evidence on which it is based.

Begging the question Arguing off the point, changing direction. A type of logical fallacy.

Deductive reasoning Reasoning that moves from the general to the particular, from the thesis to the evidence.

Either–or reasoning Staking out two extremes as the only alternatives and, therefore, excluding anything in between. A type of logical fallacy.

False analogy An analogy that does not stand up to logic. A type of logical fallacy.

False authority Citing an expert on one subject as an expert on another. A type of logical fallacy.

Hasty generalization Reasoning based on insufficient evidence, usually too few examples. A type of logical fallacy.

Inductive reasoning Reasoning that moves from the particular to the general, from the evidence to the thesis.

Logical fallacy An error in reasoning, a logical flaw that invalidates the argument.

Non sequitur Literally, it does not follow. No apparent link between points. A type of logical fallacy.

Persona The character of the writer that comes through from the prose.

Post hoc reasoning Assuming a causal relationship where a temporal one exists. A type of logical fallacy.

Shifting definition Changing the definition of a key term, a form of begging the question. A type of logical fallacy.

Straw man Attacking and destroying an irrelevant point instead of the main subject.

POINTERS FOR USING ARGUMENT

Exploring the Topic

1. **What position do you want to take toward your subject?** Are you arguing to get your audience to adopt your thesis or to go further and take action? What is your thesis? What action is possible?

2. **How is your audience apt to respond to your assertion if you state it baldly?** How much background do you need to provide? Do you need to use definition? What arguments can the reader bring against your assertion?

3. **What examples can you think of to illustrate your topic?** Are all of them from your own experience? What other sources can you draw on?

4. **How can you appeal to your reader's emotions?** How can you use example, description, and narration to carry your emotional appeal?

5. **How can you appeal to your reader's reason?** How can you use example, cause and effect, process, comparison and contrast, analogy, or division and classification to strengthen your logic?

6. **What tone is most appropriate to the kind of appeal you want to emphasize?** Does your persona fit that tone? How can you use persona to support your argument?

Drafting the Paper

1. **Know your reader.** Estimate how familiar your reader is with your topic and how, if at all, the reader may react to it emotionally. Keeping those ideas in mind, review how the various patterns of development may help you contend with your audience's knowledge and attitudes, and decide whether your primary appeal should be to emotion or to reason.

   Description, narration, and example lend themselves particularly well to emotional appeal; process, cause and effect, comparison and contrast, analogy, example, and division and classification are useful for rational appeal. Use definition to set the boundaries of your argument and its terms as well as to clear up anything the reader may not know.

(Continued)

Pointers for Using Argument *(Continued)*

2. **Know your purpose.** Depending on the predominant appeal you find most appropriate, your essay will argue a position using reason, though you may appeal to emotion to a lesser extent; you are trying to get your reader not only to understand your major assertion but also to adopt it and perhaps even to act on it. Short of that, a successful writer of argument must settle for the reader's "Well, I hadn't thought of it that way" or "Maybe I should reconsider."

   The greatest danger in argumentative writing is to write to people like yourself, ones who already agree with you. You need not think of your audience as actively hostile, but to stay on the argumentative track, it helps to reread constantly as you write, playing the devil's advocate.

3. **Acknowledge the opposition.** Even though your reader may be the ideal—someone who holds no definite opposing view and indeed is favorably inclined toward yours but hasn't really thought the topic through—you should bring out one or two of the strongest arguments against your position and demolish them. If you don't, the reader may, and there goes your essay. The ideal reader is also the thinking reader who says, "Yes, but...."

4. **Avoid logical pitfalls.** Logical fallacies can crop up in unexpected places; one useful way to test them is to check your patterns of development. If you have used examples, does your generalization or assertion follow? Sometimes the examples are too few to support the assertion, leading to a hasty generalization; sometimes the examples don't fit, leading to begging the question or arguing off the point or misusing authority; and sometimes the assertion is stated as an absolute, in which case the reader may think of an example that is the exception, destroying your point.

   If you have used analogy, double-check to see that the analogy can stand up to scrutiny by examining the pertinent aspects of the things compared. If you have used cause and effect, you need to be particularly careful. Check to see that the events you claim to have a causal relationship do not have a temporal one instead; otherwise, you fall into the post hoc fallacy. Also examine causal relationships to make sure that you have not merely assumed the cause in your statement of effect. If you claim "poor teaching is a major cause of the high dropout rate during the freshman year in college," you must prove that the teaching is poor; if you don't, you are arguing in a circle or begging the question.

Non sequiturs can also obscure cause-and-effect relationships when an element in the relationship is missing or nonexistent. Definition also sets some traps. Make sure your definition is not only fully stated but also commonly shared and consistent throughout.

5. **Be aware of your persona.** The ethical appeal, the rational appeal, and the emotional appeal are fundamental concepts of argument, and it is the persona, together with tone, that provides the ethical appeal. To put it simply, you need to be credible.

If you are writing on an issue you feel strongly about and, for example, are depending primarily on an appeal to reason, you don't want to let your dispassionate, logical persona slip and resort to name-calling (formally known as arguing ad hominem or ad populem). That's obvious.

Not so obvious, however, is some slip in diction or tone that reveals the hothead behind the cool pen. Your reader may feel manipulated or use the slip to discount your entire argument, all because you lost sight of the ethical appeal. Tone should vary, yes, but never to the point of discord.

6. **Place your point where it does the most good.** Put each of your paragraphs on a separate piece of paper so that you can rearrange their order as you would a hand of cards. Try out your major assertion in different slots. If you have it at the beginning, try it at the end and vice versa. Or extend the introduction so that the thesis comes closer to the middle of the paper. See which placement carries greater impact.

You may want to organize your material starting with examples that lead up to the position you wish to attack and to the conviction you are arguing for; in that case your thesis may occur somewhere in the middle third or at the end of the paper. On the other hand, you may want to use deduction—starting with the opposition, stating your position, and then spending 90 percent of the remaining essay supporting your case. Remember that you want to win your reader over, so put your thesis where it will do the greatest good.

Dance, Dance, Revolution

Barbara Ehrenreich

Essayist, novelist, journalist, activist, Barbara Ehrenreich has written extensively on almost every imaginable subject, though politics and the media are her prime targets. At last count, she has written 14 books in addition to being a regular contributor to Time, Harpers, *and* The Nation *as well as numerous other magazines. She has her own blog, and her work also appears in the electronic magazine* Z. *Her voice is often heard on* Today, Nightline, *and National Public Radio, among other radio and television shows and stations. Ehrenreich turned to writing after earning a PhD in biology from The Rockefeller University. About her career change, she says "Sure, I could have had more stability and financial security if I'd stuck to science or teaching. But I chose adventure and I've never for a moment regretted it." For a full account of her life and work, check out http://barbaraehrenreich.com/. There you'll find her complete list of publications, but perhaps her best known book is* Nickel and Dimed: On (Not) Getting by in America *(2001). Her most recent book is the satiric commentary* This Land Is Their Land: Reports from a Divided Nation *(2008). The following essay however, is more closely related to her scholarly* Dancing in the Streets: A History of Collective Joy *(2007) and was published in* The New York Times *on June 3, 2007.*

What to Look For Ehrenreich was bothered by what she thought was an unfair regulation, so in tackling it she places the activity the regulation is aimed at into a much larger historical context. As you read Ehrenreich's essay, keep track of the immediate and historical contexts for her argument so you can understand what they add to her credibility. Like Ehrenreich, you may want to set your personal opinion in a larger context so that it becomes a general stand, not a personal beef.

1   Compared with most of the issues that the venerable civil liberties lawyer Norman Siegel takes up, this one may seem like the ultimate in urban frivolity: Late last month, he joined hundreds of hip-hoppers, salsa dancers, Lindy Hoppers and techno-heads boogying along Fifth Avenue to protest New York City's 80-year-old restrictions on dancing in bars.

2   But disputes over who can dance, how and where, are at least as old as civilization, and arise from the longstanding conflict between the forces of order and hierarchy on the one hand, and the deep human craving for free-spirited joy on the other.

3   New York's cabaret laws limit dancing to licensed venues. They date back to the Harlem Renaissance, which had created the unsettling prospect of interracial dancing.

4   For decades, no one paid much attention to the laws until Mayor Rudolph Giuliani, bent on turning Manhattan into a giant mall/food court, decided to get tough. Today, the city far more famous for its night life than its Sunday services has only about 170 venues where it is legal to get up and dance—hence last month's danced protest, as well as an earlier one in February.

5   Dust-ups over dancing have become a regular feature of urban life. Dance clubs all over the country have faced the threat of shutdowns because the dancing sometimes spills over into the streets. While neighbors annoyed by sleepless nights or the suspicion of illegal drug use may be justified in their concerns, conflict over public dancing has a long history—one that goes all the way back to the ancient Mediterranean world.

6   The Greeks danced to worship their gods—especially Dionysus, the god of ecstasy. But then the far more strait-laced Romans cracked down viciously on Dionysian worship in 186 B.C., even going on to ban dancing schools for Roman children a few decades later. The early Christians incorporated dance into their liturgy, despite church leaders' worries about immodesty. But at the end of the fourth century, the archbishop of Constantinople issued the stern pronouncement: "For where there is a dance, there is also the Devil."

7   The Catholic Church did not succeed in prohibiting dancing within churches until the late Middle Ages, and in doing so perhaps inadvertently set off the dance "manias" that swept Belgium, Germany and Italy starting in the 14th century. Long attributed to some form of toxin—ergot or spider venom—the manias drove thousands of people to the streets day and night, mocking and menacing the priests who tried to stop them.

8   In northern Europe, Calvinism brought a hasty death to the old public forms of dancing, along with the costuming, masking and feasting that had usually accompanied them. All that survived, outside of vestiges of "folk dancing," were the elites' tame, indoor ballroom dances, fraught, as in today's "Dancing With the Stars," with anxiety over a possible misstep. When Europeans fanned out across the globe

in the 18th and 19th centuries, the colonizers made it a priority to crush the danced rituals of indigenous people, which were seen as savagery, devil worship and prelude to rebellion.

9   To the secular opponents of public dancing, it is always a noxious source of disorder and, in New York's case, noise. But hardly anyone talks about what is lost when the music stops and the traditional venues close. Facing what he saw as an epidemic of melancholy, or what we would now call depression, the 17th-century English writer Robert Burton placed much of the blame on the Calvinist hostility to "dancing, singing, masking, mumming and stage plays." In fact, in some cultures, ecstatic dance has been routinely employed as a cure for emotional disorders. Banning dancing may not cause depression, but it removes an ancient cure for it.

10   The need for public, celebratory dance seems to be hardwired into us. Rock art from around the world depicts stick figures dancing in lines and circles at least as far back as 10,000 years ago. According to some anthropologists, dance helped bond prehistoric people together in the large groups that were necessary for collective defense against marauding predators, both animals and human. While language also serves to forge community, it doesn't come close to possessing the emotional urgency of dance. Without dance, we risk loneliness and anomie.

11   Dancing to music is not only mood-lifting and community-building; it's also a uniquely human capability. No other animals, not even chimpanzees, can keep together in time to music. Yes, we can live without it, as most of us do most of the time, but why not reclaim our distinctively human heritage as creatures who can generate our own communal pleasures out of music and dance?

12   This is why New Yorkers—as well as all Americans faced with anti-dance restrictions—should stand up and take action; and the best way to do so is by high stepping into the streets.

ORGANIZATION AND IDEAS

1. What paragraph or paragraphs introduce Ehrenreich's essay? How well does it relate to what follows? Given the rest of the essay, is the introduction too short or too long? How so?

2. Summarize the arguments—both religious and secular—Ehrenreich presents against dancing. Her historical accounts are based on general knowledge, which is why she sees no need to document them. Do any surprise you, and if so why? What would be the effect of documentation?

3. To what extent does cause and effect play a role in the essay? Where in the essay is it most prominent?
4. Consider the positive claims Ehrenreich makes for dancing. To what extent do you find them credible? Do you agree?
5. In paragraph 12, the essay concludes with a call to action. What do you think of it?

TECHNIQUE AND STYLE

1. To what extent does Ehrenreich take account of objections to her thesis?
2. Reread the essay with an eye out for Ehrenreich's diction. What words strike you as formal? Informal? What does her choice of words add to or detract from the essay?
3. Given your answers to the previous question, how would you describe Ehrenreich's tone? How serious is she?
4. It's possible to read the essay as a call for a Dionysian take-to-the-woods free-for-all. To what extent is that interpretation valid?
5. You can also read the essay as setting out two extremes—repression or anything goes. If it's possible that Ehrenreich also implies but does not state a middle ground, what then is her subject? Her thesis?

SUGGESTIONS FOR WRITING

Journal

1. How well do you think the title fits the essay? Explain your opinion.
2. To what extent does dance play a role in your life? If it plays no role at all, explain why.

Essay

1. Throughout history, as Ehrenreich explains, various forces have disapproved of dance, sometimes to the extent of banning it. The same is true of other forms of artistic expression. Use the Web to research a particular case of censorship, evaluating the strength of the arguments involved. Choose a particular example from one of the following categories or another of your own choosing.
   books
   paintings
   dances
   song lyrics
   plays
2. From the 1920s on (and probably before), various dances have become "the rage." You might think of the Charleston or any of the more recent ones of the 1960s on to the present. Some dances have regional

popularity, such as western line dancing, and some have ethnic roots as in the polka. Use the Web to research a particular kind of dance so you can analyze the positive and negative responses it generates. You may find yourself arguing for its greater acceptance or promoting its popularity or declaring it downright silly, and so on. You'll probably have no problem finding an argumentative position.

Veiled Insult

Anne Applebaum

After finishing her undergraduate degree at Yale University, Ann Applebaum was awarded a Marshall scholarship to the London School of Economics and then studied at St. Antony's College at Oxford University before beginning her career in journalism in the late 1980s. Living in Poland and later in London, she covered the upheavals in Eastern Europe for The Economist, *wrote a column for London's* Evening Standard, *and became the deputy editor of the British magazine* The Spectator. *By 2002 she was living in Washington, D.C., and a member of* The Washington Post's *editorial board. Between East and West: Across the Borderlands of Europe, Applebaum's first book, was published in 1995 and won the Adolph Bentinck Prize for European nonfiction.* Gulag: A History *(2003), her second book, provides a detailed history of the Soviet Union's concentration camp system, an account that earned a Pulitzer Prize for general nonfiction. Concentrating on foreign affairs, she now writes a weekly column for* The Washington Post, *where the following essay appeared on October 24, 2006.*

What to Look For   Before you read Applebaum's essay, think about the role religious freedom plays in your life and in the lives of others whose religions differ from yours. Then as you read the essay, notice how Applebaum tries to deal with the subject.

1   Quite a long time ago, having briefly joined the herd of 20-something backpackers that eternally roams Southeast Asia, I found myself in Bali. Like all of the other 20-somethings, I carefully

read the Lonely Planet backpacker's guide to Indonesia and learned, among other things, that it was considered improper for women to wear shorts or trousers when entering Balinese temples. I dutifully purchased a Balinese sarong and, looking awkward and foreign, wore it while visiting temples. I didn't want to cause offense.

2   I thought of that long-ago incident during a visit last week to London, where a full-fledged shouting match has broken out over Muslim women who choose to wear the veil. This particular argument had begun because a teaching assistant in Yorkshire refused to remove her veil—a *niqab,* which covers the whole body except for the eyes—in the presence of male teachers, which was much of the time. She was fired; she went to court—and a clutch of senior British politicians entered the fray.

3   Jack Straw, the former foreign secretary, called the full-face veil "a visible statement of separation and of difference." Tony Blair, the prime minister, added that he could "see the reason" for the teaching assistant to be suspended.

4   What followed was predictable: accusations of racism, charges of discrimination and disagreement about whether the veil was even a valid topic of discussion. If Blair and Straw were really concerned about Muslim women, shouldn't they be more interested in under-age marriages, or wife beating, or something more important?

5   The short answer is, yes, probably. But the curious fact is that the veil, as a political issue, won't go away. The French have banned not only the full veil but head scarves in state schools. Some German regions have banned the head scarf for civil servants too, and they are not permitted in Turkish universities at all. Slowly, the issue is coming to the United States: Just this month a Michigan judge dismissed a small-claims court case filed by a Muslim woman because she refused to remove her full-face veil while testifying.

6   Critics call the veil a symbol of female oppression or rejection of Western values. Defenders say that it is a symbol of religious faith and that it allows women to be "free" in a different sense—free from cosmetics, from fashion and from unwanted male attention. Debate about the veil inevitably leads to discussions of female emancipation, religious freedom and the assimilation, or lack thereof, of Muslim communities in the West.

7   And yet, at a much simpler level, surely it is also true that the full-faced veil—the *niqab, burqa* or *chador*—causes such deep reactions in the West not so much because of its political or religious symbolism but because it is extremely impolite. Just as it is considered rude

to enter a Balinese temple wearing shorts, so, too, is it considered rude, in a Western country, to hide one's face. We wear masks when we want to frighten, when we are in mourning or when we want to conceal our identities. To a Western child—or even an adult—a woman clad from head to toe in black looks like a ghost. Thieves and actors hide their faces in the West; honest people look you straight in the eye.

8   Given that polite behavior is required in other facets of their jobs, it doesn't seem to me in the least offensive to require schoolteachers or civil servants to show their faces when dealing with children or the public. If Western tourists can wear sarongs in Balinese temples to show respect for the locals, so too can religious Muslim women show respect for the children they teach and the customers they serve by leaving their head scarves on, but removing their full-faced veils.

9   It would, of course, be outrageous if Tony Blair or the French government were to ban veils altogether—just as it is outrageous that Saudi Arabia bans churches and even forbids priests from entering the country. But just because authorities persecute Christians and Jews in some parts of the Muslim world, that doesn't mean we need to emulate them. In their private lives, Muslim women living in the West should be free to use veils or head scarves as they wish. But freedom to practice religion in the West shouldn't imply freedom to hold jobs that impinge on that practice. An Orthodox Jew should not have an absolute right to work in a restaurant that is open only on Saturdays. A Quaker cannot join the Army and then state that his religion prohibits him from fighting. By the same token, a Muslim woman who wants to cover her face has no absolute right to work in a school or an office where face-to-face conversations are part of the job.

10   It isn't religious discrimination or anti-Muslim bias to tell her that she must be polite to the natives, respect the local customs, try to speak some of the local patois—and uncover her face.

ORGANIZATION AND IDEAS

1. To what extent is the essay organized around the particular and the general? Trace how Applebaum uses the two throughout her essay.
2. Applebaum's essay depends heavily on example. Choose one that stands out as necessary and effective and explain why it is so.
3. Paragraphs 6 and 7 address the veil as symbol. What other associations do you have with the veil? Might those other associations have a place in the essay? Why or why not?

4. Trace the references to freedom in the essay. What kinds of freedoms does Applebaum mention? Does she discuss them fully enough?

5. What is Applebaum's thesis and how effective is its placement?

TECHNIQUE AND STYLE

1. Reread the essay paying particular attention to the links between paragraphs. Circle the connections between one paragraph and another. What do you notice?

2. Applebaum uses an analogy in paragraph 8. Test its validity. How valid is it?

3. Paragraph 9 uses a number of comparisons. What do they add to the essay? How valid are they?

4. Think about the essay's tone, use of examples, structure, and thesis. Explain the degree to which you find Applebaum's position a balanced one.

5. In a short space, Applebaum mentions Bali, England, France, Germany, Turkey, and Saudi Arabia as well as the United States. What does she gain by these allusions?

SUGGESTIONS FOR WRITING

Journal

1. Think about a time you unintentionally violated a dress code and write about how it made you feel. To what extent was the code fair?

2. Consider the pun in the essay's title. Explain the ways in which the pun may relate to Applebaum's tone.

Essay

1. The word *manners* may bring to mind tea cups, fussiness, and a la-di-dah attitude, but it is also used to describe accepted or expected behavior that smoothes social interaction. Think about the manners that are exhibited in various situations and argue for an appropriate code. Suggestions:
football games
basketball games
movie theaters
rock concerts
city driving
Your tone could range from serious to sarcastic or ironic.

2. Our Constitution guarantees freedom of religion, but it has also been used to justify some practices well outside society's norms—practices such as animal sacrifice, the use of hallucinogenics, and polygamy. Use the Web to research one such practice so you can analyze the validity of the arguments for and against it.

Should the Drinking Age Be Lowered?

John Cloud

Controversy is nothing new for John Cloud. He was a senior writer at
Washington City Paper, *a weekly that covers what's going on in D.C.
including book and music reviews and upcoming events but also, as
the paper declares on its Web site, "profiles, investigative pieces,
polemical essays, 'Talk of the Town' type articles, and stories about
local institutions." While at the paper, Cloud wrote pieces that fit all
those categories, experience that has served him well at* Time, *where
he started as a staff writer in 1997 and is now features editor. You
may have seen Cloud's name on the front of* Time, *as he has written a
fair number of cover stories on topics as varied as gay teens, euthanasia, the drug Ecstasy, and the controversial political commentator
Anne Coulter. "Should the Drinking Age Be Lowered?" Cloud's essay
that follows, was published in* Time *on June 6, 2008.*

What to Look For   You may well find yourself writing an essay in response to a specific proposal, which is the situation that prompted Cloud
to write the following essay. When you read the essay, notice how Cloud
provides the reader with general background information and how
he addresses the proposal and its authors directly. You can apply those
techniques to your own writing.

1   Every year around this time, millions of American kids graduate
from high school, throw massive parties and get drunk. Police end
up arresting a lot of these kids, causing them legal trouble for
months or even years. So, every year around this time, there's
a new debate about whether we should lower or even abolish the
legal drinking age.

2   What's different this time is that an entire organization—a conspicu-
ously sober group led by a former college president—now exists to
promote the idea that drinking should be lowered from 21 to 18. John
McCardell Jr., an esteemed historian of the American South and former
head of Middlebury College, founded Choose Responsibility in 2006 to
argue in favor of licensing 18-to-20-year-olds to drink after they have

completed an exhaustive 42 hours of instruction in the history, chemistry, psychology and sociology of alcohol—which could even include sitting in on an AA session for three hours.

3   McCardell has won some favorable news coverage, and when I first e-mailed him last year, I told him his idea sounded persuasive. After all, in almost every other legal and cultural respect, you're an adult at 18. You can vote, adopt children, sign up for Iraq or become a commercial pilot at 18. Treating alcohol differently helps turn it into a holy grail of adulthood. In a 224-page white paper he co-authored, McCardell also argues that raising the minimum age to 21—as states did after the federal government threatened to withhold highway funds in 1984—"forced alcohol consumption behind the closed doors of [dorms] and fraternity basements. Always unsupervised, done in secret and too often excessive, this style of drinking has no doubt been responsible for the alarming rise in rates of so-called 'binge' drinking seen at colleges."

4   McCardell's argument seems logical, but it falls apart once you look at the statistics on underage drinking. First of all, while binge drinking is a serious problem, the data do not show that it has gotten worse since states raised their drinking age. As researchers John Schulenberg of the University of Michigan and Jennifer Maggs of Penn State point out in a 2002 *Journal of Studies on Alcohol* paper, "during the past two decades, despite many social, demographic, political and economic changes—and despite dramatic shifts in cigarette and illicit drug use—rates of frequent heavy drinking among those ages 19 to 22 have shifted little." According to the University of Michigan's Monitoring the Future study, the proportion of those 19- to 22-year-olds who reported consuming five or more drinks in a row in the two weeks prior to being surveyed actually fell from 40.7% in 1984 to 38.1% in 2006. And no researchers have documented an increase in the percentage of alcohol-poisoning deaths among college students, although the raw number has probably increased with the growing college population.

5   There's a more basic problem: If the drinking age is lowered to 18, who is to provide the supervision that McCardell suggests? Surely not bar owners who want to sell them as many drinks as possible. It's unclear why shifting the venue of drinking from frat houses to bars will help solve the problem of hard-core student drinking.

6   Finally, lowering the drinking age to 18 would stop infantilizing college students, but it would probably kill more of them in traffic accidents. In 2006, 2,121 people ages 16 to 20 died in alcohol-related

fatalities on U.S. roads, according to data compiled for me by the National Highway Traffic Safety Administration; in 1984, the figure was 4,612. McCardell has argued that improvements in seat-belt use and car safety partly explain these gains, but traffic fatalities unrelated to alcohol have increased 21% in that age group during the same period (the raw numbers are 2,915 in 1984 and 3,537 in 2006).

7   Choose Responsibility supporters have also claimed that other countries that haven't raised their drinking ages—including Canada and the United Kingdom—saw their drunk-driving fatalities drop even faster than in the U.S. But that's simply not true. In 1984, 45% of U.S. drivers killed in accidents turned out to have been legally drunk. That percentage was just 32% in 2006. By contrast, the percentage of drivers killed in Great Britain who were drunk actually rose slightly, from 19% in 1989 to 21% in 2005.

8   McCardell is right that the U.S. has an odd and dysfunctional relationship with alcohol, and his voice is refreshing in a debate dominated by MADD pieties. But lowering the drinking age is going too far.

ORGANIZATION AND IDEAS

1. Think about the number of topics Cloud mentions in his essay—drunk high school students, McCardell's proposal, binge drinking, drunk driving, unsupervised drinking, the legal age for drinking, society's attitude toward drinking. What is his main subject and thesis? State Cloud's theses as fully as possible.

2. Paragraphs 1–3 explain the background to Cloud's argument. How thoroughly does he explain it? What would you like to know more about and why?

3. Cloud relies on using topic sentences for several of his paragraphs. Where does he use them and how well do they function?

4. McCardell's proposal involves a fairly stiff addition to the college curriculum (paragraph 2). How realistic is it? To what degree would it help solve the problem?

5. Cloud and McCardell agree "the U.S. has an odd and dysfunctional relationship with alcohol." To what extent does that statement ring true?

TECHNIQUE AND STYLE

1. Reread the essay paying particular attention to Cloud's appeals to reason, emotion, and persona. Which one predominates? How effective is that choice?

2. Given what you answered to the previous question, how fair is Cloud? How balanced is his line of argument?

3. Try testing Cloud's reasoning against the logical fallacies outlined in the chapter's introduction. What do you find?

4. Go through the essay so you can list Cloud's sources. How reliable are they? How fair? How thorough is his research?

5. Think about the way Cloud constructs his argument, his use of sources, and his appeals. Describe his tone as fully as possible.

SUGGESTIONS FOR WRITING

Journal

1. Cloud states "lowering the drinking age to 18 would stop infantilizing college students, but it would probably kill more of them in traffic accidents." To what extent does the present law "infantilize" college students?

2. If the legal age for drinking were lowered, what would be the effect on your campus? Describe what you think would probably occur.

Essay

1. Think of an action that was considered acceptable in the past but today is either questionable or unacceptable. Fifty years ago, for instance, no one thought much about the hazards of smoking, nor of cholesterol levels, nor of needing to inspect meat. Segregation was acceptable, as were other forms of racism. Choose a subject and think about the ethics involved and how present knowledge has changed how we live. Other suggestions:

the sale of cigarettes

the advertising of alcoholic beverages

the popularity of natural foods

the sale of diet products

2. The combination of economic downturn, global warming, and finite fossil fuels may well lead to a number of proposed regulations. Mandatory mileage limits for cars are already on the books, and there's been some discussion of a mandatory—and lower—national speed limit. Consider a problem that we may face in the next five to ten years and think about possible regulations that could be proposed to lessen or solve that problem. The possible regulations you come up with may be as realistic or far-fetched as you like. Once you have some ideas to work with, choose one and research it so you can construct an argument in favor of it or against it. If you like, you could write a satiric essay.

Old Enough to Fight, Old Enough to Drink

Debra J. Saunders

Debra J. Saunders has written extensively on a variety of hot issues—the "supersize" financial bailout, the race card, medical ethics, animal rights, assisted suicide, just to name a few—all of which reflect her passionate interest in politics. After working as a writer and researcher first for a Republican lobbying firm in California and then for a Republican media consulting firm in Boston, Saunders became a columnist and editorial writer for the Los Angeles Daily News. *She now writes a column for the* San Francisco Chronicle *three times a week and her work is syndicated, appearing in* The Wall Street Journal, National Review, *and* Reason Magazine, *among others. On the Web, you can find her work at http://www.rasmussenreports.com and the Heritage Foundation's http://townhall.com/; or you might see her on television's* The News Hour, CNN, *or* Politically Incorrect. *She is also the author of* The World According to Gore *(2000). The following essay appeared on September 14, 2008, in* Rasmussen Reports, *"one of the few political sites to attract roughly equal numbers of Republicans, Democrats, and unaffiliated voters."*

What to Look For   It's possible to think of an argumentative essay as an invitation to a conversation, and one way to involve the reader is to be aware of your tone, the attitude you have toward your subject and your reader. Look for examples of Saunders' tone so that you can think about how to shape your own.

1   At age 18, an American can enlist in the military, vote, sign a contract, get married, have an operation—hey, in California, a 14-year-old can have an abortion without telling her parents—but he cannot buy a beer. Not legally, anyway.

2   It makes absolutely no sense, and it is shameful that my generation, which won the right to vote at age 18, continues to infantilize people who are allowed to make life-and-death decisions on every issue, save one. We believe in rights—except for college-age kids—even if they are serving in the military.

3   Enter the Amethyst Initiative, pushed by former Middlebury College President John McCardell and signed by more than 100 college presidents, which is pushing for Washington "to reopen public debate over the drinking age." According to McCardell, it is time for Washington to reconsider a 1984 measure, signed by President Ronald Reagan, that withheld 10 percent of highway funds from states that had a legal drinking age lower than 21.

4   The reason for the Amethyst Project—named for a gemstone believed to be "an antidote to the negative effects of intoxication"—is simple. Many college officials do not believe that the 21-year-old drinking age works. They believe that most students break the law. Worse, McCardell argues, they believe that the age fosters a "culture of dangerous, clandestine binge-drinking."

5   Does the law work? How many kids break it? More than half of 18-to-20-year-olds, according to the Department of Health and Human Services' latest survey on drug and alcohol use, reported that they drank alcohol in the last month alone, despite legal prohibitions. College students were more likely to drink than their same-age peers not attending college. So apparently it doesn't work. I submit that there is something wrong—something that breeds contempt—with a law that most people break.

6   The primary opposition to the initiative comes from Mothers Against Drunk Driving. MADD argues that if the drinking age is lowered, then more high school students will drink. That may well be true. Although it does seem that teens have scant trouble finding alcohol—or illegal drugs—as it is. The same national study found that close to 30 percent of 16- and 17-year-olds drank alcohol in the past month, while 13 percent smoked marijuana.

7   MADD also argues that the 21-year-old drinking age saves lives. Amethyst Initiative's McCardell argues that there was no big dip in fatalities when the drinking age was raised. Instead, there has been a small steady decline in drunk-driving fatalities over the years as MADD's work rightly has stigmatized drunk driving—the term "designated driver" came into use in the 1980s—and improved car safety has saved lives as well.

8   MADD Chief Executive Officer Chuck Hurley notes that several studies have found that the 21-year-old drinking age saves lives. As the Associated Press reported, a survey of research from the United States and other countries by the Centers for Disease Control and Prevention concluded that the 21-year-old drinking age has saved lives.

9   By that account, then, raising the drinking age to 25 or 30 or 40 would save lives, too. But there is this thing called freedom. And freedom should apply to men and women old enough for military service, old enough to get married and old enough to have had an abortion (four years before).

10   There is something nasty in the way MADD takes on the critics. "Parents should think twice before sending their teens to these colleges or any others that have waved the white flag on underage and binge-drinking policies," MADD President Laura Dean-Mooney warned. This is MADD's way of trying to stifle debate.

11   MADD execs also have charged that university presidents want to rethink the drinking age to make their lives easier—as if they don't care about students—or to protect against legal liability. Now maybe the argument that lowering the age will reduce binge drinking is just plain wrong, but it also is false to argue that the 21-year-old limit has stopped teen drinking.

12   How can we trust 18-year-olds to vote or run for office, but not to legally buy a beer?

ORGANIZATION AND IDEAS

1. Paragraphs 1 and 2 set out the problem and Saunders' stand. How well do they function as an introduction?
2. Saunders' thesis is obvious, but her reasons behind it are a bit less so. List those reasons and the paragraphs in which they are presented. How valid are they?
3. Paragraphs 6–11 discuss the views of Mothers Against Drunk Driving (MADD). How fairly does Saunders present those views?
4. Paragraph 11 imputes suspect motives to the Amethyst Project's proposal. To what extent do you think those motives are accurate? What evidence can you find to support your opinion?
5. Reexamine the last paragraph. How easy is it to turn around Saunders' point and argue that 18-year-olds should not be allowed to vote or run for office? To what extent is Saunders' question rhetorical?

TECHNIQUE AND STYLE

1. Reread paragraphs 1 and 2. To what extent do they set the author's tone? How would you describe that tone?
2. Evaluate the sources Saunders uses to construct her argument. Should she have used more? What other sources might have helped support her thesis?
3. In paragraph 9, Saunders' first sentence draws an analogy. How valid is it?

4. Reexamine the last sentence in paragraph 9 and review the list of "Useful Terms" on p. 242. Which, if any, apply to Saunders' line of thinking? How so?
5. Consider Saunders' tone and line of thinking. Does her essay appeal primarily to emotion? Reason? Persona? What evidence can you find to support your opinion?

SUGGESTIONS FOR WRITING

Journal

1. The biographical information about Saunders explains that she is a conservative. To what extent does her position on the legal age for drinking fit that image?
2. Both the essay and the Amethyst Initiative take for granted that underage drinking is a problem on college campuses. Think about your own campus. How much of a problem is it?

Essay

1. Ask any advisor or counselor at a college or university about problems, and that person will probably reel off a list, among them:
   exhaustion
   drugs
   binge drinking
   cheating
   eating disorders
   Select one of these topics or another of your own choosing, narrow your subject, research it, take a position, and then write an essay using sources to support that position.
2. In paragraph 1, Saunders points out the number of actions an 18-year-old can take legally. Choose one of them and argue that it should or should not remain legal for this age group.

College Life

Chip Bok

It's hard to pick up a newspaper, flip to the editorial pages, and not see a political cartoon by Chip Bok. You may also see his work in magazines such as Newsweek, Time, *and* The Week, *and among the Sunday collections in* The New York Times. *He was declared Editorial Cartoonist of the Year by* The Week *in 2007, has been honored by the National Cartoonists Society, and received the H. L. Mencken Award as well as being named a finalist for the Pulitzer Prize (1997). Since 1987, he has been the editorial cartoonist for the* Akron Beacon Journal, *though his work is syndicated and runs in over 100 other newspapers. His cartoons have been collected in two books—*Bok!: The 9.11 Crisis in Political Cartoons *(2002) and* The Recent History of the United States in Political Cartoons: A Look Bok *(2005). And in 2008 he collaborated with White House correspondent Helen Thomas by illustrating the children's book* The Great White House Breakout. *The following cartoon was published on August 25, 2008.*

The Other Coast

Adrian Raeside

The Other Coast *is the name of Adrian Raeside's comic strip, a name that makes sense given that Raeside was born in New Zealand, moved to England as a teenager, and then later settled in Canada, where he now draws for the Victoria, British Columbia,* Victoria Times Colonist. *His work is syndicated and appears in over 150 newspapers both in Canada and the United States as well as Japan and Russia. An animator as well as editorial cartoonist, Raeside has worked extensively on animated children's shows for Turner Broadcasting and Children's Television Workshop and has written scripts for a number of animated series. In addition, he has illustrated and written a number of children's books. You can check out his humor in his books with titles such as* There Goes the Neighbourhood: An Irreverent History of Canada *(1992),* The Demented Decade *(1993), and* This Is Your First Rock Garden, Isn't It?: An Other Coast Collection *(2005). Better still, take a look at his Web site: http://www.raesidecartoon.com/bio/index.html. The following cartoon was published on August 22, 2007.*

The Other Coast

FOR DISCUSSION

1. Who is depicted in Bok's cartoon? Why might he have chosen those figures?
2. Why might Raeside have chosen Lindsay Lohan and Paris Hilton? The woman sitting on the sofa?
3. What does each drawing contribute to the debate over under-age drinking?

4. How does each drawing contribute a different perspective to the essays by Cloud and Saunders?

5. Consider each cartoon as a political statement on the issue of abusive drinking. What thesis would you give to each and why?

SUGGESTIONS FOR WRITING

Journal

Of the two, which cartoon do you prefer and why? Make specific reference to the drawings to support your point.

Essay

Make a short list of subjects that interest you, choose one or two, and then bring up http://www.cartoonistgroup.com. On both sides of the Web page, you'll see search engines. On the left, all you need to do is type in the cartoonist or topic you're interested in; on the right, you'll see ways to search the catalogue. For each of the categories—Who, What, When, Where, Why—you'll see a list that concludes with "and more." Click that to see the complete file of headings in the group. Once you've brought up the cartoons that relate to your topic, look around to see what appeals to you. Perhaps the work of a particular cartoonist appeals to you, or maybe it's a subject that draws you in. At that point you'll probably be able to come up with a working thesis and chase down the drawings to support your point.

Guest Workers and the U.S. Heritage

Jay Bookman

Jay Bookman holds degrees in history and journalism from Pennsylvania State University. After writing for newspapers in Washington, Nevada, and Massachusetts, he joined the staff of The Atlanta Journal-Constitution *and is now that paper's deputy editorial page writer. His columns appear on the editorial page twice weekly and are carried by other papers as well. His interests range from national and state politics to technology and the environment, the latter leading to his book* Caught in the Current: Searching for Simplicity in the Technological Age *(2004). Bookman's work has earned him recognition from various environmental groups such as the Wilderness Society and the National Wildlife Federation, and he has also received the Aldo Leopold Award, as well as the Scripps Howard and National Headliner awards. For his editorial work, he won a Eugene Pulliam Fellowship from the Society of Professional Journalists. The essay below appeared in the Austin* American-Statesman *on April 4, 2006.*

What to Look For When you think about an issue that you want to take an argumentative stand on, you might try the approach that Bookman uses: analyzing the problem and the possible solutions. He discusses various solutions others have proposed, finds them unsatisfactory, and concludes with his own.

1   If the American people decide that 12 million illegal immigrants should be removed and sent back home, fine, we can try to do that.

2   The process would be hard and expensive and brutally inhumane at times, and it could never be entirely successful. But if we hardened our hearts and emptied our wallets, we could probably come somewhat close to achieving that goal.

3   Of course, banishing those millions from our borders would also mean that we would do without the labor they now provide in industries from construction to hotels and restaurants to agriculture to food processing. Some Americans—generally the most rabid and extremist

among us—are ready to make that deal anyway, and there are politicians in Washington willing to pander to that crowd, at least in theory.

4   Others, however, are trying to find a way to retain the labor that illegal immigrants provide without offering them the right to live here permanently, let alone the right to pursue citizenship. It's an effort to solve a politically tough problem by cutting the baby in half, placating anti-immigrant fervor without denying American business the cheap, docile work force it relies upon.

5   That is in essence the proposal championed by President Bush, who advocates "legalizing" millions of immigrants now here illegally, but only on a temporary basis. After working several years, the temporary "guest workers" would be forced to return to their home countries to be replaced by new temporary workers.

6   That proposal has been condemned by extremists—most of them in Bush's own party—as offering "amnesty" to those who broke the law in coming here, as if punishment were more important than solving the problem. The more serious problem with that approach is practical; it assumes that workers will return home once their legal status has expired, and that's unlikely to happen.

7   It's also important to think about the guest worker approach in moral terms, in terms of the values that we claim to honor as Americans.

8   Under a guest worker policy, we will let the immigrants come here by the millions, but only temporarily. We will let them mangle their hands in our poultry plants and salt our farmlands with the sweat off their brows and break their backs at our construction sites and raise our children as nannies and clean our homes as maids, all at cut-rate wages.

9   But we will not allow them to dream—for themselves or their children—of sharing in the future they help to build here.

10   In other words, we are willing to let them serve us but not join us; they must by law be held apart and beneath us. We will import them to serve as a perpetually rotating servant class, and we will do so even while pretending to still honor that most American of principles, "that all men are created equal."

11   That system of second-class citizenship—far from slavery, but far from the full range of human rights as well—has precedent in American history. In colonial times, more than half of those who immigrated from Europe came here not as free people but as indentured servants.

12   In return for the cost of passage to the New World, they agreed to be legally bound to an employer for a number of years, unable

to marry without permission and with no say over where they lived or how they worked. They could even be sold to another boss.

13 But even back then, when the period of bonded indenture ended—usually after seven years—the servant was freed and allowed to take his or her place as a full citizen.

14 In reality, there is nothing all that complicated about drafting a practical, humane policy on illegal immigration. It would have three basic components:

- Tighter border security, to cut off as much as possible the supply of illegal workers coming into this country;
- Much more effective enforcement against illegal employers, to reduce as much as possible the demand for illegal workers;
- A way to deal effectively and humanely with the illegal immigrants already here.

15 Any proposed solution that does not include all three components is neither workable nor serious. But in a consideration that is just as important, any proposal that condemns millions to a permanent menial class, even while profiting from their labor, is beneath us as a country and a betrayal of all we are supposed to represent.

ORGANIZATION AND IDEAS

1. What paragraph or paragraphs introduce the essay? How effective is that introduction?
2. Paragraphs 8–10 discuss the drawbacks of a guest worker program. What are they? How are they related to American "values"?
3. Bookman draws an analogy between a guest worker program and indentured servitude. Explain the degree to which the analogy is accurate.
4. State Bookman's thesis in your own words. What words or sentences did you draw on in Bookman's essay to form your statement?
5. In paragraph 14, Bookman spells out three "basic components" of a "practical, humane policy on illegal immigration." To what extent is his overall argument weakened by his not fleshing out the third component?

TECHNIQUE AND STYLE

1. Take a good look at the verbs in paragraph 8. What effects do you think Bookman wants to achieve by choosing those verbs?
2. Where in the essay do you find examples of loaded language? What effect does it have on you?

3. Read the last paragraph out loud with your ear tuned to the way it sounds. What alliteration do you find? What purpose does it serve?

4. How would you characterize Bookman's persona? Given what he says in the essay and how he says it, what sort of person does he appear to be?

5. Reread the essay, marking the various places where Bookman appeals to emotion, reason, and his own persona. Which appeal is dominant? What evidence supports your view?

SUGGESTIONS FOR WRITING

Journal

1. Choose a sentence from the essay that strikes you as particularly effective and explain why you find it so.

2. What other titles can you think of for the essay? Which do you prefer and why?

Essay

1. Immigration is such a hot topic that it has spun off any number of related issues. Listed below are some of the questions raised in the course of the debate:

Should American citizens be required to have and carry identity cards?

Should English be the official language of the United States?

Should the official policy on asylum be modified?

Should we build a wall on the entire U.S./Mexican border?

Is deportation an effective solution for illegal immigration?

Choose one of the topics or a similar one of your own, research it, and gather enough evidence so that you can make your own argument.

2. In the heat of debate, *amnesty* can mean different things to different people. Use your library and other resources to discover how the word has been used in the past and how it is used in the current debate over immigration. Write an essay in which you argue for the "true" interpretation of the word.

We Don't Need 'Guest Workers'

Robert J. Samuelson

Any time you pick up Newsweek, *you will see Robert Samuelson's regular column on economics, but before joining the magazine in 1984, he was a reporter for* The Washington Post *and still contributes a column to that newspaper, one that also appears in the* Los Angeles Times *and* The Boston Globe. *There's hardly a journalism award that he hasn't won: the John Hancock Award for Best Business and Financial Columnist (1993), Gerald Loeb Award for Best Commentary (1993 and 1986), National Headliner Award for Feature Column on a Single Subject (1993 and 1992), as well as others. He is also the author of two books:* Untruth: Why the Conventional Wisdom is (Almost Always) Wrong *(2001) and* The Good Life and Its Discontents: The American Dream in the Age of Enlightenment *(1997). The following essay was published on March 22, 2006, in* The Washington Post.

What to Look For   Like Samuelson, you will be doing a lot of research to back up your argument, but research, particularly if it involves statistics, needs to be made interesting. One way to do that is by varying your tone and diction. As you read Samuelson, look for the ways he uses informal language.

1   Economist Philip Martin of the University of California likes to tell a story about the state's tomato industry. In the early 1960s, growers relied on seasonal Mexican laborers, brought in under the government's "bracero" program. The Mexicans picked the tomatoes that were then processed into ketchup and other products. In 1964 Congress killed the program despite growers' warnings that its abolition would doom their industry. What happened? Well, plant scientists developed oblong tomatoes that could be harvested by machine. Since then, California's tomato output has risen fivefold.

2   It's a story worth remembering, because we're being warned again that we need huge numbers of "guest workers"—meaning unskilled

laborers from Mexico and Central America—to relieve U.S. "labor shortages." Indeed, the shortages will supposedly worsen as baby boomers retire. President Bush wants an open-ended program. Sens. Edward M. Kennedy (D-Mass.) and John McCain (R-Ariz.) advocate initially admitting 400,000 guest workers annually. The Senate is considering these and other plans.

3   Gosh, they're all bad ideas.

4   Guest workers would mainly legalize today's vast inflows of illegal immigrants, with the same consequence: We'd be importing poverty. This isn't because these immigrants aren't hardworking; many are. Nor is it because they don't assimilate; many do. But they generally don't go home, assimilation is slow and the ranks of the poor are constantly replenished. Since 1980 the number of Hispanics with incomes below the government's poverty line (about $19,300 in 2004 for a family of four) has risen 162 percent. Over the same period, the number of non-Hispanic whites in poverty rose 3 percent and the number of blacks, 9.5 percent. What we have now—and would with guest workers—is a conscious policy of creating poverty in the United States while relieving it in Mexico. By and large, this is a bad bargain for the United States. It stresses local schools, hospitals and housing; it feeds social tensions (witness the Minutemen). To be sure, some Americans get cheap housecleaning or landscaping services. But if more mowed their own lawns or did their own laundry, it wouldn't be a tragedy.

5   The most lunatic notion is that admitting more poor Latino workers would ease the labor market strains of retiring baby boomers. The two aren't close substitutes for each other. Among immigrant Mexican and Central American workers in 2004, only 7 percent had a college degree and nearly 60 percent lacked a high school diploma, according to the Congressional Budget Office. Among native-born U.S. workers, 32 percent had a college degree and only 6 percent did not have a high school diploma. Far from softening the social problems of an aging society, more poor immigrants might aggravate them by pitting older retirees against younger Hispanics for limited government benefits.

6   It's a myth that the U.S. economy "needs" more poor immigrants. The illegal immigrants already here represent only about 4.9 percent of the labor force, the Pew Hispanic Center reports. In no major occupation are they a majority. They're 36 percent of insulation workers, 28 percent of drywall installers and 20 percent of cooks. They're drawn here by wage differences, not labor "shortages."

In 2004, the median hourly wage in Mexico was $1.86, compared with $9 for Mexicans working in the United States, said Rakesh Kochhar of Pew. With high labor turnover in the jobs they take, most new illegal immigrants can get work by accepting wages slightly below prevailing levels.

7   Hardly anyone thinks that most illegal immigrants will leave. But what would happen if new illegal immigration stopped and wasn't replaced by guest workers? Well, some employers would raise wages to attract U.S. workers. Facing greater labor costs, some industries would—like the tomato growers in the 1960s—find ways to minimize those costs. As to the rest, what's wrong with higher wages for the poorest workers? From 1994 to 2004, the wages of high school dropouts rose only 2.3 percent (after inflation) compared with 11.9 percent for college graduates.

8   President Bush says his guest worker program would "match willing foreign workers with willing American employers, when no Americans can be found to fill the jobs." But at some higher wage, there would be willing Americans. The number of native high school dropouts with jobs declined by 1.3 million from 2000 to 2005, estimates Steven Camarota of the Center for Immigration Studies, which favors less immigration. Some lost jobs to immigrants. Unemployment remains high for some groups (9.3 percent for African Americans, 12.7 percent for white teenagers).

9   Business organizations understandably support guest worker programs. They like cheap labor and ignore the social consequences. What's more perplexing is why liberals, staunch opponents of poverty and inequality, support a program that worsens poverty and inequality. Poor immigrant workers hurt the wages of unskilled Americans. The only question is how much. Studies suggest a range "from negligible to an earnings reduction of almost 10 percent," according to the CBO.

10   It's said that having guest workers is better than having poor illegal immigrants. With legal status, they'd have rights and protections. They'd have more peace of mind and face less exploitation by employers. This would be convincing if its premise were incontestable: that we can't control our southern border. But that's unproved. We've never tried a policy of real barriers and strict enforcement against companies that hire illegal immigrants. Until that's shown to be ineffective, we shouldn't adopt guest worker programs that don't solve serious social problems—but add to them.

ORGANIZATION AND IDEAS

1. Samuelson opens his essay with an example. How does it tie into the rest of the essay? How effective is it?
2. Reread paragraph 4, noting the causal relationships. What are the effects of poverty?
3. Where in the essay does Samuelson consider arguments that can be used against his points? How does he counter them?
4. Samuelson's argument rests on economic analysis. How effective is it?
5. Where in the essay is Samuelson's thesis? What effect does he achieve by that placement?

TECHNIQUE AND STYLE

1. How would you describe Samuelson's tone? What examples can you find to support your opinion?
2. Paragraph 3 consists of one sentence. What effect does it achieve?
3. The essay brims with facts and figures. How well does Samuelson judge his reader's tolerance for pure information? How clearly does he present it?
4. Reread the essay, marking examples of Samuelson's use of appeals. Which dominates? What evidence supports your opinion?
5. If Samuelson's essay were written for an academic audience instead of a popular one, all the information would be documented in notes. Opinion essays in newspapers, however, don't use notes but must present facts and figures credibly. How well does Samuelson do that?

SUGGESTIONS FOR WRITING

Journal

1. What fact or figure does Samuelson use that surprises you and why?
2. What do you associate with the word *immigrant?* After you've written a paragraph or two, reread what you've written and sum it up in one sentence. You then have a starting place for an essay.

Essay

1. Many arguments have been put forward as reasons to control illegal immigration:
    to protect national security
    to protect jobs and wages
    to prevent increased pressure on health services and public schools
    to prevent "back-door citizenship" (citizenship being granted automatically to children born in the US)
    to preserve the English language

Choose one of these reasons and research it so that you can amass enough information to form an educated opinion you can then defend in an essay.

2. Samuelson's concluding paragraph suggests that illegal immigrants, lacking the "rights and protections" accorded to American citizens, are sometimes abused by their employers. Use research to explore the truth of that idea. You might start by picking a type of job that attracts illegal immigrants: house and garden work, restaurant jobs, construction, fruit and vegetable harvesting, and the like.

All These Illegals

Darrin Bell

Darrin Bell is best known for Candorville, *an aptly named comic strip featuring a diverse inner-city cast. Writing as an African American, he depicts tough issues—race and poverty among them—in a way that is both honest and upbeat, and as a result the strip has a wide appeal. Now syndicated by the Washington Post Writers Group,* Candorville *is carried by newspapers such as the* Los Angeles Times, *the* Chicago Tribune, *and the* Detroit Free Press, *as well as* Al Dia, *a Spanish language paper published in Dallas. Bell grew up in Los Angeles, earned a degree in Political Science at the University of California, Berkeley, and now lives and works in Berkeley. His work has been published in two collections:* Another Stereotype Bites the Dust: A Candorville Collection *(2006) and* Candorville: Thank God for Culture Clash *(2005). Working with the writer Theorn Heir, Bell also draws the comic strip* Rudy Park. *The strip included here was published on April 10, 2006.*

© 2006, Darrin Bell. Distributed by the Washington Post Writers Group. Reprinted with Permission.

Americans and Jobs

Steve Kelley

Steve Kelley's home base is the New Orleans Times-Picayune, *but his cartoons are syndicated and appear in many other papers, often showing up in the weekly collections gathered by* The New York Times, Newsweek, *and* The Week. *A graduate of Dartmouth College, Kelley's first job in journalism was at the* San Diego Union-Tribune. *While there, he helped start a program to raise money for the San Diego Child Abuse Prevention Fund. Since then, he has started "1,000 Laughs for 1,000 Smiles," to raise money for Mexican children in need of plastic surgery. Kelley has won numerous awards for his cartoons, including the Best of the West and National Headliner awards. The following cartoon was published on March 29, 2006.*

By permission of Steve Kelley and Creators Syndicate.

FOR DISCUSSION

1. To what extent are Kelley's characters "typical" Americans?
2. To what extent are Bell's characters typical? Stereotypical?
3. How does each drawing narrow the debate over immigration?
4. How does each drawing contribute a different perspective to the essays by Bookman and Samuelson?
5. Consider each cartoon as a political statement on the issue of immigration. What thesis would you give to each and why?

SUGGESTIONS FOR WRITING

Journal

Of the two, which cartoon do you prefer and why? Make specific reference to the drawings to support your point.

Essay

Perhaps a particular current issue interests you, or perhaps you're curious about how a certain political figure is portrayed, or maybe you want to know more about a political cartoonist. Can the cartoonist, for example, be labeled *liberal?* And if so, what sort of liberal and what positions does he or she take? Or think about how any prominent political figure is drawn by different artists. What is exaggerated? What is implied? Use a search engine to find cartoons or comic strips that deal with a current topic, political figure, or artist. More than likely, once you have brought up a site, you will be able to narrow a search so that you can explore the pertinent cartoons or comic strips. As you explore your topic, you will start to form a thesis that can be used for your essay, an essay that uses your description of the drawings and some examples of them to support your point.

Multiple Modes

10

Two Topics, Six Views

ON REALITY AND TELEVISION ● ● ● ●

The relationship between television and reality has always been an uneasy one, and the advent of reality television shows has made that relationship more complicated. Talent shows, sitcoms, contests (of wits, strength, and/or endurance), and their like clog the channels with spin-offs and wannabes. And we watch them. And we sometimes wonder why. *Why* is the focus of the three essays that follow, and taken together they provide a kind of conversation about reality shows—what they represent and why we watch them.

The "conversation" takes place among authors who differ in age, experience, and perspective. Anna Quindlen started her career as a journalist, first as a reporter for *The New York Times,* moving on to become the *Times'* deputy metropolitan editor and then columnist, winning a Pulitzer Prize for her commentary in 1992. Since that time, she has concentrated on writing novels, though she still has a regular column, "Voices," in *Newsweek.* Quindlen has written more than 14 books, including two for children, and is perhaps the only person to hit the *Times'* best-seller list in three categories—fiction, nonfiction, and self-help. Her essay "Watching the World Go By" was published in 2001 and appears in her collection *Loud and Clear* (2005).

James Poniewozik is currently *Time* magazine's media and television critic, appearing in print and on his television blog http://mobile.time.com/item.jsp?key=tu_bl. His background in electronic media as a columnist for *Salon.com* and as a contributor to National Public Radio's "On the Media" has given him much to write about. His brief biography at Time.com describes his subjects as "ranging from advertising to Internet radio to TV shelter shows to the cultural significance of eBay and *Antiques Roadshow.*" Poniewozik's articles have appeared in publications as varied as *Fortune* and *Rolling Stone*. The one included here appeared in *Time* on November 20, 2006.

Amelia Meyer has a professional writing career to look forward to. At present she is a fourth-year student at the University of Virginia, majoring in American studies. For the past year and a half she has been writing opinion columns for the University's *Cavalier Daily,* covering University-related topics as well as popular culture. "Queens of the Hills" was her last column of the Spring 2008 semester.

Watching the World Go By

Anna Quindlen

1   Never watched *Survivor*. Never will. What's the point? I've eaten bugs inadvertently myself, dozing in the hammock by the pond on a muggy summer evening. And anyone who wants to watch two pitched and petty rival factions go at one another can just wander between the purchasing and accounting departments of any company. Add up the physical challenges and the head games, and the whole thing sounds like nothing more than gym class meets sophomore mixer, no scarier than high school. (Although in the last analysis, nothing is scarier than high school.) I don't scare easy. I've lived through a kitchen renovation in an old house with uneven floorboards, and Donald Trump is building a skyscraper at the end of my block. Here on Temptation Island, where multimillionaire divorce lawyers roam free, survivors are those who pass the co-op board.

2   People named Kimmi and Colby and Amber (who chooses the participants, the writers for *One Life to Live*?) balancing on rafts, living on goat brains, turning brown in the outback? This is a stunt, not survival. Liz Taylor and Debbie Reynolds doing a TV movie and making fun of Eddie Fisher, Debbie still with that tight-lipped good-girl look—that's surviving. Bill Clinton taking an overdose of stupid pills, making an endless string of what we moms call "bad choices," then being lionized on the streets of Harlem after he decides to seek salvation and office space in an all-black neighborhood—that's surviving.

3   Yet how quickly the voyeurism of sofa slugs has become, not only a national obsession but an expected staple of the weekly program schedule. Only three decades ago America was shocked and amazed by the Loud family of Santa Barbara, California, who permitted a documentary crew to plaster their imperfect lives on public television in a series called *An American Family*. Today the fractured marriages of ordinary folk are severed in the seedy real-life setting of *Divorce Court*, and the people who bring you *Trauma: Life in the ER* find themselves blurring the genital area of a patient while the camera comes in tight on his severed leg.

4   A very wise trial attorney, knowing of my unslakable appetite for episodes of *Law & Order* (particularly during the classic Chris Noth years) once remarked that a televised trial is as much like the real thing as a wedding is like a marriage. All the boring bits are excised,

leaving only the high drama. And that's the same relationship between reality and reality TV. The broadcast version covers only the peaks and valleys, the breakups and the big events. The magic moment of birth without the tedium of toilet training. The white dress and the cutaway, not the socks on the bedroom floor. MTV's *The Real World* features more pitched arguments and aberrant hookups in a few weeks than most of us experience in a lifetime.

5   Conventional wisdom is that TV is the purview of those with nothing better to do. But this boom in the vicarious is instead the hallmark of a people with not enough time on their hands, people who have a to-do list instead of a life, people for whom the download can never be quick enough. An entire nation living at warp speed has no time for tedium. What could be easier than cutting out the middleman of our own daily existence and instead watching the high points of life on tape? All the passion, none of the pain or perspiration. When Bob Vila builds a deck, it gets built in only an episode, and the wood never warps.

6   Perhaps *Survivor* satisfies a stunted yen for adventure, or maybe its tribes are just stand-ins for the Machiavellian maneuvering of virtually every workplace, the intrigue without the bad coffee. It doesn't seem like particularly real reality television, although it's become the standard-bearer of the form. *A Baby Story,* on TLC, in which you get to see the precise moment when a woman says to her husband, "I hate you, I want the epidural" is reality TV. Or *Cops,* in which law-abiding Americans learn that suspects will never, ever quietly put their hands behind their backs for the cuffs (and that most police officers are way out of shape). Or even *The Operation,* which is a completely no-frills look at the miracles of medicine. Guess what? Mitral valve replacement surgery is as boring as watching paint dry.

7   Which leads us to the most terrifying reality show on television, more terrifying than watching Judge Judy yell at a grandmother who let her dog off the leash, more terrifying than seeing two girls with bad bleach jobs fight over the sexual favors of a round-shouldered guy with acne and a mullet cut on Ricki Lake, more terrifying than the salad-to-dessert C-SPAN broadcast of Katherine Harris giving a lunch speech in front of a portrait of Pat Nixon. *Trading Spaces* lets you watch as neighbors swap homes and, with the help of two annoying decorators who describe window treatments as fun, and a hunky carpenter who's always around (all right, it's only partly real), redo a room in the house next

door. The episode in which the cheerful married couple painted the bedroom of the single father black to give it a manly, sophisticated look is not for the easily frightened.

8   Once there were visions of television uniting people, making the rich understand the problems of the poor, the poor understand the problems of the rich. (See: *Dynasty.*) A global community would develop around the cathode-ray tube. Instead it has come to this: bad bridesmaids' dresses, small-claims court, and stitches in some kid's lip up close and personal. And a black bedroom with this poor guy standing in the doorway making that face people make when they've gotten novelty sweatshirts for Christmas, the face that says "it's awful" so much better than words alone can say. Reality television is the twenty-first-century equivalent of astronaut food: Just point and click, and it's as though you're really alive. "I hate television. I hate it as much as peanuts. But I can't stop eating peanuts," Orson Welles once said. Pass the snacks and settle back. And if your kids want to talk or your mother calls just say, "Shhhh—they're about to vote someone off the island." Because isn't that what life is really all about?

Ugly, the American

James Poniewozik

1   Few prime-time TV characters are more American than Betty Suarez. On ABC's hit comedy-soap *Ugly Betty,* she's a fashion-magazine assistant who is distinctly unfashionable—chunky sweaters, frizzy hair, bear-trap braces—but succeeds through good old Yankee values like perseverance, optimism and hard work. Smart and sweet-hearted, she embodies the Puritan-Shaker-Quaker principle of valuing inner good over outer appearance. She's as Norman Rockwell as a chestnut-stuffed turkey. The actress who plays her is even named America Ferrera.

2   And yet—if you listen to some politicians and pundits—she should have been booted out of the country years ago. Betty's father is an illegal immigrant from Mexico. To hear Lou Dobbs and Pat Buchanan tell it, our fellow citizens are boiling with resentment

against people like Betty. Taking our kids' spots in college! Helping themselves to our orthodontia! Stealing low-paid magazine jobs that rightfully belong to American trust-fund babies!

3   So why do some 14 million people a week watch and root for her? Because it's easier to hate a straw man—or a straw Mexican—than a person, even a fictional one. And because, as our pop culture shows, Americans' attitude toward foreigners is more complex than the build-a-fencers would make it.

4   On its face, the political debate is about illegal immigration—law, security and fairness. But this immigration panic, like past ones, taps into fears not limited to illegals. Who gets to say what American culture is? Is there enough room—and prosperity—to go around? *Ugly Betty*'s overarching story is metaphorically about the same battle. Betty is an outsider at *Mode* magazine not just because she dresses badly but also because of things that have to do directly with her ethnicity. She grosses out her skinny, preening, (mostly) Anglo co-workers by bringing empanadas for lunch. Her features are broad and unmistakably Mesoamerican. (Ferrera is strikingly pretty in real life.) On her first day at work, she wears a hideous poncho with GUADALAJARA emblazoned on it.

5   Betty's scheming co-workers resent her in the same way immigration demagogues do: she's an interloper. Yet she succeeds—and even wins over some of her *Mode* enemies—for exactly that reason. Like generations of immigrants, legal or not, she brings fresh eyes, a tireless work ethic and a different perspective to revitalize a tired institution. (Like Borat, she's in the tradition of the outsider who helps America see itself.) Ironic, amid the effete fashionistas, that she's the one the audience identifies with as an everyday American.

6   It's no coincidence that *Ugly Betty* the series is itself an immigrant, a remake of a worldwide-sensation telenovela franchise. That's what makes our pop culture so vital: from TV to music to fashion, it is constantly transfused by foreigners who are able to out-American Americans.

7   Take reality TV. It embodies everything there is to love and despise about this country—ambition and greed, free-spiritedness and vulgarity, boldness and shamelessness. But it is an American staple that was pioneered overseas, much like pizza and gunpowder. *American Idol* is British. *Big Brother,* Dutch. *Survivor,* Swedish and imported by Mark Burnett, a Brit. And every week on reality shows, Americans embrace foreigners with Emma Lazarene openness—Heidi Klum and Simon Cowell, East European and Latin hoofers on *Dancing with the*

Stars, Mexican boxers on *The Contender* and a Siberian drag queen on *America's Got Talent.*

8   Reality TV may be so hospitable to immigrants because it's a fun house mirror of the immigrant experience. You leave your comfort zone and prove your worth with little more than gumption and (maybe) talent. Wherever you come from, you embrace a new, anything-goes culture that values chutzpah over tradition and propriety. Emigré Burnett's shows, like *The Apprentice,* are full of Horatio Algerisms about industry and opportunity—not unlike *Ugly Betty.*

9   Political observers suggest that immigration law will be one of the areas where a Democratic Congress and a Republican White House may be able to reach consensus. Before they do, they should flick on a TV. They would see that you can pass laws and put up walls but it is much harder to erect a fence around your culture. (Just ask the French.) That while borders need to be protected, new blood is what makes this country the maddening, fantastic free-for-all that it is. And that what makes Betty ugly is, in the long run, what makes us America the beautiful.

Queens of the Hills

Amelia Meyer

1   On Tuesday mornings, in the dining halls, in the dorms, even in the bathrooms, the standard chatter revolves around a single question: "Did you watch 'The Hills' last night?" Okay, so maybe I'm exaggerating a bit about the show's popularity, and maybe for some, chatter actually revolves around academics rather than reality television. But chances are that if you mention "The Hills" to a crowd of people, you are likely to spark up an interesting conversation.

2   "The Hills" has garnered an amazing level of popularity in the past few years as television viewers have loyally followed L.A. princess Lauren Conrad and her gossipy friends, if friends is what you can call them. We refer to the characters purely on a first-name basis, not because they are as real to us as our own friends, but because they are so unreal that we speak about them like we do any fictional character on television.

3   Yet this week's edition of *The New Yorker* features a scathing review of the much-loved MTV reality show in which Nancy Franklin criticizes "Hills" viewers for their superficiality and gullible innocence. Franklin fails to find any redeeming qualities in the show, writing as if she were a cultural anthropologist entering the land of vapidity. She concludes her article in an expected fashion, citing the immaturity and naiveté of teenagers and young adults as the only possible explanation for the show's success.

4   She characterizes this generation of young people as materialistic and, to put it bluntly, dumb. For why on earth would any sane human being with the slightest grounding in reality actually sit in front of a television and watch these women live their fantastically spoiled lives? How could watching Audrina's constantly empty expression or Heidi's ever-changing face—the poor girl is a poster child for plastic surgery— make for quality TV? I can tell you how.

5   What Franklin fails to realize is that most people who watch "The Hills" don't for one second buy the fakeness. We don't think these girls continue to land their dream jobs in L.A. on sheer talent; we don't think Heidi's plastic face looks in any way real; and most importantly, we don't wish we could be Lauren. We all know better, and that is why we watch.

6   What appeals to us most about the show is that it allows us all, for one brief thirty-minute period a week, to come together and feel good about ourselves. It allows us to bask in the knowledge that even if we just failed a midterm or forgot a friend's birthday, we are not the fake, materialistic, spoiled brats we watch every Monday night at 10 P.M. We are—and we will remain—something more.

7   "The Hills" is simply one in a long line of reality shows intended to appeal to young audiences. What once began with "The Real World" morphed into an army of shows that were passed off by producers as reflections of some sort of American cultural reality. Yet somewhere along the way, this attempt to present a reality became subsumed by the goal to simply entertain. Reality television is now just another fictional genre, and everyone knows it.

8   In other words, "The Hills" is not meant to give anyone "a sense of what it's like to be a young person in Los Angeles," as Franklin believes it to be. Instead, the show is meant to give us all something to laugh at as we stand confounded by its absolute ridiculousness.

9   Perhaps more than that, and perhaps unintentionally, the show and others like it have given us some sort of common ground upon which we can all stand united. In a somewhat twisted way,

"The Hills" shows us that despite our vastly different interests, backgrounds, and career goals, there is something we all share. Our common identity comes in the fact that every time Spencer strokes his own ego or Lauren whines about her love life, we can look at someone else—anyone else—and know that we are both thinking the same exact thought.

10   Watching "The Hills" is a way of reassuring ourselves that we are not alone. It is a way of holding onto our sanity, comforted in the knowledge that no one is actually that vain.

11   So next time our generation's intelligence is questioned, we can rest assured that watching "The Hills" does not mean that we are stupid or that we dream someday of being Lauren or Heidi. In fact, it means the opposite, that as we watch those characters, we also keep watch of ourselves, always making sure we are firmly grounded in a reality that can never be duplicated on television. Out of absurdity comes clarity, and out of artificiality comes truth.

ON FREEDOM, CENSORSHIP, AND EDUCATION ● ● ● ●

For the past 27 years, the last week in September has been declared Banned Books Week, an event sponsored by the American Library Association along with a host of other organizations including the American Booksellers Association, American Society of Journalists and Authors, and National Association of College Stores among them. To look at the Library Association's list of top 100 books banned or challenged in 2007 is to see a lot of famous names. But censorship doesn't stop there. At a time when the Columbine and Virginia Tech shootings are still fresh memories, school and university authorities are understandably wary, a wariness that carries over to the rights of students, faculty members, and writers: Who or what might be "dangerous"? What may offend? The three essays included here present some answers and together provide varied perspectives on different aspects of censorship: Ursula Le Guin writes about a proposed banning of her book, Anna Quindlen tells of the mangling of her prose, and Michael Chabon speaks out on behalf of students.

Ursula Le Guin's name is familiar to anyone who reads science fiction—notably *The Left Hand of Darkness* (1969), the six *Earthsea* novels—though she also writes poetry, children's books, short stories, screenplays, fantasy, young adult novels, and essays. Put all those genres together, and the result is 50 books. She has been awarded almost as many prizes and honors, among them the National Book Award, five Hugo Awards for science fiction, five Nebula Awards for science fiction/fantasy, and many, many more. Her most recent novel takes the reader to Virgil's Italy before the founding of Rome and into the mind and times of Lavinia, Aeneas' second wife whose name is the title of the novel (2008). But it's the reception of Le Guin's novel *The Lathe of Heaven* (1971) that prompted her to write the essay that follows. It was written originally for the "Forum" section of the newspaper *The Oregonian* in May 1984 and has been reprinted in her collection *Dancing at the Edge of the World* (1989).

A brief biographical note about Anna Quindlen appears on page 276. Her essay "With a No. 2 Pencil, Delete" first appeared in June 2002 and is reprinted in her collection *Loud and Clear* (2005). For more information about Quindlen, check out her Web site: http://www.annaquindlen.com.

Like Ursula Le Guin, Michael Chabon has been honored with a Hugo Award and Nebula Award, both for his most recent novel *The Yiddish Policeman's Union* (2007), an imaginative comic noir mystery/thriller. Chabon's first novel *The Mysteries of Pittsburgh* (1988) was written for his master's degree in creative writing at the University of California at Irvine, and his list of publications suggest he hasn't stopped writing since. All told, he has published seven novels, two short story collections, and *Maps and Legends* (2008), a compilation of essays. His novel *The Amazing Adventures of Kavalier & Clay* (2000) received a Pulitzer Prize and reflects his off-beat interest in comic books, a subject he knows something about—he has written for DC Comics and coauthored the story for *Spider-Man 2*. He is also involved in the screen version of *The Amazing Adventures of Kavalier & Clay,* due out in 2009. The piece that follows appeared as an op-ed in the April 13, 2004, *New York Times.*

Whose Lathe?

Ursula Le Guin

1   In a small town near Portland late this spring, a novel, *The Lathe of Heaven*, was the subject of a hearing concerning its suitability for use in a senior-high-school literature class. I took a lively interest in the outcome, because I wrote the novel.

2   The case against the book was presented first. The man who was asking that it be withdrawn stated his objections to the following elements in the book: fuzzy thinking and poor sentence structure; a mention of homosexuality; a character who keeps a flask of brandy in her purse, and who remarks that her mother did not love her. (It seemed curious to me that he did not mention the fact that this same character is a Black woman whose lover/husband is a White man. I had the feeling that this was really what he hated in the book, and that he was afraid to say so; but that was only my feeling.)

3   He also took exception to what he described as the author's advocacy of non-Christian religions and/or of non-separation of Church and State (his arguments on this point, or these points, were not clear to me).

4   Finally, during discussion, he compared the book to junk food, apparently because it was science fiction.

5   The English Department of the school then presented a carefully prepared, spirited defense of the book, including statements by students who had read it. Some liked it, some didn't like it, most objected to having it, or any other book, banned.

6   In discussion, teachers pointed out that since it is the policy of the Washougal School District to assign an alternative book to any student who objects on any grounds to reading an assigned one, the attempt to prevent a whole class from reading a book was an attempt to change policy, replacing free choice by censorship.

7   When the Instructional Materials Committee of the district voted on the motion to ban the book, the motion was defeated twenty votes to five. The hearing was public and was conducted in the most open and democratic fashion. I did not speak, as I felt the teachers and students had spoken eloquently for me.

8   Crankish attacks on the freedom to read are common at present. When backed and coordinated by organized groups, they become

sinister. In this case, I saw something going on that worried me a good deal because it did not seem to be coming from an outside pressure group, but from elements of the educational establishment itself: this was the movement to change policy radically by instituting, or "clarifying," guidelines or criteria for the selection/elimination of books used in the schools. The motion on which this committee of the school district voted was actually that the book be withdrawn *"while guidelines and policies for the district are worked out."* Those guidelines and policies were the real goal, I think, of the motion.

9   Guidelines? That sounds dull. Innocent. Useful. Of course we have to be sure about the kinds of books we want our kids to read in school. Don't we?

10   Well, do we? The dangerous vagueness of the term "guidelines and policies for the district" slides right past such questions as: Who are "we"? Who decides what the children read? Does "we" include you? Me? Teachers? Librarians? Students? Are fifteen-to-eighteen-year-olds ever "we," or are they always "they"?

11   And what are the guidelines to be? On what criteria or doctrines are they to be based?

12   The people concerned with schools in Oregon try, with ever decreasing budgets, to provide good, sound food in the school cafeterias, knowing that for some students that's the only real meal they get. They try, with ever decreasing budgets, to provide beautiful, intelligent books in classes and school libraries, knowing that for many students those are the only books they read. To provide the best: everyone agrees on that (even the people who vote against school levies). But we don't and we can't agree on what books are the best. And therefore what is vital is that we provide variety, abundance, plenty—not books that reflect one body of opinion or doctrine, not books that one group or sect thinks good, but the broadest, richest range of intellectual and artistic material possible.

13   Nobody is forced to read any of it. There is that very important right to refuse and choose an alternative.

14   When a bad apple turns up, it can be taken out of the barrel on a case-by-case, book-by-book basis—investigated, defended, prosecuted, and judged, as in the hearing on my *Lathe of Heaven*.* But this

---

*Currently (1987) a textbook written for Oregon schools called *Let's Oregonize* is going through this process on the state level. The arguments against it were brought by environmentalists and others who found it tendentious and biased towards certain industries and interests. From my point of view it certainly sounds like a rather bad apple. But it is getting a scrupulously fair hearing.

can't be done wholesale by using "guidelines," instructions for censorship. There is no such thing as a moral filter that lets good books through and keeps bad books out. Such criteria of "goodness" and "badness" are a moralist's dream but a democrat's nightmare.

15   Censorship, here or in Russia or wherever, is absolutely antidemocratic and elitist. The censor says: You don't know enough to choose, but we do, so you will read what we choose for you and nothing else. The democrat says: The process of learning is that of learning how to choose. Freedom isn't given, it's earned. Read, learn, and earn it.

16   I fear censorship in this Uriah Heepish guise of "protecting our children," "stricter criteria," "moral guidance," "a more definite policy," and so on. I hope administrators, teachers, librarians, parents, and students will resist it. Its advocates are people willing to treat others not only as if they were not free but were not even worthy of freedom.

With a No. 2 Pencil, Delete

Anna Quindlen

1   You can imagine how honored I was to learn that my work was going to be mangled for the sake of standardized testing. I got the word just after a vigilant parent had discovered that statewide English tests in New York had included excerpts from literary writers edited so heavily and so nonsensically that the work had essentially lost all meaning. Isaac Bashevis Singer, Annie Dillard, even Chekhov—the pool of those singled out for red-penciling by bureaucrats was a distinguished one, and I found myself a little disappointed that I had not been turned into reading comp pablum.

2   But the State of Georgia was more accommodating. The folks at the Educational Testing Service, one of America's most powerful monopolies and the entity responsible for the SATs, were preparing something called the Georgia End-of-Course Tests and wanted to use an excerpt from a book I'd written called *How Reading Changed My Life*.

3   In the sentence that read "The Sumerians first used the written word to make laundry lists, to keep track of cows and slaves and household goods," the words "and slaves" had been deleted.

4   And in the sentence "And soon publishers had the means, and the will, to publish anything—cookbooks, broadsides, newspapers, novels, poetry, pornography, picture books for children" someone had drawn a black line through the word "pornography" and written "EDIT!" in the margin.

5   I got off easy. In the Singer excerpt on the Regents exam, which was about growing up a Jew in prewar Poland, all references to Jews and Poles were excised. Annie Dillard's essay about being the only white child in a library in the black section of town became almost unintelligible after all references to race were obliterated. The New York State Education Department's overheated guidelines are written so broadly that only the words "the" and "but" seem safe. "Does the material require the parent, teacher or examinee to support a position that is contrary to their religious beliefs or teaching?" the guidelines ask. "Does the material assume that the examinee has experience with a certain type of family structure?" As Jeanne Heifetz, an opponent of the required Regents exams who uncovered the editing, wrote, "Almost no piece of writing emerges from this process unscathed." Nor could any except the most homogenized piece of pap about Cape Cod tide pools.

6   "The words 'slave' and 'pornography' deal with controversial issues that could cause an emotional reaction in some students that could distract them from the test and affect their performance," wrote the ETS supernumerary snipping at my sentences.

7   This was in a week when students likely heard of another suicide bomber in Israel, the gunpoint abduction of a teenager in Utah, and the arrest of a rap star for appearing on videotape having sex with underage girls. And they're going to be distracted by the words "slaves" and "pornography"?

8   That's the saddest thing here: not the betrayal of writers by bureaucrats, but the betrayal of kids by educators. Everyone complains that teenagers don't read enough good stuff; the lists of banned books in school libraries are thick with quality, with Steinbeck and Margaret Atwood. Everyone complains that students are not intellectually engaged; controversial issues are excised from classroom discussions and those staggeringly boring textbooks. Everyone complains that kids are not excited about school; the point of school increasingly seems to be mindless and incessant testing that doesn't even have the grace to be mildly interesting. By the standards of the Regents tests, *The Catcher in the Rye* is unacceptable. ("Does the material require a student to take a position that challenges

parental authority?") So is *To Kill a Mockingbird* and *The Merchant of Venice.*

9   Here is the most shocking question among the New York State Education Department guidelines: "Does the material assume values not shared by all test takers?" There is no book worth reading, no poem worth writing, no essay worth analyzing, that assumes the same values for all. That sentence is the death of intellectual engagement.

10   The education officials in New York have now backed down from their cut-and-paste-without-permission position, faced with an angry mob of distinguished writers. But what do the kids learn from this? That the written word doesn't really matter much, that it can be weakened at will. That no one trusts a student to understand that variations in opinion and background are both objectively interesting and intellectually challenging. That some of the most powerful people involved in their education have reduced them to the lowest common denominator.

11   I like kids, have a brace of them around here, and I'm damned (EDIT!) if I'm going to abet some skewed adult vision of their febrile emotional state. Unlike those in New York, the people preparing tests for the State of Georgia at least had the common courtesy to ask permission to mess with my stuff. I declined. It's not that one or two words are particularly precious; I have hacked away at my own sentences to get them to fit tidily in this space. But not to make pablum for students who deserve something tastier.

Solitude and the Fortresses of Youth

Michael Chabon

1   Earlier this month my local paper, the *San Francisco Chronicle,* reported that a college student had been expelled from art school here for submitting a story "rife with gruesome details about sexual torture, dismemberment and bloodlust" to his creative writing class. The instructor, a poet named Jan Richman, subsequently found herself out of a job. The university chose not to explain its failure to renew Ms. Richman's contract, but she intimated that she was being punished for having set the tone for the class by assigning a well-regarded if disturbing short story by the MacArthur-winning novelist David Foster Wallace, "Girl with Curious Hair." Ms. Richman had been troubled enough by the student's work to report it to her superiors in the first place, in spite of the fact that it was not, according to the *Chronicle,* "the first serial-killer story she had read in her six semesters on the faculty at the Academy of Art University."

2   Homicide inspectors were called in; a criminal profiler went to work on the student. The officers found no evidence of wrongdoing. The unnamed student had made no threat; his behavior was not considered suspicious. In the end, no criminal charges were brought.

3   In this regard, the San Francisco case differs from other incidents in California, and around the country, in which students, unlucky enough to have as literary precursor the Columbine mass-murderer Dylan Klebold, have found themselves expelled, even prosecuted and convicted on criminal charges, because of the violence depicted in their stories and poems. The threat posed by these prosecutions to civil liberties, to the First Amendment rights of our young people, is grave enough. But as a writer, a parent and a former teenager, I see the workings of something more iniquitous: not merely the denial of teenagers' rights in the name of their own protection, but the denial of their humanity in the name of preserving their innocence.

4   It is in the nature of a teenager to want to destroy. The destructive impulse is universal among children of all ages, rises to a peak of vividness, ingenuity and fascination in adolescence, and thereafter

never entirely goes away. Violence and hatred, and the fear of our own inability to control them in ourselves, are a fundamental part of our birthright, along with altruism, creativity, tenderness, pity and love. It therefore requires an immense act of hypocrisy to stigmatize our young adults and teenagers as agents of deviance and disorder. It requires a policy of dishonesty about and blindness to our own histories, as a species, as a nation, and as individuals who were troubled as teenagers, and who will always be troubled, by the same dark impulses. It also requires that favorite tool of the hypocritical, dishonest and fearful: the suppression of constitutional rights.

5   We justly celebrate the ideals enshrined in the Bill of Rights, but it is also a profoundly disillusioned document, in the best sense of that adjective. It stipulates all the worst impulses of humanity: toward repression, brutality, intolerance and fear. It couples an unbridled faith in the individual human being, redeemed time and again by his or her singular capacity for tenderness, pity and all the rest, with a profound disenchantment about groups of human beings acting as governments, court systems, armies, state religions and bureaucracies, unchecked by the sting of individual conscience and only belatedly if ever capable of anything resembling redemption.

6   In this light the Bill of Rights can be read as a classic expression of the teenage spirit: a powerful imagination reacting to a history of overwhelming institutional repression, hypocrisy, chicanery and weakness. It is a document written by men who, like teenagers, knew their enemy intimately, and saw in themselves all the potential they possessed to one day become him. We tend to view idealism and cynicism as opposites, when in fact neither possesses any merit or power unless tempered by, fused with, the other. The Bill of Rights is the fruit of that kind of fusion; so is the teenage imagination.

7   The imagination of teenagers is often—I'm tempted to say always—the only sure capital they possess apart from the love of their parents, which is a force far beyond their capacity to comprehend or control. During my own adolescence, my imagination, the kingdom inside my own skull, was my sole source of refuge, my fortress of solitude, at times my prison. But a fortress requires a constant line of supply; those who take refuge in attics and cellars require the unceasing aid of confederates; prisoners need advocates, escape plans, or simply a window that gives onto the sky.

8   Like all teenagers, I provisioned my garrison with art: books, movies, music, comic books, television, role-playing games. My secret

confederates were the works of Monty Python, H. P. Lovecraft, the cartoonist Vaughan Bodé, and the Ramones, among many others; they kept me watered and fed. They baked files into cakes and, on occasion, for a wondrous moment, made the walls of my prison disappear. Given their nature as human creations, as artifacts and devices of human nature, some of the provisions I consumed were bound to be of a dark, violent, even bloody and horrifying nature; otherwise I would not have cared for them. Tales and displays of violence, blood and horror rang true, answered a need, on some deep, angry level that maybe only those with scant power or capital, regardless of their age, can understand.

9   It was not long before I began to write: stories, poems, snatches of autobiographical jazz. Often I imitated the work of my confederates: stories of human beings in the most extreme situations and states of emotion—horror stories; accounts of madness and despair. In part—let's say in large part, if that's what it takes to entitle the writings of teenagers to unqualified protection under the First Amendment—this was about expression. I was writing what I felt, what I believed, wished for, raged against, hoped and dreaded. But the main reason I wrote stories—and the reason that I keep on writing them today—was not to express myself. I started to write because once it had been nourished, stoked and liberated by those secret confederates, I could not hold back the force of my imagination. I had been freed, and I felt that it was now up to me to do the same for somebody else, somewhere, trapped in his or her own lonely tower.

10   We don't want teenagers to write violent poems, horrifying stories, explicit lyrics and rhymes; they're ugly, in precisely the way that we are ugly, and out of protectiveness and hypocrisy, even out of pity and love and tenderness, we try to force young people to be innocent of everything but the effects of that ugliness. And so we censor the art they consume and produce, and prosecute and suspend and expel them, and when, once in a great while, a teenager reaches for an easy gun and shoots somebody or himself, we tell ourselves that if we had only censored his journals and curtailed his music and video games, that awful burst of final ugliness could surely have been prevented. As if art caused the ugliness, when of course all it can ever do is reflect and, perhaps, attempt to explain it.

11   Let teenagers languish, therefore, in their sense of isolation, without outlet or nourishment, bereft of the only thing that makes it all

CREDITS

Page 23: "Summer Wind" by Verlyn Klinkenborg from the *New York Times,* July 18, 2008. Copyright © 2008 The New York Times. All rights reserved. Used by permission and protected by the Copyright Laws of the United States. The printing, copying, redistribution, or retransmission of the Material without express written permission is prohibited.

Page 25: "The Bridge" by Jason Holland. Reprinted by permission of the author.

Page 29: "Tommy" by Kelly Ruth Winter, originally published in *Brevity,* Issue 25. Used by permission of the author.

Page 32: "You'll Love the Way We Fly" by Lori Jakiela. Originally appeared in *Brevity.* Used by permission of the author.

Page 36: "El Hoyo" by Mario Suárez for *Arizona Quarterly,* Summer 1947, vol. III, no. 2. Copyright © by the Arizona Quarterly. Reprinted by permission.

Page 48: "A Fowl Trick to Play on a Lawn Tractor" by Peter Dexter from *Paper Trails* by Peter Dexter. Copyright © 2007 by Peter Dexter. Reprinted by permission of International Creative Management, Inc.

Page 52: "Learning, then College" by Meg Gifford from the *Baltimore Sun,* May 19, 2003. Copyright © 2003 Baltimore Sun. Reprinted with permission of the Baltimore Sun in the format Textbook via Copyright Clearance Center.

Page 55: "The Night of the Oranges" by Flavius Stan from the *New York Times,* December 24, 1995. Copyright © 1995 by the New York Times Co. Reprinted by permission.

Page 59: "Time to Look and Listen" by Magdoline Asfahani from *Newsweek,* December 2, 1996. Copyright © 1996 by Newsweek, Inc. Reprinted by permission of Newsweek, Inc.

Page 63: "Footprints on the Flag" by Anchee Min. Copyright © 2001 by Anchee Min. First appeared in *The New Yorker.* Reprinted by permission of the author and the Sandra Dijkstra Literary Agency.

Page 67: Used with the permission of Ann Telnaes and the Cartoonist Group. All rights reserved.

Page 75: "Sweatin' for Nothin'" by Michael Barlow. Reprinted by permission of the author.

Page 79: "Have Fun" by Allison Silverman from the *New York Times Magazine,* April 8, 2007. Used by permission of The New York Times Syndication Sales Corp.

Page 83: "Stop Ordering Me Around" by Stacey Wilkins from *Newsweek,* January 4, 1993. Copyright © 1993 by Newsweek, Inc. Reprinted by permission of Newsweek, Inc.

Page 87: "A Black Fan of Country Music Tells All" by Lena Williams from the *New York Times,* June 19, 1994. Copyright © 1994 by the New York Times Co. Reprinted by permission.

Page 92: "Bananas for Rent" by Michiko Kakutani from *New York Times* Magazine, November 1997. Used by permission of The New York Times Syndication Sales Corp.

Page 102: "Chocolate Equals Love" by Diane Ackerman from *Parade,* February 9, 2003. Copyright © 2003 by Diane Ackerman. Reprinted by permission of William Morris Agency, LLC on behalf of the Author.

INDEX